COLD CASE RESEARCH

RESOURCES FOR UNIDENTIFIED, MISSING, AND COLD HOMICIDE CASES

COLD CASE RESEARCH

RESOURCES FOR UNIDENTIFIED, MISSING, AND COLD HOMICIDE CASES

SILVIA PETTEM

FOREWORD BY JAMES TRAINUM

CRC Press
Taylor & Francis Group
Boca Raton London New York

CRC Press is an imprint of the
Taylor & Francis Group, an **informa** business

Cover image: Unidentified gravestone in the Evergreen Cemetery, Leadville, Colorado. (Photo by author)

CRC Press
Taylor & Francis Group
6000 Broken Sound Parkway NW, Suite 300
Boca Raton, FL 33487-2742

First issued in paperback 2020

ISBN-13: 978-1-4398-6169-1 (hbk)
ISBN-13: 978-0-367-77853-8 (pbk)

Library of Congress Cataloging-in-Publication Data

Pettem, Silvia.
Cold case research : resources for unidentified, missing, and cold homicide cases / Silvia Pettem.
p. cm.
Includes bibliographical references and index.
ISBN 978-1-4398-6169-1 (hbk. : alk. paper)
1. Cold cases (Criminal investigation) I. Title.

HV8073.P445 2012
363.25'952--dc23 2012015717

Visit the Taylor & Francis Web site at
http://www.taylorandfrancis.com

and the CRC Press Web site at
http://www.crcpress.com

In memory of the victims

Contents

Section III

RESOURCES FOR EXPANDED RESEARCH

Case Histories and Profiles

List of Figures

Foreword

Early on in my 27-year career with the Metropolitan Police Department of Washington, DC, I had the extremely good fortune to be assigned to the Repeat Offender Project. Tasked, as the name suggests, with the investigation of repeat offenders, the crimes we investigated ran the gamut of criminal offenses from shoplifting rings and white-collar crimes to fencing operations, drugs, and murder. I gained a wide variety of investigative experience, going places and meeting people I never would have in any other profession. A case may have necessitated taking a basic class in accounting, another with learning the ins and outs of many alternative lifestyles. During one rather schizophrenic phase in my life, I spent my mornings working undercover as a heroin addict at a drug treatment center attempting to identify the suspects involved in a contract hit. In the afternoon I posed as a graduate student at a local university. This background in the investigation of such a wide assortment of crimes served me well when I finally ended up in Homicide in late 1993.

I always believed that good homicide detectives did not investigate homicide. Instead, they investigated the crime that led up to the homicide. If you had a murder that occurred during a burglary, and you didn't have any experience investigating burglary, then you were starting off "behind the eight-ball." And, if most of your prior investigative experience consisted of drug cases, then your investigative "tool box" might have lacked some of the essentials needed to bring the homicide to closure. Here is where my experience came into play, because my learning curve was not as steep as it could have been.

All of this changed when I was transferred to the Cold Case Unit. The normal challenges offered by any homicide case were still there; however, these were combined with a lack of a master searchable database of cases, a lack of a systematic review and case selection process, and, to make matters worse, there never was enough manpower or money to correct these additional problems. Tasked with developing a case review protocol, I reached out to other agencies to learn from both their successes and mistakes. The results of my efforts are detailed in Chapter 2. Conquering these organizational and logistical issues was relatively easy, however, compared to overcoming the bane of all cold case investigations: missing documentation and missing witnesses. In tackling these problems, my learning curve suddenly looked more like Mount Everest during a blizzard.

I once read an article that described cold case detectives as the "Indiana Joneses" of the Homicide Unit. If only it was that exciting! I would even settle for the clean and organized file room portrayed by television in the series "Cold Case;" that is, each case neatly arranged and the documentation complete in well-marked boxes. In going to the Cold Case Unit, I had traded a life of executing search warrants and chasing suspects to one of reviewing microfilm files (when I could find a viewing machine that worked) for hours. I remember trying to locate a witness with minimal identifying information (for some reason, "back in the day," my predecessors didn't think it was important to capture dates of birth), and rummaging through the dark and dank basements of retired detectives for "their" copies of old files. The Indiana Jones image quickly became that of the quintessential spinster librarian.

Not that there is anything wrong with spinster librarians! In fact, a librarian came to my aid much like Indiana Jones. In an old serial murder case from the 1970s, it became necessary to try to reconstruct a now-vanished Washington, DC neighborhood and to identify everyone who lived there all those years ago. I had no idea where to begin and spent hours on false starts. By chance I happened to mention my plight to a research librarian from the Washingtoniana Room of the Martin Luther King Library. Taking great pity on me, she took me by the hand and educated me about historical property records and maps, old telephone directories, and numerous other resources that helped us tease out the necessary information. Later, during other investigations, I relied on volunteers with specialized research skills and interns to help perform these critical and often labor-intensive tasks.

The reality is that cold case investigators need to be at home with both the old and the new. The current generation of investigators is very much at home with the Internet and computers, but they lack, and often have little patience for, old-fashioned research skills. Old guys like me know the old ways, but we are uncomfortable with computers and databases. And rapidly developing technology, especially in the field of the forensic sciences, often leaves both groups in the dust.

Enter Silvia Pettem: historical researcher and author. In 1996, while participating in an event jointly hosted by two historical organizations in Boulder, Colorado, she first learned of the 1954 murder of a then-unidentified woman, "age about 20 years," who was buried in a Boulder cemetery. The more Pettem researched the old case, the more fascinated she became with the identity of the unknown woman. Although Pettem had no prior police experience, she was able to team up with the local sheriff's office in a quest to put a name to this unidentified victim. Pettem's unprecedented work, detailed in her book *Someone's Daughter: In Search of Justice for Jane Doe,* combined not only dogged old-fashioned research with the power of the Internet, but it also included the extensive use of the media and the latest advances in forensic science. The result was a positive identification of the victim, bringing resolution to the victim's family and advancing the cold case investigation by leaps and bounds.

In this book, *Cold Case Research: Resources for Unidentified, Missing, and Cold Homicide Cases,* Pettem does more than give cold case investigators the benefit of her experience and the lessons learned from her investigation of the Boulder Jane Doe case. Working with experts from around the country and taking a thinking-outside-the-box approach, Pettem has helped fill major gaps in traditional cold case investigation training and techniques.

However, when it comes to embracing new ideas and techniques, law enforcement can be a hard sell. Our "BS" meters are extremely sensitive. It is just not enough to tell us that this new-fangled procedure or database is a good thing; we want proof. Through the generous use of profiles and case histories, Pettem not only gives concrete examples of how these research resources, practices, and strategies save time, she also explains how they actually work in the real world. More important, the book is structured to be a handy resource guide in and of itself. Through use of a checklist at the end of Chapter 1, the book allows the investigator to rapidly identify the material that addresses his or her specific cold case problem. Unlike most investigative references that collect dust on an investigator's desk, *Cold Case Research* is destined to become a much dog-eared guidebook, as my advance copy already has become.

Several chapters of the book are devoted to the investigation of missing persons and the unidentified dead, a topic not usually covered in cold case investigation training. Tens of thousands of persons go missing under suspicious circumstances each year. In many jurisdictions, no body equals no homicide, with the result that these cases often do not receive the level of attention or documentation they deserve. The seriousness of this problem within my own agency struck home when my work led me to missing persons cases where it was obvious that the missing person had been murdered. At the time, no tracking system existed for any of these cases, and the investigative documentation was often deplorable. Most of these cases were not classified as homicides, so the file and evidence retention periods were much shorter, leading to their premature destruction.

Pettem provides law enforcement agencies with practical recommendations, as well as the tools and techniques needed to help rectify these problems. But, she takes it a step further. In addition to a section in Chapter 9 on prosecuting "no body homicides," she presents, in Chapter 1, the case history of "Surette Clark and Little Jane Doe" as an example of how an agency successfully prosecuted a murder case in which the victim had not, at the time, been found, thus denying to the killer what used to be the first step to the commission of the perfect crime: the disappearance of the victim.

At first glance, some of the chapters in the book may not seem to belong. What do volunteers and contact with the victim's next-of-kin have to do with historical research and modern databases? This is where creative thinking comes into play. My own experience taught me the value of incorporating both volunteers and interns into a cold case unit. In these cash-strapped times, they are manpower, a vital and often untapped resource that brings so much to the table. From simple file organization to performing complex case reviews and data entry, volunteers and interns perform the tedious and time-consuming tasks that can free up investigators to perform the necessary street work. Many cold case units across the country would be lost without them, and Pettem provides numerous examples of how they can be incorporated: from large intern programs like I ran, to small, part-time volunteer units.

Co-victim programs that use advocates as liaisons with the family members of homicides are another untapped resource for cold case units that often are overlooked in these times of belt-tightening. Too often, investigators do not realize the impact that these cases still have on family members, even decades after the event. A few years ago, I sat in the living room of a family whose relative was a child victim of a 1970 serial murderer. To the family, it was as if the murder occurred only yesterday. On their end, family members received some comfort that the case was still under investigation. On my end, I received a wealth of information, including old newspaper clippings from now defunct papers, and other details and leads that were either not documented or were lost from the case files. A well-run co-victim program not only provides comfort and assistance to the family and friends of the missing and murder victims, it can create allies who can help get units the resources and support they need.

Similarly, it is largely because of grass-roots victim advocacy groups that Washington, DC was able to get its own forensic laboratory. Pettem offers several examples of successful programs of different types across the country. For instance, in her chapter on the use of volunteers, she does not offer a one-program-fits-all approach, but instead, she provides samples of different approaches that can be adapted to an agency's unique needs.

Pettem's experience as a writer and newspaper columnist, along with several accounts of those in law enforcement in various parts of the country, allows her to tackle a topic almost taboo to cops and coroners and the rest of us: the media. From the first days of the police academy, we are taught to avoid, at all cost, the media, the "gotcha" reporters, the skewers of facts. But cold case investigations can create strange bedfellows. The media and their archives are important sources of old information, and, if used properly, sources of new information as well. Again, using case studies, Pettem explores the positive use of all sorts of media from social media on the Internet to mainstream reporting in cold case investigations. She offers tips that help take the fear out of working with the media, as well as producing stories that will maximize the potential of new leads coming in.

During my career in law enforcement, I have attended more conferences, training sessions, and seminars than I care to count. From most I was at least able to take away a little something. But once in a while, I would attend one that was an eye-opener—one that taught me new tricks and investigative approaches—and I could not wait to get back to work in order to apply what I had learned. This book has affected me the same way. For the investigator, Pettem's work will undoubtedly jump-start many a stalled investigation and keep others moving forward. For cold case unit managers, it opens up a world of new opportunities: the opportunity to expand the capacities of their units, take advantage of free resources, and to institute changes that address the outdated attitudes, policies, and procedures that, in the past, prevented some cases from being solved. At the same time, *Cold Case Research* promises to keep other cases from going cold in the future.

Detective James Trainum, retired
Metropolitan Police Department
Washington, DC

Preface

The definition of a cold case varies from agency to agency, but the National Institute of Justice currently defines it as "any case whose probative investigative leads have been exhausted."* Therefore, cold cases can range from those that are a few months old to others that go back for decades. This is a book of resources for cold case research, with profiles and case histories that illustrate how these resources have successfully been applied. To get started, browse through the checklist in Chapter 1, or pick a chapter from the Table of Contents.

"To know even one life has breathed easier because you have lived. This is to have succeeded," is a quotation that has been attributed to several authors, including nineteenth-century American essayist and poet, Ralph Waldo Emerson.† It is my sincere hope that *Cold Case Research: Resources for Unidentified, Missing, and Cold Homicide Cases* will help investigators solve their cases, and that their solutions will, ultimately, bring justice to the victims. That is why we do what we do.

Silvia Pettem
Boulder, Colorado

* Sidebar to Charles Heurich, "Cold Cases: Resources for Agencies, Resolution for Families," *National Institute of Justice (NIJ) Journal*, 260 (July 2008).

† Ralph Waldo Emerson Society, http://emerson.tamu.edu/Ephemera/Success.html

Acknowledgments

The concept for this book came from Richard H. Walton, EdD, associate professor of criminal justice, Utah State University Eastern and author of *Cold Case Homicides: Practical Investigative Techniques.* Walton suggested that a book on research methodology was needed, and that I should write it, a daunting prospect at the time.

Once underway, I sought advice from law enforcement friends who helped me brainstorm the topics to include. Jefferson County Sheriff's Office Investigator Cheryl Moore invited me to her home, where we spent a hot summer afternoon hammering out the initial outline. Former Westminster Police Department Senior Criminalist Tom Adair, Boulder County Sheriff's Office Division Chief Phil West, and Boulder Police Department Deputy Chief David Hayes all took the time to give me the benefit of their joint expertise, and each contributed many more excellent suggestions.

Walton then introduced me to retired Detective James Trainum (Metropolitan Police Department, Washington, DC) who became my chief advisor. He generously read the chapters as I wrote them, and he provided a welcomed peer review as he shared his own experiences and helped in shaping the book as a whole. I will miss his early morning e-mails.

In fact, one of the best parts of writing *Cold Case Research* has been the people I have interacted with along the way. Those mentioned throughout these acknowledgments gave freely of their time to inform me of their work. Family members of victims told me, a complete stranger, their very personal stories. All were eager to share their collective wealth of knowledge, the basis for the profiles and case histories spread throughout the following pages.

Two of the profiles are on Jefferson County's Investigator Cheryl Moore and Colorado Springs Detective Ron Lopez and the outstanding work they are doing in their respective agencies. Thank you to both of you, as well as to Sarah Chaikin, who enjoys a unique role as the Cold Case Program Coordinator of the Victim Assistance Unit at the Denver Police Department.

Thanks, too, to longtime friend Todd Matthews (now the communications manager for NamUs), who I finally met face to face at a national NamUs Training Academy. That was where I met Detective Lopez, as well as Investigator Matthew Lunn, of the Arapahoe County Coroner's Office. The three of us now teach the NamUs portion of the 16-hour training class, "Cold Case Investigations—Strategies and Best Practices," sponsored by the

Colorado Bureau of Investigation, thanks to retired Lieutenant Jonathyn Priest (Denver Police Department) and CBI's Criminal Intelligence Analyst, Audrey Simkins.

My heart, obviously, is with the victims, and I wish to particularly thank the families who shared their stories with me. Stephanie Clack told me about the disappearance of her oldest sister Paula Beverly Davis, and James H. Davis, MD (no relation), Coroner of Montgomery County, Ohio, explained his agency's role and use of NamUs in identifying Paula as a Jane Doe murder victim. Clack and another sister, Alice Beverly, now work as victim advocates for the organization, Missouri Missing. Co-founder Marianne Asher-Chapman gave me her comments, as well.

A special thank you goes, too, to Regina Mayo, who lost her husband, Gary Mayo, in a drowning accident. She asks that he be remembered as a man who lived life to the fullest. Following a Vidocq Society meeting in Philadelphia, I met with Hal G. Brown, deputy director of the Delaware Office of the Chief Medical Examiner and Forensic Sciences Laboratory. I appreciated the time that he and his assistant, Phillip Petty, spent with me discussing their agency's role in identifying Gary Mayo's partial remains.

Sharron Bullis, sister of murder victim Bonita Raye Morgan, kindly corresponded with me and continues to offer her decades-long perspective on unsolved homicides at annual conferences of Families of Homicide Victims and Missing Persons. The organization's director, Howard Morton, who lost a son to homicide, filled me in on what families want from law enforcement.

I am grateful, too, for learning a new (to me, anyway) perspective when I corresponded with the sister of the killer of a Navajo child, Surette Clark. The sister asked that, in this book, her name be withheld, but her bravery led the way to providing justice for Clark. The case was one of several of retired Detective Ed Reynolds (Phoenix Police Department), who shared with me some of his early-day experiences with his agency's Cold Case Squad. Thanks, too, to Detective Stuart Somershoe (Phoenix Police Department), who put me in contact with Detective Reynolds and provided more information on the Clark case.

Cold cases include homicides, the unidentified, and missing persons, and each case, in each category, is different. Investigator Kevin Parmelee (Somerset County Prosecutor's Office, and formerly with the Piscataway Police Department in New Jersey) is to be commended for using DNA from a PKU (phenylketonuria) test, leading the way in the use of this overlooked primary reference sample to identify a missing teenager, Ben Mauer.

Thanks, too, to part-time chief Chad Weaver (employed part-time by both the Hutsonville and Robinson police departments, in rural Illinois) for sharing his enthusiasm in the use of TLO's online investigative system to track down another missing person: a sexual predator. Meanwhile, Florida Department of Law Enforcement Special Agent Tommy Ray initiated the use of Cold Case Playing Cards that, thanks to him, are now spreading across the country and have led to the arrests and convictions of several killers.

I also appreciated hearing from Investigator Darrell Harris (Marin County Sheriff's Office–Coroner Division). Former cold case volunteer Mark C. Friedman tipped me off to the agency's identification of a John Doe as Joseph Coogan. Even though I learned of the Coogan family's reaction secondhand, their gratitude shines through. I hope that Roland Halpern, and his son, Koa Halpern, will someday find similar resolution in their search for Joseph Halpern.

Historical researchers are not to be overlooked either. Michael C. Dooling is the first person to take a serious look at the likely related disappearances of three young women in New England; and Virginia resident Micki Lavigne creatively used a combination of keywords in a Google search to find a woman who had been missing for more than a half century. John R. Piearson took the time to show me the graves of the unidentified in the Evergreen Cemetery in Leadville, Colorado, and he and Karen Anne Nicholas are working with me to give them back their names.

If there were a volunteer of the year award, however, it would probably go to Milli Knudsen, who has forged new ground—and shared her organizational skills—as a civilian in the Cold Case Unit of the New Hampshire Department of Justice, Office of Attorney General. Other volunteers are eager to share very different skills, as noted by retired Postal Inspector Tom Hall, one of Oregon's Cold Case Cowboys, as well as Gene and Sandy Ralston (Ralston & Associates), who aid law enforcement by performing underwater search and recovery missions.

In the preparation of this book, I also consulted with Professor Mary Dodge, PhD (director of Criminal Justice Programs, University of Colorado, Denver), retired Detective Dixie Grimes (Denver Police Department), retired Captain Tom McLellan (Fort Collins Police Department), Professor Michael L. Radelet, PhD (sociology, University of Colorado, Boulder), Derek Regensburger (legal studies instructor, criminal justice, Everest College), and N. Prabha Unnithan, PhD (professor of sociology, also director of the Center for the Study of Crime and Justice, Colorado State University, Fort Collins).

Additional input came from the following professionals: Justice Solutions Director Diane Alexander; former Assistant United States Attorney (Washington, DC) Thomas A. "Tad" DiBiase; LexisNexis Solutions Consultant and former FBI ViCAP Crime Analyst Samantha Gwinn; Chief Investigator of the Twentieth Judicial District (Colorado) Jane Harmer; Senior Crime Analyst Diana Havlin; Supervisory Special Agent, retired, R. Stephen Mardigian (National Center for the Analysis of Violent Crime, FBI); Cold Case Investigative Research Institute Director Sheryl McCollum; attorney Joseph K. Reynolds; United States Attorney's Office (Washington, DC) Victim Advocate Marcey Rinker; crime analyst Suzanne Stiltner (ViCAP

NamUs Coordinator, FBI); archivist and librarian Carol Taylor; and—from the Vidocq Society—Frederick Bornhofen (chairman of the board and case management director) and William Fleisher (commissioner).

Many other people have also contributed to *Cold Case Research*, and I offer my apologies to those I may have missed. Investigator Lunn reviewed the NamUs chapters, and Dr. Steven C. Clark and Randy Hanzlick, MD (chief medical examiner, Fulton County, Georgia) read over the section on NamUs's background and evolution. Robert C. Davis kindly shared the *Rand Corporation Reports on Cold Case Investigations*, which he co-authored. Detective Bryan Franke (Longmont Police Department) and computer forensic analyst Jeremy Shavin (Boulder County Sheriff's Office) let me pick their brains on search engines and databases. Detective Stephen Furr (Charlotte-Mecklenburg Police Department) told me of his agency's cold case squad, a model for the country. And I appreciated the help of photo librarian Faye Haskins, of the Washingtoniana Division of the District of Columbia Public Library, in selecting a photograph from the library's archives.

Thanks, too, to the other individuals and institutions (not mentioned elsewhere) who contributed illustrations: *Ahwatukee News*, Boulder *Daily Camera*, Beverly family, Alan Cass, Colorado State Archives, Florida Department of Law Enforcement, Robert Freitas, Jennifer Kitt, Library of Congress, Judah Lifschitz, Maricopa County Recorder, Montgomery County Coroner's Office, National Archives, National Institute of Justice, Richard Nixon Presidential Library and Museum, *North Platte Telegraph*, E.W. Scripps Co., Visit Denver, and Diane Wetzel.

Ken Hunter, CEO of TLO, personally and graciously gave me a two-day tour of the investigative system company's headquarters in Boca Raton, Florida. Along with Randy Huff, with whom I continue to correspond, other TLO employees who contributed to this book include Wally Abrams, Derick Anderson, founder Hank Asher, Sybille Brown, Lynn Dallmer, Derek Dubner, Kevin Flanagan, Janette Harris, Caren Holmes, Erika Husemann, Skye Kamakani, Joyce Lewis-Bass, former Mississippi Attorney General Mike Moore, Mitch Nixon, COO Steve Racioppo, Bettye Samuels, James Samuels (NCMEC manager domiciled at TLO), Christine Schmitt, Bill Shrewsbury, and Bill Wiltse.

I also would like to acknowledge members of the Boulder Police Department. As a volunteer in the Detectives Section, I appreciate the professionalism of my co-workers and the opportunity they have given me to work with them. Thanks go to Chief Mark Beckner, Deputy Chief David Hayes, Deputy Chief Greg Testa, Commander Kimberly Stewart, Detective Sergeant Rob Bustrum, Detective Sergeant Melissa Kampf, Detective Sergeant Tom Trujillo, Detective Ruth Christopher, Detective Tom Dowd, Detective Kurt Foster, Detective Jeremy Frenzen, Detective Chuck Heidel,

Detective Colleen Wilcox, Legal Advisor Bob Keatley, and Police Records Specialist Jennifer Bragg.

To my associates at the Taylor & Francis Group/CRC Press, I wish to thank Becky Masterman for her faith in me to write *Cold Case Research*, and to Kathryn Younce, Iris Fahrer, and Bev S. Weiler for patiently working with me through all the details.

Last, special thanks go to my husband, Ed Raines, my sounding board and best friend.

About the Author

Silvia Pettem is a longtime historical researcher, newspaper columnist, and author of more than a dozen books. After decades of work for individuals, businesses, and governments, her life took a new turn in 1996, when she stumbled upon the gravestone of a Jane Doe, a murder victim from 1954. A few years later, Pettem applied her research skills to both old-fashioned detective work and the power of the Internet by entering into a successful partnership with her local sheriff and forensic experts of the Vidocq Society to determine the young woman's identity. Pettem chronicled their work in *Someone's Daughter: In Search of Justice for Jane Doe.*

In 2008, the Boulder County Sheriff's Office gave Pettem a Sheriff's Commendation Award for doing the "lion's share of the research" on the Jane Doe case. Two years later, the Vidocq Society presented her with its Medal of Honor.

While continuing to volunteer for the Sheriff's Office, Pettem is now an associate member of the Vidocq Society, a volunteer in the detectives section of the Boulder Police Department, a NamUs Academy graduate, and a NamUs instructor in classes sponsored by the Colorado Bureau of Investigation, expanding her expertise and working with colleagues all over the country. She wrote *Cold Case Research: Resources for Unidentified, Missing, and Cold Homicide Cases* in order to aid other investigators as they grapple with cold cases of their own.

Tools and Techniques

I

Challenges and Checklist

1

In 1964, Mick Jagger and his British rock band, the Rolling Stones, wowed American audiences on the *Ed Sullivan Show* with the group's new hit song, "Time Is On My Side." The Stones were singing about a lost love, but the premise was the same—time can be an ally—especially when working cold cases, due to advances in technology as well as new information that often is revealed when relationships, loyalties, and associations change.

Changing relationships, for instance, can bring forward new witnesses. But witnesses age, and cold case investigators—who also age and retire and never have enough time in the day—are challenged with shortened windows of opportunity in which to solve the cases that have new leads, as well as go after missing gaps from the past proactively. Today's cold case investigators have found that they need to be Internet savvy and make the best use of the rapidly changing research methodologies of the twenty-first century, but they also have to be time travelers and open the door to the past. If their cold cases go back a decade or more, they know that it helps to learn, or relearn, the nearly forgotten skill sets and methodology of classical historical researchers.

Much has been written elsewhere about prioritizing cold cases, as well as the collection and preservation of physical evidence, which are not the subject of this book. Instead, the purpose of *Cold Case Research: Resources for Unidentified, Missing, and Cold Homicide Cases* is to provide cold case investigators with research resources that will save them time and money, along with examples of practices and strategies that work.

Use the checklist at the end of this chapter to put at your fingertips the very latest (as well as the traditional) research tools you need to aid in the arrest and conviction of criminals, give resolution to families, and bring justice to victims.

Case History: Surette Clark and Little Jane Doe

In 1993, a Canadian woman could no longer keep quiet about a crime she believed her brother had long ago committed in Arizona. The woman's decision to contact police led to her brother's arrest and conviction for the murder of his 4-year-old stepdaughter, Surette Clark, even though Surette's body had not, at the time, been found. All through the trial, and for years afterwards, the remains of a female child, known only as "Little Jane Doe," lay unclaimed in a nearby agency's evidence room.

Forty years after the girl's murder, after the convicted killer had served his time in prison and was released on parole, a DNA match finally identified the remains as Surette's. Her story combines a homicide investigation with an identification, and it also illustrates the following facts:

- The passage of time can change family relationships.
- Incorrect race (or even sex, in some cases) can set a case back for years.
- Interagency cooperation is essential.
- Revisited cold cases can be solved.

In Surette's case, there was nothing that anyone could have done to speed up the passage of time, but the child might never have been identified if investigators in both Tempe and Phoenix, Arizona, had not pulled this cold case off their evidence room shelves and worked on it together.

The investigation into Surette's remains began on Saturday March 24, 1979, with two rockhounds who were hunting for specimens along the edge of the then-dry Salt River bottom, west of the Mill Avenue Bridge, in Tempe. When the men began to overturn rocks, they unexpectedly stumbled upon the skeleton of a child. Then they called the police.

Three days later, a story titled, "Child's Skeleton Found in Tempe," made modest headlines on page 2 of Section B of the *Arizona Republic*. At first, investigators could not determine the sex or the exact age of the child, but they estimated the individual to have been between five and seven years old. Clothing was found, but no identification. There were no missing-child reports that fit. A patch of brown hair was still attached to the skull, but the condition of the child's remains indicated that he, or she, had been buried for at least a year, or up to thirteen more years, as the shallow grave was lined with copies of the *Arizona Republic* dated June 6, 1966 and October 2, 1966.

Of the skeleton, Tempe Police Captain Richard Christensen told a reporter, at the time, "It didn't wash up. The water never got that high. It was laid up against a bridge support, and it had been buried wrapped in a blanket."[1] Officers searched the area and found additional small bones that they said were part of the same remains. Inspection of the skeleton revealed a broken jaw, but it was unknown whether it had been broken before or after the child's death. "We will be sending the bones to the medical school in Tucson," added Christensen, "and they should be able to give us a better idea of the age and, possibly, the cause of death. We really can't call it a murder at this point."[2]

On the day that the story of the child's skeleton ran in the newspaper, much larger headlines proclaimed that Egypt and Israel had signed a treaty ending 30 years of hostility. A front-page photo of a beaming President Jimmy Carter showed him clasping the hands of Egypt's Anwar Sadat and Israel's Menachem Begin. But what of the unidentified child left under a bridge in Arizona? How many cars had passed overhead before the remains were found? And who, and where, were his or her parents?

These questions haunted police as the unidentified child's remains sat on an evidence shelf for the next 18 years in the Tempe Police Department. Little did their detectives know that in 1971, and far away in Canada, a short-order cook named Wayne Clifford Roberts had confessed to his brothers that he had "accidentally" killed his wife's daughter from a previous marriage.

Decades passed; then in 1993 Roberts's sister, also a Canadian resident, learned of the child's death and the possibility that her brother had killed Surette Clark. The girl was born in Tuba City, Arizona, on the Navajo Indian Reservation, on June 21, 1966. Stated Roberts's sister in a recent interview, "I guess I put everyone on the spot when I decided we could no longer be quiet and take the risk that another child could be hurt by Wayne."[3] The sister then contacted the local Children's Aid Society in Ontario, which called Arizona police and set in motion Roberts's extradition and a November 1996 trial in Arizona.

The year 1993 (when Roberts's sister came forward) was also the year that the Phoenix Police Department created its Cold Case Unit, and Detective Ed Reynolds (see Figures 1.1 and 1.2) was the department's first cold case investigator. The Illinois native had moved to Phoenix shortly after he graduated from high school, and he joined the police department in 1979. Ten years later he became a detective, and was assigned to the homicide division in 1992. The following year, in the newly formed Cold Case Unit, Reynolds was working on the murder of Jeanne Tovrea, and would soon be handed the Diane Keidel case, when the murder of Surette Clark landed in his lap.[4]

Although Roberts had confessed to family members, Surette's stepfather had not, technically, confessed to the Phoenix Police (the county attorney did not want to litigate the Miranda issues), and they still did not have Surette's remains.[5] In correspondence with the author, now-retired Detective Ed Reynolds stated, "The difficult part was convincing the Canadian 'Crown' to extradite him for a murder with no body." Reynolds, however, did a good job of showing Roberts's predisposition for extreme child abuse, just before the murder, by finding very old medical records of a then-recent visit to an American Indian hospital emergency room when he had beaten Surette and taken her in for treatment. Added Reynolds, "Just getting those records was a real tough job."[6]

Figure 1.1 Surette Clark's murderer was behind bars, but the child's remains had not yet been found when Detective Ed Reynolds and the other members of the Phoenix Police Department's Cold Case Squad posed for the press in 1998. From left, the detectives are Tom Gabriel, Frank DiModica, Ed Reynolds, and Robert Brunansky. (Photo by Todd Lillard. Reprinted from the *Ahwatukee Foothills News,* 14 October 1998. With permission.)

Figure 1.2 Detective Ed Reynolds had time to relax in 2008, the year he retired after 30 years with the Phoenix Police Department. He recently reflected, "I had a wonderful career, and I miss it." (Photo courtesy of Ed Reynolds.)

Detective Reynolds personally arrested Roberts in Calgary and brought him to Arizona. Then, with evidence from Roberts's siblings as well as his former wife (who had divorced him prior to his arrest), Roberts was convicted of Surette's murder and sent to the Arizona State Prison. The court was convinced that Roberts, as stepfather, had violently punished Surette for an act of disobedience while her mother was at work. Prosecutors determined that Roberts had forced his former wife—the child's mother—to remain silent, before fleeing with her to Canada. At the time, Surette's mother was seven months pregnant with the couple's first child.[7]

Independent of the arrest and conviction of Wayne Roberts, the Tempe police received a federal grant, in 1997, to re-examine their unsolved cases. They hired former Phoenix homicide investigator, Charles Hodges, a colleague of Detective Reynolds, to create a forensic sculpture of the still-unidentified child found in 1979. By then, medical examiners had determined that the skeleton most likely belonged to a 4-year-old Caucasian girl, but her body was so badly decomposed that the cause and manner of death remained unknown. Possibly, she had suffered a broken neck. In Hodges's new position as criminal investigator for the Maricopa County Attorney's Office, the sculptor spent 40 hours in his basement workshop creating a "likeness" of the girl he called "Little Jane Doe."

Hodges started by placing 25 tissue-depth markers on her skull, then he filled in her facial features with clay in the hopes that the reconstruction would lead to the young girl's identification. Quoted in the *Arizona Republic* on May 10, 1997, Hodges stated, "I never kid myself that I've made a perfect likeness. When you have it done, just like with a composite drawing, you say, 'Who does this remind you of?' not, 'Who does this look like?' It won't look exactly like the person it once was. But it can be close enough for someone to recognize the face and call us and finally identify the victim. And that's all we want."[8] (See Chapter 15 for more on facial reconstructions.)

"I work a lot of cold cases," Hodges continued. "A body is found, no identification, no relatives come forward, and police hit a dead end. Sometimes years pass, but for one reason or another, the case is reopened. Detectives need to put features on the victim's remains and hope [that] circulating the picture of the reconstructed face will jog someone's memory."[9] Eight years later, with a face but still no name, Tempe Police Detective John Thompson told another reporter, "It's always difficult when we can't determine how someone died, but it's even more frustrating when we don't know who the victim was. If nothing else, this little girl deserves to be identified as someone other than 'Little Jane Doe.' "[10]

Roberts served 13 years in the Arizona State Prison (plus one and one-half years of pretrial time in a Phoenix jail) for the second-degree murder of Surette Clark. All throughout the trial, Surette's remains continued to elude investigators. While Hodges and the police continued to try to identify "Little Jane Doe," Roberts's sister searched missing persons' websites in the hopes of finding some mention of the little girl. The sister had read about the child's skeleton that was found in Tempe, but she (and, presumably, the police as well) did not believe the skeleton was Surette's, because both police and news reporters stated that the child's remains were Caucasian when, in fact, they were Navajo.[11] The search for Surette's body had become part of Roberts's trial. Detective Ed Reynolds suggested the possibility that the child was buried near the trailer home where Roberts and his wife had once lived, but the ground was not dug up during the trial because a shopping center then covered the site.

In December 2009, Roberts, out of prison on parole, reportedly returned to Canada, and "Little Jane Doe" still remained unidentified. Then, when the Phoenix Police Department's Missing and Unidentified Persons Unit was working on a separate Jane Doe case, Phoenix detectives requested a list of unidentified child victims from the National Center for Missing and Exploited Children (NCMEC). "This brought the [Little] Jane Doe case to light," stated Detective Stuart Somershoe, of the department's Missing and Unidentified Persons Unit. "NCMEC helped put two and two together and pushed Tempe to do a DNA comparison."[12]

In May 2010, the Phoenix Police Department detectives approached Tempe Police Detective Tom Magazzeni, and the two departments worked together. Before long, they began to see similarities between Surette's disappearance and "Little Jane Doe" 's murder. In addition to NCMEC, also involved in the investigations were the Arizona Department of Public Safety Crime Lab and the Maricopa County Medical Examiner's Office. "Looking at the reports," Tempe Detective Magazzeni said in a statement released to the press, "the cases matched, the time line matched and the victim's description matched."[13] In August 2010, DNA comparison,with genetic evidence gathered from both Surette's mother and her biological father, confirmed the identity of the little girl, murdered 40 years earlier, in 1970.

A few months after Surette's identification, her cremated remains were sent to Canada to be reunited with her mother and her extended family and buried in a grave with her own name, at last. Along with Surette Clark's name, are her mother's memories: a "sweet" little girl, with dark brown hair neatly held in place with a barrette and last photographed on a two-wheeled bicycle with training wheels in the Arizona desert.[14] Although closure in any murder case is unattainable, this resolution in one family's tragedy is the best ending possible.

Time as an Ally

As described in the above case study on Surette Clark, a family member (or a newly surfaced or previously hostile witness, or even someone who was just plain scared) may, at a later date, decide the time is right to talk to police. Time—sometimes decades—can give people an opportunity to mature, to overcome former fears, and to develop a different sense of right and wrong.

In August 2009, the Colorado Bureau of Investigation (CBI) requested the Center for the Study of Crime and Justice, Department of Sociology at Colorado State University, to analyze data from 233 surveys distributed to all local law enforcement agencies in Colorado. The Center's final report, "Analysis of the Cold Case Survey of Law Enforcement for the Colorado Bureau of Investigation," substantiated the importance of new witnesses. As one of a series of questions, the authors asked investigators in the state's police departments and sheriffs' offices to think back to their last resolved homicide that was more than three years old, and to relate the crucial factor that broke that case. With a completion rate of 91.7%, the leading response was "previously unavailable witness," followed by "receiving help from an outside agency" and "the assignment of different investigators to the case."[15]

In the case of Surette Clark, the murderer's sister was the precipitating new witness, and her testimony was supplemented with that of the child's mother and others in their family. As noted previously, initial outside agencies included the University of Arizona College of Medicine and the Maricopa County Attorney's Office, followed by the Arizona Department of Public Safety Crime Lab, the Maricopa County Medical Examiner's Office, and the National Center for Missing and Exploited Children. Both the Phoenix and Tempe Police Departments had investigators new to their respective cases. One of the Tempe Police Department's stumbling blocks, however, was the unfortunate misidentification of Clark's remains as Caucasian, rather than Navajo. The correct racial classification may not have been forensically possible at the time of the child's murder, but the misinformation should serve as an example to today's investigators that what appear to be facts in cold cases must always be questioned. (See Chapter 7, "Entering and Searching in the NamUs System," for similar examples of misidentifications of remains.)

The Surette Clark case also demonstrates that new ways to solve cold cases are continually becoming available. For instance, the NamUs System, with its federally funded dual databases for missing and unidentified persons, was put into use in 2009, the same year that old-fashioned police work identified "Little Jane Doe." If NamUs had existed years ago—and if both the missing person and the unidentified remains had been entered—Surette

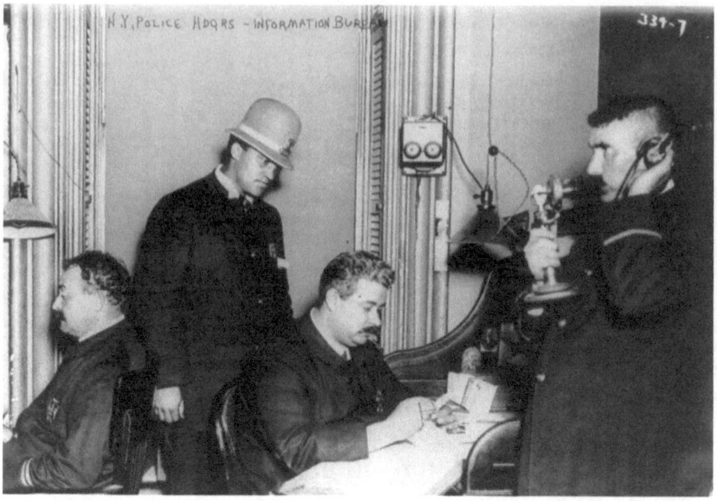

Figure 1.3 Then: In 1908, officers of the New York Police Department made use of the latest twentieth-century technology while at work in the agency's "Information Bureau." (Photo courtesy of Bain News Service, Library of Congress.)

Clark's identity might have been determined much sooner, and prosecutors would have had a body during the murder trial of Wayne Clifford Roberts. (See Chapters 6 and 7.)

Although it took a long time to bring justice to the little Navajo child in Arizona, time was on her side. Cold case research is a hot topic. Today's investigators live in an exciting technological era, with many new investigative tools now available and on the horizon. See Figures 1.3 and 1.4 for "then" and "now" comparisons.

Checklist: To Help in Navigating the Chapters

For Tips on People Searching, See

- Chapter 3, "TLO, The Latest Online Investigative System," for the profile "TLO Revolutionizes Investigations in Rural Illinois Agencies," as well as "TLOxp® User Tips."
- Chapter 4, "Additional Options for People Searches," including Google and the Social Security Death Index.
- Chapter 11, "Newspaper Research: Online and Off," for locating new witnesses and searching for names for missing persons lists.
- Chapter 12, "Published and Public Records," to aid in determining family relationships.

Figure 1.4 Now: A century later, Detective Chris Mammarella (a forensic computer examiner in the Boca Raton Police Department) works in the law-enforcement area of TLO, where specialized hardware and software enable him to recover computer files without altering the original data. (Photo courtesy of TLO.)

To Determine Family Relationships and Next of Kin, See

- Chapter 3, "TLO, The Latest Online Investigative System," for contact information for possible relatives and likely associates.
- Chapter 4, "Additional Options for People Searches," for public search engines that can help in narrowing down similarly named people and changes in women's names, as well as for the Social Security Death Index, useful in determining when and where people died in order to find their obituaries.
- Chapter 11, "Newspaper Research: Online and Off," on finding obituaries that often give names and addresses of next of kin.
- Chapter 12, "Published and Public Records," for recorded documents, and how they can help in determining changes in women's names.
- Chapter 16, "Taking Advantage of the Media," for tips on the investigative use of social media, where some people lay out their family relationships for the world to see.

To Identify John and Jane Does, See

- Chapter 1, "Challenges and Checklist," for the case history, "Surette Clark and Little Jane Doe."
- Chapter 2, "Agency Organization: Cold Case Units," for the profile, "Investigator Cheryl Moore's 'Unit of One' Produces Results," on the identification of Lisa Kay Kelly.

- Chapter 5, "Dealing With Databases," for a Marion Police Department dispatcher's use of the Doe Network in the identification of Chad Griffith.
- Chapter 6, "NamUs: Connecting the Missing and Unidentified," for the case histories of Paula Beverly Davis and Englewood Jane Doe, and "Gary Mayo and Partial Remains."
- Chapter 7, "Entering and Searching in the NamUs System," on both the NamUs-MP database on missing persons and the NamUs-UP database on unidentified remains.
- Chapter 8, "PKU Cards Retain Overlooked Data," for the case history, "DNA from PKU Identified Ben Mauer."
- Chapter 9, "The Plight of the Missing and Unknown," for suggestions for reconstructing case files of John and Jane Does, starting with newspaper articles, followed by database searches.
- Chapter 16, "Taking Advantage of the Media," for the case history, "John Doe Identified as Joseph Coogan."

To Search for Missing Persons, See

- Chapter 2, "Agency Organization: Cold Case Units," for the profile, "Detective Ron Lopez's Proactive Investigations Pay Off."
- Chapter 4, "Additional Options for People Searches," for the case history, "Google Search Used to Find Missing Woman with Changed Identity."
- Chapter 5, "Dealing with Databases," for a guide to some of the databases that may be helpful in cold case research, including NCIC, the Doe Network, and ViCAP.
- Chapter 6, "NamUs: Connecting the Missing and Unidentified," for the case histories of Paula Beverly Davis and Englewood Jane Doe, as well as "Gary Mayo and Partial Remains."
- Chapter 7, "Entering and Searching in the NamUs System," on both the NamUs-MP database on missing persons and the NamUs-UP database on unidentified remains.
- Chapter 8, "PKU Cards Retain Overlooked Data," for the case history, "DNA from PKU Identified Ben Mauer."
- Chapter 9, "The Plight of the Missing and Unknown," for examples of missing-person scenarios that include missing under suspicious circumstances and presumed dead, as well as a motive to disappear, walking away, committing suicide, and natural and accidental deaths. See also the case history, "Joseph Halpern Disappeared into Thin Air," which describes how a family member uncovered his uncle's decades-old missing persons files.
- Chapter 11, "Newspaper Research: Online and Off," for tips on searching for names for missing persons lists.

For Law Enforcement and Medical Examiners/Coroners at Work, See

- Chapter 1, "Challenges and Checklist," the case history, "Surette Clark and Little Jane Doe," in which Phoenix Detective Ed Reynolds brought justice to a Navajo child.
- Chapter 2, "Agency Organization: Cold Case Units," for current practices for reopening cold cases, qualities of a good cold case investigator, and the formations of cold case squads/units, with current examples: "Investigator Cheryl Moore's 'Unit of One' Produces Results," and "Detective Ron Lopez's Proactive Investigations Pay Off."
- Chapter 3, "TLO, The Latest Online Investigative System," for the profile of part-time Chief Chad Weaver in "TLO Revolutionizes Investigations in Rural Illinois Agencies."
- Chapter 6, "NamUs: Connecting the Missing and Unidentified," for two case histories. Montgomery County Coroner James H. Davis is featured in "Paula Beverly Davis and Englewood Jane Doe," and Deputy Director of the Delaware Office of the Chief Medical Examiner Hal G. Brown, is featured in "Gary Mayo and Partial Remains."
- Chapter 8, "PKU Cards Retain Overlooked DNA," for Investigator Kevin Parmelee and "DNA from PKU Identified Ben Mauer."
- Chapter 9, "The Plight of the Missing and Unknown," for former Assistant United States Attorney, Thomas A. (Tad) DiBiase on the prosecution of no-body homicides, as well as Victim Advocate Marcey Rinker's comments on why it is important to have a presumed dead missing person declared legally dead.
- Chapter 14: "Contact with Co-Victims," for the profile of Sarah Chaikin, Cold Case Program Coordinator of the Victim Assistance Unit at the Denver Police Department, "Victim Advocate Is Integral Member of Denver's Cold Case Unit."
- Chapter 16, "Taking Advantage of the Media," for the case histories featuring Investigator Darrell Harris of the Marin County Sheriff's Office–Coroner Division in "John Doe Identified as Joseph Coogan," as well as "Special Agent Tommy Ray Has Ace Up His Sleeve" on cold case playing cards.

For Contributions of Historical Researchers, See

- Chapter 4, "Additional Options for People Searches," for Micki Lavigne's work in the case histories, "Google Search Used to Find Missing Woman with Changed Identity," as well as "Find, Then Print, Sensitive Information."

- Chapter 10, "Historical and Geographical Context," for Michael C. Dooling's work in the case history, "Different States, Same Highway," as well as "Locating a Long-Forgotten Crime Scene."
- Chapter 13, "Volunteers: How They Can Help," for Milli Knudsen's volunteer work in the Cold Case Unit of the New Hampshire Department of Justice, Office of Attorney General.

To Dig into the Past, See

- Chapter 10, "Historical and Geographical Context," for maps, photographs, and other historical resources needed to "revisit" the time and scene of the crime when reconstructing a case file.
- Chapter 11, "Newspaper Research: Online and Off," used for placing a crime in historical context and for developing timelines.

To Bring in New Leads and Witnesses, See

- Chapter 1, "Challenges and Checklist" and Chapter 2, "Agency Organization: Cold Case Units," for examples of how changes in relationships can bring forward new witnesses.
- Chapter 16, "Taking Advantage of the Media," for interacting with the public through newspaper articles, cold case websites, social media, and cold case playing cards.

To Establish Better Relationships with Co-Victims, See

- Chapter 14, "Contact with Co-Victims," for the use of a victim advocate in a cold case unit, suggestions from co-victims, and resources for co-victims.

To Prosecute Cold Case Homicides, See

- Chapter 9, "The Plight of the Missing and Unknown," for recommendations by former Assistant United States Attorney Thomas A. (Tad) Dibiase on no-body cases. (For a case history on a no-body case, see "Surette Clark and Little Jane Doe" in Chapter 1.)
- Chapter 11, "Newspaper Research: Online and Off," for locating new witnesses, as well as finding articles that are helpful in determining if a suspect or witness was telling the truth when he or she claimed to have read about the case, at the time of the crime, in a newspaper.

To Save Time and Money, See

- Chapter 3, "TLO: The Latest Online Investigative System," for the most up-to-date data that is free to law enforcement.
- Chapter 6, "NamUs: Connecting the Missing and Unidentified," for free forensic services, including odontology, anthropology, and fingerprint and DNA analyses.
- Chapter 13, "Volunteers: How They Can Help," for the use of volunteers in cold case research, including the profile, "New Hampshire's Milli Knudsen in Win–Win Situation" (also, Chapter 2, "Agency Organization: Cold Case Units," for student interns and volunteers with the Metropolitan Police Department in Washington, DC).
- Chapter 15, "Cold Case Review Teams and Information-Sharing Resources," for pro bono help on cold cases and agencies that share resources.

Endnotes

1. Staff. "Child's skeleton found in Tempe," *Arizona Republic*, March 27, 1979.
2. Staff. "Child's skeleton found in Tempe," *Arizona Republic*, March 27, 1979.
3. Sister of Wayne Clifford Roberts (name withheld upon request). E-mail correspondence with author, January 24, 2011.
4. Jackson, Steve. *No Stone Unturned: The True Story of NecroSearch International, the World's Premier Forensic Investigators* (New York: Kensington Books, 2002), 203.
5. Reynolds, Ed. Detective. E-mail correspondence with author, November 3, 2011.
6. Reynolds, Ed. Detective. E-mail correspondence with author, October 31, 2011.
7. Reynolds, Ed. Detective. E-mail correspondence with author, October 31, 2011.
8. Staff. "Lost Face Reappears; Expert Reconstructs Unknown Victims," *Arizona Republic*, May 10, 1997.
9. Staff. "Lost Face Reappears; Expert Reconstructs Unknown Victims," *Arizona Republic*, May 10, 1997.
10. Nelson, Katie. "Little Victim Still Without an Identity," *Arizona Republic*, July 1, 2005.
11. Sister of Wayne Clifford Roberts (name withheld upon request). E-mail correspondence with author, January 25, 2011.
12. Somershoe, Stuart. Detective. E-mail correspondence with author, October 7, 2011.
13. Russo, Stephanie. "Tempe Police Identify Child's Body After 40 Years," *Arizona Republic*, August 5, 2010.
14. Sister of Wayne Clifford Roberts (name withheld upon request). E-mail correspondence with author, January 25, 2011.

15. Naday, Alexandra; Unnithan, N. Prabha; Shelley, Tara; and Hogan, Michael. "Analysis of the Cold Case Survey of Law Enforcement for the Colorado Bureau of Investigation" (Fort Collins, Colorado: Colorado State University, Center for the Study of Crime & Justice, Department of Sociology, 2009), 1.

Agency Organization: Cold Case Units

2

There are many reasons why cases go cold. Some of the most obvious include missing files, lack of evidence, overworked detectives, lack of money, few or no witnesses, or lack of cooperation between jurisdictions. Maybe the district attorney refused to file, or the case was not an easy one in the first place. In the 1950s, homicide clearance rates were high. The majority of victims knew their murderers, making perpetrators easier for police to identify. From 1960 to 1995, however, along with an increase in the use of illegal drugs, the number of murders in the United States increased dramatically. Many of these cases involved shootings where little physical evidence was left at the scene other than, possibly, shell casings. More and more victims were killed by strangers, and clearance rates plummeted.

Facing a backlog of unsolved cases, agencies began to tackle the problem by forming cold case squads, or units. Leading the way were the Miami-Dade Police Department, in Miami, Florida; the Metropolitan Police Department, in Washington, DC; and the Phoenix Police Department, in Phoenix, Arizona. (See Chapter 1, "Challenges and Checklist" for Detective Ed Reynolds's work in the Phoenix Police Department's Cold Case Unit, created in 1993.[1])

Miami-Dade Police Department's Cold Case Squad

In the early 1980s, the Miami-Dade Police Department (then called the Metro-Dade Police Department) put together an ad hoc squad composed of one sergeant and two detectives to review the unsolved murder of a 12-year-old girl. After the arrest and conviction of two individuals responsible for her murder, the team reviewed and closed several other unsolved homicides. According to the agency's website, a *Miami Herald* reporter wrote a series of articles covering the cases and referred to the team as the "Cold Case Squad," the name eventually adopted by the Homicide Bureau.[2]

Sergeant David W. Rivers took over the squad in 1988.[3] In his undated report on its formation, he wrote, "As detectives transferred in and out of the section, their cases sat open and un-worked. If a lead came in, then a detective, in rotation at the time and with cases of his own, had to first become completely familiar with the case. Secondly, as time permitted, [he had to] follow up on the information. The problem with that concept is there was never enough time." At first the squad was designed to be proactive in its choice of cases, but Rivers noted that it soon became reactive to incoming leads.[4] Whichever way a case was chosen, however, Rivers recommended the following steps in initiating a review of a cold case homicide:

- Consult with a district attorney regarding the statute of limitations.
- Locate and establish the availability of all physical evidence, and determine how advances in technology can be applied.
- Involve a prosecutor as soon as possible.
- Try to determine who has benefited the most from the death of the victim.
- Redo all background checks on suspects, subjects, witnesses, and anyone involved in the crime. Look for criminal arrests, changes in associations, and changes in personal relationships.
- Contact the victim's family and try to involve them (unless, of course, they are the suspects).
- Begin interviews with peripheral witnesses and associates.
- Before interviewing major witnesses, determine if their situations have changed, that is, in jail, on probation, or, possibly, straightened up their lives.[5]

Sergeant Rivers wrote his report after his team closed more than 100 cases. He recommended that detectives in cold case squads be left entirely alone to work on old unresolved homicides and added, "If they are constantly being put into rotation, or having to work current cases, then their effectiveness will be greatly reduced."[6]

Metropolitan Police Department's Cold Case Squad

In 1988, the same year that David Rivers became the sergeant in charge of the Metro-Dade Police Department's Cold Case Squad, the District of Columbia had the distinction of becoming the nation's murder capital (see Figure 2.1). At the time, homicides in Washington, DC spiraled to 369, a rate of 50.5 homicides per 100,000 residents.[7] As the cases piled up on the shelves of the Metropolitan Police Department (MPD), detectives found that they could not keep up with their caseloads, and many of the cases remained unsolved. Even homicides with good leads got relegated to the back burner as soon as fresh cases landed on the investigators' desks.

In 1992, the MPD and the FBI joined forces to clear the glut of unsolved homicides in the city by establishing a Cold Case Homicide Squad with six dedicated homicide detectives and one dedicated detective sergeant. Then

Figure 2.1 On April 19, 1972, U.S. President Richard M. Nixon greeted members of the Metropolitan Police Department on the White House lawn. At the time, Washington, DC's Freeway Phantom killer had strangled five of his six victims. For more on the Freeway Phantom, see Chapter 11. (Photo courtesy of the Richard Nixon Presidential Library and Museum.)

they added FBI agents experienced in violent crime investigations. In the squad's first five years, it closed 157 previously unsolved homicides.[8]

The 1980s and 1990s were an era when record-keeping was just beginning to enter the computer age. At the time, most of the records at the MPD were paper logs, but some investigators had created computer databases for specific purposes, such as attempting to link female murders. The software systems, however, had become outdated, leaving the next generation of investigators with drawers full of unreadable floppy disks. (See Chapter 10, "Historical and Geographical Context.") Then, beginning in 2004 and under the direction of now-retired MPD Detective James Trainum, the department began a systematic review of all unsolved homicides back to 1970.

"At the time, cold case reassignment was often based on the 'squeaky wheel' approach—the family who complained the most had their loved ones' cases investigated," stated Trainum in recent correspondence. "One of the main reasons for the review was to allocate resources to solvable cases. We knew that there were probably a lot of cases out there with high solvability factors, and that the victims—prostitutes, drug users, drug dealers, and the homeless and the unidentified—did not have anyone advocating for them, and we were right." Trainum also was amazed at the number of cases that had been closed by arrest but resulted in dismissals before trial, calling the revelation "law enforcement's dirty little secret." He began treating those cases as if they were open, looking at the same solvability factors there, as well.[9]

From 2004 to 2010, graduate student interns, who were trained in the basics of homicide investigation, assisted Trainum in reviewing the cases. "When the interns started, the various components of the case files, such as fingerprints, all had separate tracking numbers," Trainum stated. "One of the interns' first tasks was to identify those tracking numbers and enter at least the basic information on each homicide—date, location, victim, suspect, motive, and mode of death—into easily searchable databases. These included the Washington Area Computer Intelligence Information System (WACIIS)—the MPD's internal case management system—as well as in the Violent Criminal Apprehension Program (ViCAP)." Trainum emphasized to his team that if they could not match a new clue to a crime, then the clue was worthless.[10]

Although many of the interns stayed on as volunteers, some of the work was done by one intern in one semester, and then was worked on the next semester by another, so the databases helped to link their cases together. The databases even revealed ties between some of the victims and their killers in closed cases, to cases that were still open. Along with identifying and listing the tracking numbers, the interns also summarized the facts of their cases. "This was important because it had not been done in the past," said Trainum. "Previously, a detective new to the case had to review the entire file to find out what was going on. Now all the detectives had to do was access either WACIIS or ViCAP and review the summaries to give them an idea of what the cases were about. It saved our investigators lots of time and energy."[11]

In addition, the interns entered and summarized evidence on spreadsheets with the following information:

- Item numbers assigned by crime scene technicians
- Item numbers assigned by the lab technicians
- A brief description of the item
- A brief description of the item's origin
- Lists of results from different labs, including firearms, fingerprints, serology, and DNA

The spreadsheets also listed the tracking numbers, when available, for items at evidence control. Trainum found that detectives are usually visual people and charts can cut through all of the confusion of lab reports to show investigators exactly what was recovered and what was or was not done. "On one occasion we were able to see where the trace evidence results dovetailed in with the DNA evidence results, resulting in an arrest," he said. "The original detective had been unable to make that connection."[12]

Additional Cold Case Squads and Units

Agencies in other parts of the country, primarily in large cities, also formed cold case squads or units. In 2003, the Charlotte-Mecklenburg Police Department in Charlotte, North Carolina, started its cold case homicide unit, which consists of two full-time homicide detectives who meet monthly with a six-person volunteer Civilian Review Team, comprised of several retired FBI agents, a retired New York City police captain, and a criminal justice professor. In addition, two volunteers work directly for the cold case unit.[13] (See Chapter 13, "Volunteers and How They Can Help.") Adding to the unit's success is early and frequent communication with prosecutors, as Sergeant Rivers also indicated in his report on the Cold Case Squad in Miami. Both investigators and prosecutors understand that the prosecution of cold cases sends the message to murderers and to the families of their victims that these cases will never be forgotten.[14]

The main benefits of cold case squads or units are obvious, as they reduce the backlog of unsolved cases. They bring perpetrators to justice, take dangerous criminals off the streets, and bring resolution to the victims' families. Few agencies, however, have organized volunteers or have the staff or resources to incorporate cold case units. Some have "units of one." Two outstanding examples of individuals making a difference in their respective agencies are Investigator Cheryl Moore and Detective Ron Lopez. Investigator Moore is the only dedicated cold case investigator in the Jefferson County Sheriff's Office, in Golden, Colorado. An hour's drive south, in Colorado Springs, in the Colorado Springs Police Department, is Detective Ron Lopez. Although he has four volunteers, he is the sole dedicated sworn detective for missing persons. On the following pages are both Moore's and Lopez's profiles.

Profile: Investigator Cheryl Moore's "Unit of One" Produces Results

On March 24, 1989, sightseers on Lookout Mountain, in unincorporated Jefferson County, Colorado, found a woman's body. Seven months later, in the same geographical area, college students panning for gold in Clear Creek Canyon found the body of another woman. Both had been murdered. Also in 1989, then-22-year-old Cheryl Moore signed on as a rookie deputy with the Jefferson County Sheriff's Office, in Golden, Colorado. Little did she know at the time that cold case homicides would become her life's work.

The victim found in the canyon was identified as 28-year-old Lanell Williams, and her remains were returned to her family. The county buried the other victim in the Golden Cemetery under a modest gravestone with the inscription: "Jane Doe 1989, Known Only to God, May Her Soul Rest in Peace." No one knew who killed the women, and there was no indication that anyone even considered them related. DNA technology, at the time, was not sufficient to produce the evidence needed to determine a suspect, let alone file charges. By the time anyone carefully looked again at these murders, 16 years had passed, and the women's cases had gone cold.

Today, the solitary murderer of both women is in prison, Jane Doe has her real name on a new gravestone, and Investigator Cheryl Moore is the Jefferson County Sheriff's Office's sole Cold Case Unit, a unit of one. She is convinced that she has the ideal job, working in a position that she requested and that her supervisor gave, specifically, to her.

Moore grew up in Lakewood, Colorado, and had a cousin in law enforcement. "I always knew that being a cop was what I wanted to do," she said when meeting with the author over a cup of coffee.[15] After police academy training, Moore served in the county jail and on patrol, and in 1996 worked her way up to investigations and then to persons cases. In 2002, Moore asked her sergeant if she could work on one cold case between her normal duties. There were 50 to choose from, and she picked Melanie "Suzy" Cooley, a former Nederland, Colorado, high school senior with long dark hair. In April 1975, a road maintenance worker had found her bludgeoned body in Coal Creek Canyon. She had been beaten repeatedly over the head with a rock. "That case called to me," said Moore. "I needed it, and it needed me. I will do everything in my power on the case before I die."[16]

As Moore made progress on the still-unsolved case, she became hooked on cold case research. In 2005, and because of Moore's work, the Jefferson County Sheriff's Office created a new position, that of a dedicated cold case investigator. Moore kept her previously assigned cases (including a recent homicide and numerous sex assaults), but all of the others were dumped on her desk. "At first I was overwhelmed," she said. "The case files were in a hodgepodge of notebooks that had piled up for more than 50 years. I knew, realistically, that I couldn't work on too many at a time or I would spread myself too thin."[17]

Instead of initially setting out to sort the files, however, Moore found that the cases prioritized themselves. For instance, her research on a case from 1948 (for which there was only an autopsy report and a few photos) revealed that it had already been solved. Although Moore could cross that case off her list, she found others that rose to the top. Family members of one of the victims had recently initiated publicity, so Moore become familiar with that file so she would be ready for any new tips that might come in. The Cooley case, too, continuously nagged for her attention. (See Chapter 14 on victims and Chapter 16 on the media.)

Four of the 50 cases were unidentified bodies and they, too, received high priority. One of Moore's first tasks with the unidentified victims was to make sure that their dental records, fingerprints, DNA, and other information were entered into existing databases. Since then—in order to cover all bases—she also has been authorized by her local coroner's office to enter its data into the NamUs system. (See Chapters 6 and 7 on NamUs.) Included in the four unidentified bodies was the Jane Doe found in 1989 on Lookout Mountain. Photos of a reconstruction of the black woman's face had been circulated, and all responses were systematically eliminated. A search based on one available partial fingerprint had not produced any results. The time had come to look at the Jane Doe case again.

Moore sent Jane Doe's fingerprint to her agency's lab to be resubmitted to the Automated Fingerprint Identification System (AFIS). At the lab, a diligent technician manipulated the parameters in order to enter the fingerprint into the system in three different ways. In just four hours, in October 2005, the technician had a hit and excitedly called Moore to tell her that she had a match. The previously unidentified fingerprint had belonged to a woman named Lisa Kay Kelly. The victim, determined to have been 33 years old when she was murdered, had been fingerprinted following arrests for shoplifting and prostitution.

"We used good old-fashioned police work to identify Kelly," said Moore, who demonstrated that she would rather "think outside the box" than prioritize cases based solely on DNA evidence.[18] The victim's identity then opened up new possibilities in investigating her murder. As Moore worked on the Kelly case, she began to see similarities in the circumstances of Kelly's murder and that of Lanell Williams, the other woman whose body had been found the same year. As was Kelly, Williams was also black, they were of similar age, and both had been involved with crack cocaine.

Moore submitted clothing and other items found with Kelly and Williams to the Colorado Bureau of Investigation (CBI) for DNA analysis. Kelly's had little to no physical evidence and did not produce results, but Williams's came back with matches to Billy Edwin Reid. His criminal record showed that in 1987 he had been paroled to Colorado on a Kansas sex assault case. Subsequently, he was rearrested for various offenses, but his DNA profile did not get into the Combined DNA Index System (CODIS) database until 2002, when he was released from prison in Kansas. In May 2006, Moore was ready to arrest Reid for the murder of Williams when Reid was pulled in on a traffic warrant in Denver. Moore then questioned him about both Williams and Kelly. Reid denied even knowing them, but in the Denver County Jail, he began talking with a fellow inmate who took detailed notes. Eventually, those notes, along with Reid's own writings, played a key role in getting him off the streets for good.

Also in 2006, the Colorado Homicide Investigators Association (CoHIA) named Moore its "Investigator of the Year." According to the association's website, the award was established to "recognize those individuals who have demonstrated excellent performance, outstanding talent, tenacity, dedication, and professionalism in the pursuit of homicide investigations." Moore's colleagues were in agreement that her cold case unit of one was producing results. While she was receiving recognition on the job, however, Moore, a cop's wife and the mother of two teenagers, continued to juggle family and career, a balancing act that she states was, and still is, stressful.

From 2006 to 2008, Moore and the prosecution team from the Jefferson County District Attorney's Office built their case against Reid.[19] In September 2008, he was convicted of first degree murder after deliberation, first degree murder—felony murder, and first degree sexual assault in the murders of both Williams and Kelly, reducing Moore's caseload. Reid also was linked to the murder of a third woman, in Denver, although no additional charges were filed. His sentencing followed, three months later, with grateful members of all three families in attendance. "These are as tough as it gets," District Attorney Scott Storey of Colorado's First Judicial District told a *Denver Post* reporter, in 2008. "The bottom line is that without Jefferson County Sheriff's Cold Case Unit, we would never have brought justice to the families of these two young women."[20] See Figures 2.2 and 2.3.

Figure 2.2 Investigator Cheryl Moore, of the Jefferson County Sheriff's Office, reflects on Lisa Kay Kelly's life and death while visiting the murder victim's grave in the Golden Cemetery, in Golden, Colorado. (Photo by author.)

Figure 2.3 A Jane Doe from 1989 to 2005, Lisa Kay Kelly now has her name on her grave, along with the inscription, "Never Lost, Always Loved." (Photo by author.)

Profile: Detective Ron Lopez's Proactive Investigations Pay Off

Detective Ron Lopez is the only sworn detective in the Homicide/Missing Persons Unit of the Colorado Springs Police Department. The city of approximately 416,000 people, which lies at the foot of Pikes Peak and is the home of the U.S. Air Force Academy, is the second-largest city, in population, in the state of Colorado. Lopez comes in early to his windowless office, where he sifts through messages and prioritizes his work for the day. His job requires him to handle the cases of suspicious missing persons immediately, that is, the ones who are injured or suicidal, as well as any cases that involve foul play. (See Figures 2.4 and 2.5.)

Then, Lopez goes to work where his passion lies: on the cold cases of missing persons. The people are real to him, and he often looks at their photographs. "I was meant to be a cop," he said in a recent interview. "I was always sticking up for the underdog. The victims—that's what it's all about. I really believe God put me in this position, and He's utilizing my skills to help people."[21]

Lopez's initial career plans, however, did not include law enforcement. The Florence, Colorado, native attended the University of Southern Colorado and started with a major in business management. While still in school, he worked as a night clerk in a local grocery store where he witnessed a break-in by a burglar doing "smash and grabs." Lopez chased him and caught him. That incident alone was enough to make Lopez change his major and his life. In 1981, at the age of 25, he joined the Colorado Springs Police Department. For nearly three decades, he

Figure 2.4 Detective Ron Lopez rolls up his sleeves and gets to work at the Colorado Springs Police Department, where he takes a proactive approach to cold missing persons cases. (Photo by author.)

Figure 2.5 Although Detective Lopez handles the Homicide/Missing Persons Unit of the Colorado Springs Police Department, the agency's Cold Case Squad is currently responsible for approximately 90 unsolved homicide cases dating back to 1949. (Photo by author.)

served as a patrol officer, then worked on a SWAT team that was part of a task force that apprehended automobile thieves. Later he worked in the department's fugitive and homicide units.

In August 2008, however, Lopez was put in charge of missing persons and now has a team of four volunteers who assist him. He is convinced that he is in the job he needs to be doing and he also has the track record to prove it, having started with a big backlog and clearing approximately 45 to 50 (three years and older) cases per year. The position was Lopez's idea, but his boss, Sergeant Charles Rabideau, jokes that the detective's work makes him look good.

Lopez's first objective in working a cold missing persons case is to determine if the person is dead or alive. If the person is alive, Lopez usually finds him or her. He checks law enforcement investigative systems such as Clear or TLO to make sure he has the person's correct date of birth and Social Security number. Then he calls his local contact in the Social Security Administration to see if there is any record of activity on the missing person's Social Security number. Lopez also asks the Colorado Department of Labor and Employment to search for both local and national activity in a wage-earner's contribution to workers' compensation. And he contacts utility companies to check on listed names on utility payments. He has had good luck, too, by searching computerized visitation records from the county jail.

Approximately 60 to 70% of the time, however, a former missing person will tell him that he or she did not want to be found and does not want his or her contact information released. Lopez respects the person's wishes and then explains to the reporting party that their missing person is alive but does not want to be contacted. That knowledge, alone, often provides the resolution that the family member had been seeking. Several of those who *did* want to be found have called or e-mailed Lopez to express their gratitude.

In the cases of missing persons not likely to be alive, Lopez turns to the federally funded NamUs system—dual databases that match missing persons with unidentified remains. He is an adamant supporter of the online databases and credits them with his success in clearing many of his cases. "If we had, earlier, the technology that we have now," he adds, "we wouldn't have a backlog of cold homicides and cold missing persons cases."[22] Because of his interest in missing persons, Lopez was one of five representatives from his state who completed a nationally run training academy to learn about and encourage others to use the system. But, even before the classes, he learned on his own to enter, search, and archive cases. (See Chapters 6 and 7.)

When entering cases, Lopez asks the reporting parties for aliases, as well as everything the families know about their missing persons that will make their cases more complete. He also tells family members to go to the site www.namus.gov themselves, to add any additional details, such as scars, tattoos, and types of jewelry that their missing person may have worn. With law enforcement access, the computerized missing persons cases, once entered, start generating possible matches. Lopez often eats his lunch at his desk, and, when he does, he pulls up missing persons' reports on NamUs and searches through the possible matches for images and descriptions that are similar to the people he hopes to find. When he does find a possible match, he contacts family members and asks their help in obtaining the missing person's dental records. He posts the records online, and runs them by NamUs's free consulting odontologist for comparisons to dental records of unidentified remains.

Many agencies treat suspicious missing persons and undetermined (but suspicious) death cases differently from homicides. They do not track them or maintain the documentation in the same way, which becomes a major problem when new clues come in down the road. Similarly, most law enforcement investigators limit their work with NamUs to entering the cases of missing persons and searching for their remains. Lopez, however, takes a proactive approach. He considers each current runaway or missing person a potential homicide, so, even when he solves a case, he enters—and then archives—that person's information into the database.

"We need to put *every* case into NamUs, even if the person is found, as he or she could turn up missing again," he said, stressing the need to keep his NamUs regional administrator (and also the National Center for Missing and Exploited Children, NCMEC, if under age 18) informed that he is archiving his cases. "Missing persons may be suicidal, and/or have health or mental issues. If a previously missing person goes missing again, all I have to do is reactivate the report." With obvious compassion for the victims, Lopez added, "We want to find the missing before they get harmed or harm themselves." And what is his advice for other detectives and investigators? "Never give up," he said. "Don't let the cases go cold in the first place."[23]

Current Practices and Good Investigators

In 2011, the Rand Corporation surveyed 1,051 law enforcement agencies nationwide (out of 5,000 surveys mailed) for its report, *Cold Case Investigations: An Analysis of Current Practices and Factors Associated with Successful Outcomes.* Its authors found that, at the time, 20% of the agencies had a protocol for initiating cold case investigations: either assigning cold cases to the original lead investigator or assigning the cases to detectives as part of their regular workload. An additional 10% had dedicated cold case investigators (such as Investigator Cheryl Moore and Detective Ron Lopez), and only 7% had a formal cold case unit.[24] As to funding, 20% of these squads or units were funded through established line items in the agencies' budgets, and a majority were made possible with grants or supplemental agency funds.[25]

The Rand Report found that systematic screening of cases for their investigative potential was most likely to occur when homicide units looked for ways to increase their clearance rates by identifying cold cases that could be cleared exceptionally.[26] Prioritization of cases, however, varied by agency. The Metropolitan Police Department reported that its cold case unit of 12 homicide investigators and one supervisor reviews 60–70 unsolved cases per year, all 36 months and older, based on the following criteria:

- Whether a suspect has been identified or could potentially be identified through DNA or fingerprint evidence left at the crime scene
- Whether eyewitnesses have been identified or a previously uncooperative witness has had a change of heart
- Whether potentially probative evidence exists that might be retested with advances in technology[27]

Reasons to reopen cold cases at the Dallas Police Department include:

- A family member or friend of the victim comes forward with new specific information either not revealed previously or that was recently obtained
- A witness contacts the department with new or previously withheld information
- An outside party contacts the department with information regarding an admission of guilt[28]

At the Baltimore Police Department, its Cold Case Unit reviews unsolved cases for potential epithelial or other DNA that can be submitted for laboratory analysis. It begins its cold case investigations when:

- New information is received on a case either from a witness or from a CODIS hit
- Detectives working new homicides become overloaded
- The department receives Maryland Public Information requests (usually made by the Innocence Project)
- New trials are ordered for cases as a result of a successful appeal[29]

When cases were cleared in the Metropolitan, Dallas, and Baltimore departments, the main reason was "new information from witnesses or information from new witnesses."[30] This was the same conclusion drawn by the Colorado State University report, as well as the resolution of the murder of Surette Clark and identification of "Little Jane Doe." (See Chapter 1.) It also was the conclusion of Sergeant Rivers's remarks in his report on the Metro-Dade (Miami-Dade) Police Department. Rivers wrote, "In virtually all of the cases closed by the Metro-Dade Cold Case Squad, the offender told at least one person about his/her involvement. Locating these witnesses can provide the final element for an arrest and ultimate conviction."[31]

Also, as indicated in the Rand Corporation's report, the majority of the country's police departments and sheriff's offices have investigators who work cold cases in addition to their regular assignments. The same is true in Colorado. According to the Colorado State University report, when the agencies were asked if they had a unit or squad that specialized in unresolved (cold case) homicide investigations, only nine of the 228 responding agencies stated that they had.[32]

As expected, two of these cold case homicide units are in the police departments of the state's largest cities: Denver and Colorado Springs. The Denver Police Department's Cold Case Unit was started in 2004 to evaluate unsolved cases within two specific units—sex crimes and homicides—that had a probability of being solved with DNA. Denver's unit currently employs eight detectives, one sergeant, and a Victim's Assistance Unit Cold Case Coordinator. (See Chapter 14.) The Colorado Springs Police Department, in addition to Ron Lopez's Missing Persons Unit, has a Cold Case Unit with one sworn investigator, six volunteers, and five special investigators. Four of the five are paid with a grant. All of the special investigators are retired cops with backgrounds in homicide investigations.

New leads and new investigative tools can bring about much-needed breaks in cold cases, but good investigators start by learning everything they can about their cases, whether they are homicides, missing persons, or unidentified remains. Review of existing materials includes patrol reports, detective notes, laboratory documents, photographs, crime scene diagrams, witness lists, lead sheets, and suspect information. Any or all of these materials are likely to bring up challenges or create questions. Was the original investigation thorough? Does the evidence still exist? Did the original investigator fail to return a telephone call or interview a witness? Are there new leads to follow?

In addition, investigators use their people-searching skills to update the contact information on their victims or co-victims, suspects, and witnesses. Have they moved, or have women married or divorced and changed their names? Are they still alive, and could they be found to reinterview and, if necessary, to put on the witness stand? Investigators have found that it helps to develop a case management system or database that allows one to enter all of the pertinent information in a searchable format. (See Chapter 5, on "ViCAP, the Violent Criminal Apprehension

Program," as well as Chapter 13, for an explanation of how this is handled in the Cold Case Unit of the New Hampshire Department of Justice, Office of Attorney General.)

Many years ago, the author interviewed a then-elderly physician who had, during his career, made house calls. Whenever the physician visited patients in their homes, he told me that he always excused himself to use the bathroom. While there, he carefully inspected the contents of his patients' medicine cabinets. Was the doctor being snoopy, or was he doing his job? The physician told me that he learned a lot about his patients in their bathrooms and considered his behavior a legitimate part of determining what kind of care they needed.

Although the above-referenced physician may not have analyzed his own situation, his curiosity and inquisitiveness would have made him a good cold case investigator. Whether the process of reviewing cold cases is undertaken by a cold case unit, a single dedicated cold case investigator, or investigators who have to drop their research every time someone commits a new crime, they all need to share the same skills. In addition to the curiosity of the visiting doctor, a good cold case investigator:

- Has a passion for his or her work
- Is persistent and highly motivated
- Keeps an open mind and is nonjudgmental
- Is patient, detail-oriented, and tenacious
- Is creative, an independent thinker, and uses deductive reasoning
- Is discreet and keeps information confidential
- Is skilled in conducting interviews
- Has strong research skills
- Is proactive and keeps up to date with developing trends and investigative tools

In the chapters that follow, the reader is acquainted with the latest online investigative systems (including TLO), tackles a whole battery of databases, further explores the revolutionary missing and unidentified persons databases of the NamUs System, and brushes up on historical and geographical context. Additional topics include techniques for researching newspapers as well as published and public records, exploring the plight of the missing and unidentified, and learning about the use of volunteers, contacts with co-victims, cold case review teams, information-sharing resources, and taking advantage of the media.

Summary

Resources in this chapter include:

- Descriptions of formations of cold case squads/units, with current examples of law enforcement at work
- Current practices for reopening cold cases
- Qualities of a good cold case investigator

Murders increased dramatically between 1960 and 1995. Facing a backlog of unsolved cases, agencies began to tackle the problem by forming cold case squads, or units. Leading the way were the Metro-Dade (now Miami-Dade) Police Department in Miami, Florida; the Metropolitan Police Department in Washington, DC; and the Phoenix Police Department in Phoenix, Arizona.

- Investigator Cheryl Moore's "Unit of One," at the Jefferson County Sheriff's Office, in Golden, Colorado, identified a Jane Doe and brought justice to her and to another victim, both murdered by the same man.
- Detective Ron Lopez, the only sworn officer in the Homicide/Missing Persons Unit of the Colorado Springs Police Department, proactively tackles and solves cold missing persons cases.
- According to recent surveys by the Rand Corporation and by Colorado State University, the main reason for clearing cold case homicides was new information from witnesses or information from new witnesses.
- A good cold case investigator has a passion for his or her work; is persistent and highly motivated; keeps an open mind and is non-judgmental; is patient, detail-oriented, and tenacious; is creative, an independent thinker, and uses deductive reasoning; is discreet and keeps information confidential; is skilled in conducting interviews; has strong research skills; and is proactive and keeps up to date with developing trends and investigative tools.

Endnotes

1. Jackson, Steve. *No Stone Unturned: The True Story of NecroSearch International, the World's Premier Forenisc Investigators* (New York: Kensington Books, 2002), 203.
2. Miami-Dade Police Department, www.miamidade.gov/mdpd (accessed December 26, 2011).
3. Baez, Javier. E-mail correspondence with author, October 4, 2011.

4. Rivers, David W. Sergeant. "Cold Case Squads" (unpublished and undated report, Metro-Dade Police Department, circa 1988–1997, p. 2).
5. Rivers, David W. Sergeant. "Cold Case Squads" (unpublished and undated report, Metro-Dade Police Department, circa 1988–1997, pp. 5–6).
6. Rivers, David W. Sergeant. "Cold Case Squads," (unpublished and undated report, Metro-Dade Police Department, circa 1988–1997, p. 8).
7. Regini, Charles L. "The Cold Case Concept," *FBI Law Enforcement Bulletin* (August 1997), 1.
8. Regini, Charles L. "The Cold Case Concept," *FBI Law Enforcement Bulletin* (August 1997), 4.
9. Trainum, James. Detective. E-mail correspondence with author, September 8, 2011.
10. Trainum, James. Detective. E-mail correspondence with author, September 8, 2011.
11. Trainum, James. Detective. E-mail correspondence with author, September 8, 2011.
12. Trainum, James. Detective. E-mail correspondence with author, September 8, 2011.
13. Furr, Stephen. Detective. E-mail correspondence with author, October 17, 2011. Also, Charlotte-Mecklenburg Police Department, Homicide Cold Case Unit, http://charmeck.org/city/charlotte/CMPD/organization/investigative/ViolentCrimes/Homicide/ColdCase/Pages/home.aspx (accessed December 26, 2011).
14. Lord, Vivian B. "Implementing a Cold Case Homicide Unit: A Challenging Task," *FBI Law Enforcement Bulletin* (74: 2, February 2005), 5.
15. Moore, Cheryl. Investigator. Interview with author, February 14, 2011.
16. Moore, Cheryl. Investigator. Interview with author, February 14, 2011.
17. Moore, Cheryl. Investigator. Interview with author, February 14, 2011.
18. Moore, Cheryl. Investigator. Interview with author, February 14, 2011.
19. Lindsay, Sue. "Jeffco Investigator Brings Drive to Job of Solving Cold Cases," *Rocky Mountain News*, January 26, 2009.
20. "Serial Killer Sentenced for Killing 2 Women," *TheDenverChannel.com*, December 11, 2008.
21. Lopez, Ron. Detective. Interview with author, June 13, 2011.
22. Lopez, Ron. Detective. Interview with author, June 13, 2011.
23. Lopez, Ron. Detective. Interview with author, June 13, 2011.
24. Davis, Robert C.; Jensen, Carl; and Kitchens, Karin E. *Cold Case Investigations: An Analysis of Current Practices and Factors Associated with Successful Outcomes* (Arlington, VA: Rand Center on Quality Policing, 2011), xi, 11–12.
25. Davis, Robert C.; Jensen, Carl; and Kitchens, Karin E. *Cold Case Investigations: An Analysis of Current Practices and Factors Associated with Successful Outcomes* (Arlington, VA: Rand Center on Quality Policing, 2011), 43.
26. Davis, Robert C.; Jensen, Carl; and Kitchens, Karin E. *Cold Case Investigations: An Analysis of Current Practices and Factors Associated with Successful Outcomes* (Arlington, VA: Rand Center on Quality Policing, 2011), 43.
27. Davis, Robert C.; Jensen, Carl; and Kitchens, Karin E. *Cold Case Investigations: An Analysis of Current Practices and Factors Associated with Successful Outcomes* (Arlington, VA: Rand Center on Quality Policing, 2011), 20.

28. Davis, Robert C.; Jensen, Carl; and Kitchens, Karin E. *Cold Case Investigations: An Analysis of Current Practices and Factors Associated with Successful Outcomes* (Arlington, VA: Rand Center on Quality Policing, 2011), 21.
29. Davis, Robert C.; Jensen, Carl; and Kitchens, Karin E. *Cold Case Investigations: An Analysis of Current Practices and Factors Associated with Successful Outcomes* (Arlington, VA: Rand Center on Quality Policing, 2011), 21.
30. Davis, Robert C.; Jensen, Carl; and Kitchens, Karin E. *Cold Case Investigations: An Analysis of Current Practices and Factors Associated with Successful Outcomes* (Arlington, VA: Rand Center on Quality Policing, 2011), 33.
31. Rivers, David W. Sergeant. "Cold Case Squads," (unpublished and undated report, circa 1988–1997, Metro-Dade Police Department, p. 4).
32. Naday, Alexandra; Unnithan, N. Prabha; Shelley, Tara; and Hogan, Michael. "Analysis of the Cold Case Survey of Law Enforcement for the Colorado Bureau of Investigation" (Fort Collins, CO: Colorado State University, Center for the Study of Crime & Justice, Department of Sociology, 2009), 1.

TLO: The Latest Online Investigative System

3

One of the most important components of a cold case investigation is searching for people—including suspects, fugitives, and witnesses—as well as those persons' relatives and associates. No matter how organized the case file, usually some amount of work needs to be completed on the front end. And, as indicated in the preceding chapters, a change in a relationship (such as a jilted girlfriend) may provide the investigator with much new information. Finding these people, however, can be a daunting task. They move, get married, get divorced, marry again, a lot of women change their names, and some of the subjects of one's searches may already be deceased.

The good news is, with each advancement in the Internet age, it is getting easier and easier to trace electronic "paper trails," and investigators today have at their fingertips the best possible tools. In 2010, when the Florida-based company, TLO ("The Last One"), went live with its product, TLOxp®, the new online investigative system quickly became well accepted by clients all over the country. Subscribers pay for the service, but there is no charge to law enforcement agencies in the United States. (When people searching, also see Chapter 4, and see obituaries in Chapter 11, and social media in Chapter 16.)

Profile: TLO Revolutionizes Investigations in Rural Illinois Agencies

Nearly all law-enforcement agencies operate on tight budgets, but small rural agencies feel the crunch the most. Examples include the police departments in Hutsonville and Robinson, small towns in east-central Illinois. Hutsonville, a town of approximately 600 people with a police force of five sworn part-time officers, lies on the Wabash River, along the state's border with Indiana.

Robinson, 10 miles to the southwest, and county seat of Crawford County, is 10 times larger and has 13 sworn officers. The majority of the area's crimes are thefts and burglaries. In January 2011, Chad Weaver (see Figure 3.1), part-time chief at Hutsonville and school resource officer in Robinson, signed on to TLOxp. After his first success of apprehending a child pornographer, Weaver became an ardent supporter. Since then, the free and far-reaching online investigative system has revolutionized the way his departments track down offenders.

"Our current success began essentially with me testing the abilities of the system," said Weaver, in e-mail correspondence with the

Figure 3.1 Part-time Chief and School Resource Officer Chad Weaver, who works for both the Hutsonville and Robinson Police Departments, is shown at his desk at the Robinson Police Department, in Robinson, Illinois. Weaver's success with TLOxp has inspired him to bring more fugitives to justice. (Photo courtesy of Chad Weaver.)

author. "I began by looking at our Crime Stoppers USA most wanted list. There I located a Robinson Police Department case from 2008—that of Edward Foltz, wanted for six counts of production and possession of child pornography with a bond of $50,000. Foltz had been investigated for photographing underage girls, with the photos beginning with the girls clothed, and as time went on the girls were less and less clothed. By the time we found this out he had photographed underage girls in bondage, indicating a clear escalation of seriousness of his crimes."[1]

"Once discovered, Foltz vanished. He had not even been charged, but he knew there would soon be a warrant for his arrest," Weaver continued. Rumors had placed him living with his sister in Texas. Weaver used his new investigative tool, primarily the people search function of TLOxp, for a fresh look and found a new and recent address in Nashville, Tennessee. Weaver attempted to verify the address by checking Department of Motor Vehicle (DMV) records for vehicles or drivers' licenses, but he was unable, through his traditional sources, to locate any information more recent than he previously had found. "I then contacted Detective Anthony Brooks with the Fugitive Division of the Metro-Nashville Police Department and provided him with all of the information I had obtained from TLOxp," said Weaver. "The very next day, Detective Brooks informed me they had arrested Foltz on our warrant. I was absolutely ecstatic! I'm fully confident that without TLOxp this man would have been on the streets for years to come."[2]

Prior to using TLOxp, the Hutsonville and Robinson Police Departments rarely conducted Internet searches and were not likely to turn up anything substantial when they did. Available to them, if needed, however, were the services of the Mid-States Organized Crime Information Center (MOCIC) and the Illinois Statewide Terrorism Intelligence Center (STIC). (See Chapter 15 for more on MOCIC, under a discussion of RISS, the Regional Information Sharing System.)

The few times the Hutsonville and Robinson departments did searches on their own, they typically used publicly accessible and free people search engines, including Intelius, AnyWho, and Google. ACCURINT® for Law Enforcement, Consolidated Lead Evaluation and Reporting (CLEAR), and other subscription-only websites used on a daily basis by many of the larger law enforcement agencies were out of reach of the small-town officials. In fact, admitted Weaver, until he signed on to TLOxp, he had never even heard of them.

Chief Weaver first learned about TLOxp from the regional planning coordinator for the Illinois Law Enforcement Alarm System (ILEAS), Illinois's statewide law enforcement mutual aid agency. ILEAS is made up of officers from all over Illinois and provides law enforcement aid on a scale that is otherwise unattainable or would take an unacceptable amount of time to locate. "The ILEAS coordinator sent me an e-mail regarding TLOxp and its invaluable resources at the convenient cost of free," stated Chief Weaver. "I subsequently registered Hutsonville to 'test the waters' before showing it to the Robinson chief. I was duly impressed."[3] Since then, the Crawford County Sheriff's Office has signed up as well.

"We have primarily been using the people search function of TLOxp, however, in our brief history I have ventured into the 411+ and vehicles," added Weaver. "Two notes of interest in those areas are the ability to search for cell phone information and the ability to search a partial license plate. We are frequently faced with a partial license plate from witness statements. While the Secretary of State has always been great to work with, having the ability in-house to search partial plates is a great tool."[4] In April 2011, three months after the Robinson Police Department signed on to TLOxp, Foltz pled guilty to child pornography charges and was sentenced to 10 years in prison.[5]

"As a result of the success of the Foltz case, there are several officers on the Robinson Police Department who have developed a strong interest in bringing more fugitives to justice," stated Weaver, only a few weeks after getting started with TLOxp. "Two other officers and myself formed an ad hoc fugitive division. In between answering calls, we are taking a new look at several old warrants. We have about 50, and each of us takes one or two and conducts an investigation until we locate the suspect or reach a dead end."[6]

"We've literally reached a dead end with three of the warrants, as we learned from TLOxp that the wanted suspects were deceased," Weaver added. "We have also located several that are outside of the extradition limits. Some of these are too far away in relation to the charges and we've closed them that way. Others with more significant charges or those which are closer to Illinois we take to the State Attorney's Office to get extradition changed to include their current location. TLOxp will be the centerpiece in these investigations and will, no doubt, be instrumental in bringing in more criminals."[7]

TLO's Beginnings

In the small towns of Hutsonville and Robinson, Illinois, law-enforcement access to TLO's product, TLOxp, has revolutionized the way these agencies conduct their investigations. For larger police departments and sheriffs' offices that routinely budget hundreds of dollars per month for paid-subscription sites, the powerful online research system is a welcome investigative tool. Among other types of information, it includes vast amounts of demographic, business, public record, criminal, and licensing data, all gathered from courthouses and news and Internet sources, as well as data purchased from data suppliers. For all that TLO does and buys to feed its enormous knowledge engine, investigators reap the rewards, all at no cost to law enforcement.

New data are continuously being added, and they are accessible anywhere an approved user has Internet access. According to CEO Ken Hunter, in early 2011 when the Hutsonville and Robinson police departments signed on to TLOxp, only 1% of the expected data were entered into the system. In subsequent correspondence with the author, Hunter acknowledged a statistic such as that can be misleading. "Since then, massive amounts of data have been added every day," he stated.

> The reality is we will never be finished gathering, loading, expanding, and refreshing the almost limitless number of sources and infinite bits of data that we will be including in our knowledge engine. Each day our data is different and has increased and, hopefully, is more accurate, more current, and more complete. Investigators should never stop checking to see if a new bit of knowledge provides the missing clue, the missing link, or the missing puzzle piece—especially in an important cold case![8]

Because use of TLOxp by law enforcement in the United States is free, even for unlimited comprehensive reports, some of the newly signed-on users question whether there is a catch. What they need to understand, however, is that TLO founder, Hank Asher, is dedicated to making the world a safer place by creating technologies, systems, and tools that protect children, people, companies, and countries from risk, fraud, and theft. In order to keep TLOxp free to law enforcement, the company charges its other subscribers, including licensed private investigators, insurance companies, financial services, attorneys, law firms, the collections industry, fraud and asset recovery operations, and large corporations.[9]

In agreement with Asher's philosophy is co-founder John Walsh, both shown in Figure 3.2. In 1981, Walsh's 6-year-old son Adam Walsh was abducted from a Florida shopping mall and then found brutally murdered. Most television viewers are familiar with Walsh's long-running show, "America's Most Wanted." Speaking of TLOxp in a promotional video, Walsh stated, "This has been mine and Hank Asher's dream for years—that the private sector could be part of the solution." Walsh added, "New types of crime and threats are emerging faster than solutions. TLO is committed to change this. We're in the process of building the largest most powerful database in the entire world. It's going to be much less safe to be dangerous."[10]

Based in Boca Raton, Florida, the private company is located in an impressive, technology-rich and security-savvy 143,000-finished-square-foot

Figure 3.2 Hank Asher, left, and John Walsh, right, are co-founders of TLO. (Photo courtesy of TLO.)

Figure 3.3 TLO's sign—complete with lightning in a bottle—marks the company's front entrance in Boca Raton, Florida. (Photo courtesy of TLO.)

facility (Figure 3.3) which at one point in its history housed the development of International Business Machines' (IBM's) original personal computer product. Remodeled individual and group offices are modern, open, and airy. Computer screens are huge, security is tight, lunch is catered, and all women receive bouquets of fresh flowers on their desks once a week.

"Hank Asher has assembled a world-class team of computer programmers from throughout the world," stated CEO Ken Hunter. "Additionally, more than 5% of the TLO employees have prior law enforcement backgrounds; including multiple federal, state, and local agencies, as well as two former Attorneys General, a judge, a sheriff, and a police computer forensic examiner. Some of these former law enforcement officials have extensive experience in high-tech online investigations."[11] Supplementing this law enforcement expertise among TLO employees is a team of active federal, state, and local investigators, forensic analysts, and prosecutors who work in a separate secure facility at TLO using online investigative tools provided by TLO to solve current cases (see Figure 3.4). This has been characterized at TLO as a "living laboratory," where the members' suggestions lead to continuous improvements in TLOxp and other online investigative tools for the benefit of all users.

The company's philosophy sets the framework for its day-to-day operations. No one counts sick days. Instead, employees who are ill are simply told to stay home. Medical deductibles not covered by the company's insurance plan are personally covered by founder Hank Asher. Similarly, TLO does not even keep track of vacation days. Instead, as CEO Hunter explains, "Employees assure that they get their work done and advise us when they need to be absent and how to reach them, if need be."[12]

Figure 3.4 Deputies Debi Phillips (sitting) and Tina Bolton (standing), from the Palm Beach County Sheriff's Office, work in the secure law enforcement area at TLO, where they access specific sophisticated software that helps them identify criminals in their jurisdiction. (Photo courtesy of TLO.)

Framed, on the wall, is the complete *TLO Human Resources Manual*, which states:

- Bring your God-given common sense to work, and use it.
- We are a tribe. Check your ego at the door.
- Don't come to work contagious. Broken limbs are fine.
- We will set the gold standard in corporate citizenship.
- We will do well by doing good . . . together.

Behind the scenes of this upbeat and progressive work environment, however, lies a serious commitment to fighting crime, in particular, the apprehension and arrest of child predators. "TLO provides very sophisticated, specialized software to law enforcement officials in much of the world to hunt those who prey on children," stated Hunter. "This online investigative tool has led to the rescue of hundreds of children." After the Internet came into public use, the already unmanageable problem of child pornography became a global pandemic where digital files could be shared in seconds and detection and prevention became many orders of magnitude more difficult. Then, when law enforcement cracked down on those who used credit cards to pay for it, the estimated 4% of adults addicted to viewing child pornography created a market in trading pornographic videos of sexual acts with children.[13]

Part of TLO's facility is also dedicated to the National Center for Missing and Exploited Children (NCMEC), the quasi-government agency that uses massive amounts of data to help law enforcement authorities track down abducted children. Asher has given the agency longtime access to his systems and, in return, he said he received "a payback for the soul."[14] (For more on NCMEC, see Chapter 15.)

Hank Asher is a self-made millionaire who taught himself programming and formed two stand-alone companies that attained a combined capitalization of $1.5 billion. First was Database Technologies (DBT) and then, in 1998, he founded Seisint, Inc., which offered his product called ACCURINT for Law Enforcement. These two data integration/management companies, DBT and Seisint, Inc., revolutionized the way public and private sectors locate and investigate individuals and businesses.[15] In 2004, Asher sold Seisint, Inc. to LexisNexis, Inc. for $775 million.[16] The sale included a five-year noncompete clause. In 2009, after Asher was legally free to compete, he started TLO.[17]

Many of TLO's data go back to the mid-1980s, or even many years before, although data from earlier time periods are less consistently available in computer form. "TLO is continually building its knowledge engine by acquiring data from a nearly unlimited number of sources, and applying its very proprietary know-how to fuse it to build knowledge and insight about people, businesses, locations and their many, many interrelationships," stated TLO's COO, Steve Racioppo. "As TLO continues to expand its knowledge base, particularly with more and more historical data, TLOxp will be even more powerful for use by investigators working on cold cases—identifying new leads and new directions from old data through the new connections and linkages that may not have previously been known or uncovered."[18] And, as John Walsh has proclaimed, "If you liked what Hank Asher did before, you'll love TLOxp. It's lightning in a bottle."[19]

TLOxp User Tips

As good as TLOxp's search capabilities and functionalities are, they are only as good as knowing how to use the system. To gain its full advantage, authorized users can read online User Tips, refer to the information buttons next to entry fields, and contact TLO's Customer and Tech Support (available around the clock by telephone, live chat, and e-mail). In addition, there are many e-training videos available for each search module that provide good overviews on the search functionalities and results, and they show the system's many tricks and hidden features. No database of public information can be 100% accurate, 100% of the time, but familiarity will yield the most accurate results. As in all people searches, the best way to get familiar with the system is to look up oneself. If there are any errors in an investigator's own information, he or she will be alerted to look for similar discrepancies when searching for other people.

After log-in, TLOxp will open to the Main Page, where users will find all of the available search modules. At the time of this writing, there are five search categories:

- People (including Advanced and Expert Searches, as well as Comprehensive Reports)
- Business Plus
- Criminal Records
- Courts
- Assets

Each of these search categories contains several different search modules that provide the ability to search for very specific information including phone numbers, e-mail and property addresses, and complete profiles of subjects and businesses.[20]

People Search Category, Advanced Searches for People

With this search, investigators will find in-depth information on their subjects including aliases and maiden names, complete address histories, possible relatives, telephone numbers, and e-mail addresses. A popular feature is the Relationship Diagram, which visualizes the subjects' connections to relatives and associates, as well as the relationships between those relatives and associates. Subjects can be found by searching with full or partial Social Security numbers, name and location information (both former and current), names and dates of birth or approximate ages, telephone numbers, e-mails, or by addresses. (For an explanation of how Social Security numbers are, and were, issued, see Chapter 4.)

People Search Category, Expert Searches for People

Expert searches offer the option to find subjects and their relationships by entering multiple names, dates of birth, ages or age ranges, states or cities, street names, communities or buildings, approximate locations, and names of relatives or associates. For instance, users may be able to find a subject by only entering a first name, an age range, and a first name of a relative, simply by knowing that the subject has a current or past address within a certain radius from a specific city. The combinations and capabilities are limitless. For example:

- Search with the first and last names of two subjects to see a list of all individuals who are related to, or associated with, both subjects, including the subjects themselves.

- Or, enter the first and last name of one subject with the first names of two other subjects to find individuals and their relationships.
- Enter a name and a series of zip codes to find lists of all subjects who live or have lived in all of the listed zip codes.
- Enter two communities and find people who have lived, or currently live, in both communities.

People Search Category, Comprehensive Reports

Also very helpful to investigators are Comprehensive Reports (accessible through any of the people-search screens), which include the following icons:

- Checkmark: Means a confirmed address, that is, one with an active landline telephone belonging to the subject or to a member of the subject's family.
- "D": Is displayed next to the name of a deceased person.
- Mapping: Is an icon that opens to a window containing a map of the address location. The map will show all of the subjects' address locations.
- Social Network: Is an icon next to e-mail addresses that display profiles from social networks.
- Shared Address: Is an icon that shows an address shared with another individual.

Once a search subject is found, the Comprehensive Report provides in-depth information about that individual, all in one place. The report also is fully customizable and can be exported into different file formats. As TLO is constantly adding new data to its system, the Comprehensive Report continues to expand its area of coverage. Subject information in the Comprehensive Report includes:

- Address summary
- Arrest history, likely and possible
- Associates, likely
- Bankruptcy history
- Cities and counties histories
- Criminal search
- Driver's license information
- E-mail addresses
- Employers, possible
- Evictions
- Florida accidents
- Hunting permits
- Judgments
- Liens

- Neighbors' telephones
- Photographs, potential subject
- Pilot licenses, also aircraft records
- Professional affiliations (may include photographs)
- Professional licenses (may include photographs)
- Property deeds (past and current), foreclosures, and assessments
- Relatives, possible
- Sex offender registrations, possible
- Telephones (landlines and cell phones)
- Trademark records
- Uniform Commercial Code (UCC) filings
- United States (U.S.) business and corporate affiliations
- Vehicle information, past and current
- Voter registrations
- Warrant history, possible
- Weapon permits

Possible relatives and associates on the Comprehensive Report include up to five degrees of separation, as follows:

- Degrees of relatives (both summary and details)
- Likely associates (both summary and details)
- Possible associates (both summary and details)
- Neighbors (most recent addresses and residences per address)
- Neighbor phones (most recent addresses and phones per address)

(See Chapter 4 for other ways to determine relationships.)

Additional Reports and Search Modules in the People Search Category

In addition to the Comprehensive Report, the more specialized Locate/Asset Report focuses on current locations and contact information, as well as current, or most recent, assets. The Super Phone Report includes mailing and e-mail addresses, best personal and work telephone numbers (scored with a percentage of probability that it is a good number to call), as well as relatives and associates.

Subject Information in the Locate/Asset Report includes:

- Best addresses to mail
- Possible e-mail addresses
- Best numbers to call for subject
- Best numbers to call subject at work

- Best first-degree relatives' listed land-line telephone numbers
- Best second-degree relatives' listed land-line telephone numbers
- Best third-degree relatives' listed land-line telephone numbers
- Likely associates' listed land-line telephone numbers
- Possible associates' listed land-line telephone numbers
- Neighbors' listed land-line telephone numbers

Business Plus Search Category

Businesses, both domestic and international, are searchable through the Business Plus Search. Information that can be found includes business telephone numbers, UCC filings, and comprehensive business reports, as well as principals, board members, former and current employees, business assets, trade lines, and even business family trees that show headquarters, subsidiaries, and business branches.

Criminal Records Search Category

Under Criminal Records, authorized users can search specifically for criminal histories, including arrests, warrants, and sex offender registrations.

Courts Search Category

This category includes search modules for foreclosures, liens, judgments, bankruptcies, and evictions.

Assets Search Category

Vehicles, properties, trademarks, and additional asset-related information can be searched in the Asset Search Category. Included is a Vehicle Wildcard, which allows the search for vehicles (and their owners/registrants) by partial tag number, vehicle category, color, and radius from a specific location. In addition, the Vehicle Wildcard Search allows authorized users to conduct searches based on the years that specific incidents occurred, enhancing the success for cold case investigations.

Summary

Resources in this chapter include:

- A law enforcement profile that explains how TLOxp was used to solve a case

- User tips on the TLOxp online investigative system

TLOxp is not the only online investigative system, but, as part-time Chief Chad Weaver, of the Hutsonville Police Department in Hutsonville, Illinois, discovered when he was able to quickly track down a fugitive, the new tool has revolutionized the way his agency does its research.

- For its product, TLOxp, TLO gathers information from courthouses, news, and Internet sources, and also purchases data from data suppliers. The company was founded by Hank Asher, who had also founded Seisint, Inc., where he developed ACCURINT for Law Enforcement.
- Investigators reap the rewards, all at no cost to law enforcement. (In order to keep it free, the company charges its other subscribers.)
- New data are continuously being added to TLOxp. According to CEO Ken Hunter, each day the data are different and have increased and, it is hoped, are more accurate, more current, and more complete. He states, "Investigators should never stop checking to see if a new bit of knowledge provides the missing clue, the missing link, or the missing puzzle piece."[21]
- The search capabilities and functionalities of TLOxp are only as good as knowing how to use the system. To gain its full advantage, users are encouraged to contact Customer and Tech Support, live chat, and e-mail, as well as watch the company's e-training videos.
- For more information on TLOxp, and how to sign up, go to www.tlo.com

Endnotes

1. Weaver, Chad. E-mail correspondence with author, February 15, 2010.
2. Weaver, Chad. E-mail correspondence with author, February 15, 2010.
3. Weaver, Chad. E-mail correspondence with author, February 15, 2010.
4. Weaver, Chad. E-mail correspondence with author, February 15, 2010.
5. Staff. "Foltz gets 10 years for child pornography," WTAY/WTYE-TOC 1570 AM radio, Robinson, Illinois (April 11, 2011).
6. Weaver, Chad. E-mail correspondence with author, February 15, 2010.
7. Weaver, Chad. E-mail correspondence with author, March 1, 2010.
8. Hunter, Ken. E-mail correspondence with author, November 20, 2011.
9. Hunter, Ken. Interview with author, September 21, 2010.
10. "Welcome to TLO" video, www.tlo.com (accessed December 26, 2011).
11 Hunter, Ken. E-mail correspondence with author, November 20, 2011.
12 Hunter, Ken. E-mail correspondence with author, November 20, 2011.
13 Hunter, Ken. Interview with author, September 21, 2010.
14. O'Harrow, Robert, Jr. *No Place to Hide* (New York: Free Press, 2006), 114.
15. Racioppo, Steve. E-mail correspondence with author, November 21, 2011.

16. O'Harrow. Robert, Jr. "LexisNexis to Buy Seisint for $775 Million," *Washington Post* (July 15, 2004): E01.
17. Hunter, Ken. Interview with author, September 21, 2010.
18. Racioppo, Steve. E-mail correspondence with author, November 21, 2011.
19. Staff. "Welcome to TLO" video, www.tlo.com (accessed December 26, 2011).
20. TLOxp User Tips (available to users after they have signed on to TLO).
21. Hunter, Ken. E-mail correspondence with author, November 20, 2011.

4 Additional Options for People Searches

As was shown in Chapter 3, "TLO: The Latest Online Investigative System," TLOxp® is *free* to law enforcement, but there are many additional online tools for investigators. They include fee-based data aggregators and many different kinds of databases, as well as search engines, defined as computer programs that crawl the web and are designed to retrieve data from documents and databases. In addition to the sampling of people search options discussed below, see also Chapter 5, "Dealing with Databases"; Chapter 6, "NamUs: Connecting the Missing and Unidentified"; Chapter 7, "Entering and Searching in the NamUs System"; and Chapter 8, "PKU Cards Retain Overlooked DNA." This chapter addresses the following:

- Google
- Some additional, and helpful, people search engines
- Social Security Death Index (SSDI)
- Ancestry.com
- Fee-based law enforcement websites
- Coplink; see the section, "Information Sharing Resources" in Chapter 15

Google

The following was a true conversation between the author (at work on her laptop) and the author's then 6-year-old granddaughter:

Child: "Do you google?"
Grandmother: Yes, sure.
Child: My Mom "googles" with salt-water.

All generations, in some way or other, are familiar with Google—or Yahoo, Bing, or other major search engines—although Google (www.google.com) is discussed here. Combined with other research techniques, the powerful search engine can turn up a lot of surprises. (See Chapter 11 for a case history that combined newspaper research with Google to find a 50-year-old missing autopsy report.) Google can be the easiest of searches or the most frustrating, depending upon how one goes about performing a search. For instance, in a recent test of a Google search for the words *cold case resources*, without quotes, the search engine looked at each of the three words independently and came up with a completely unmanageable number of 16 million hits. Quotes around the words (as in "cold case resources") restricted the search to the exact phrase and, at the time of this writing, brought the number down to 3,390, still a lot.

Some Other Google Tips to Keep in Mind

- Narrow a search further with some words in quotes and one extra word. For instance, "cold case resources" California, brings up 436 results, easier to sort through, if one is looking for cold case resources in California. To narrow the search even more, add "Los Angeles" in quotes, as in "cold case resources" California "Los Angeles."
- Searches are not case sensitive; that is, "Los Angeles" is the same as "los angeles."
- By default, the "Everything" option is highlighted on the left side of the Google results page. By clicking on other options, the above query "cold case resources" can be narrowed to the cold case resources that only include images, only include videos, only include books, only include news, and a lot more. (See Chapter 11 for the use of Google News that, along with NewsBank, can locate newspaper articles from previous decades.)
- Click on the "Show search tools" option on the left side of the Google search page to narrow a search to a specific timeframe, or click on other options that include related searches and translated foreign pages.
- Create "Google Alerts" to get e-mail updates of the latest relevant news and website results based on a choice of keywords. For instance, type in the name of a case, a person, or even oneself. To get the maximum number of hits, set up more than one alert, with different spellings, such as "Alexander Salinger" and "Alex Salinger." Whenever the name in the alert comes up in a news report or is posted on a website, notification will be sent to the e-mail address specified when setting up the alert. This can be helpful, for instance, in keeping up to date on media coverage of an individual, a specific agency, or a developing case. To get started, simply Google "Google Alert."
- Try an infinite variety of keywords, as one researcher did in finding a long-term missing person: Twylia May Embrey.

Case History: Google Search Used to Find Missing Woman with Changed Identity

Some missing persons return on their own, whereas others tragically turn up as homicides. Still other missing persons—whether fleeing the law or for personal reasons—choose to disappear, and some of them successfully change their identities. One who made that choice was Twylia May Embrey, a spunky and independent 17-year-old Nebraska farm girl. According to family lore, she told her father, in 1952, that once she graduated from high school, he would never see her again. And no one in the family ever did, although her parents, and then her siblings, and, eventually, her great-niece, continued to search, never giving up hope of finding her. During the third generation's search, a few selective keywords typed into Google revealed the woman's past, three weeks after her funeral. Although there was no long-hoped-for reunion by Twylia's then-elderly sisters, the revelation of Twylia's half-century secret life answered many of their questions.

Twylia was last seen by a former boyfriend in North Platte, Nebraska, in the summer of 1952, when she reportedly got into a large yellow Cadillac convertible with Nevada license plates.[1] No one, at the time, filled out a missing person report, as her parents assumed the teenager had run away and, one day, would return home. A few years later, when Twylia still had not come home, her parents sold their farm and drove to California, thinking that was where the young woman had gone. In the early 1980s, Twylia's oldest sister took up the search and corresponded with a private investigator who physically thumbed through hardcopies of California telephone directories, looking for the young woman's name. The sister also wrote to the Social Security Administration, enclosing a letter to be forwarded to Twylia with the news that their father had died. The government agency returned the letter, stating that it had no record of the woman's whereabouts.

In 2004, following national publicity on the exhumation of—and search for the identity of—"Boulder Jane Doe," Twylia's great-niece, Jennifer Kitt, contacted the author and asked if Twylia could have been the Jane Doe murder victim found in 1954 near Boulder, Colorado. Months later, when DNA ruled out Twylia as Jane Doe, the author joined Kitt and fellow researcher Micki Lavigne (see Figure 4.1) in following Twylia's paper trail in the hopes of either locating her or finding out what happened to her. School records and personal correspondence with one of her high school classmates led to the name of a close female friend whose telephone number was located with an online people search. The friend told the author, during a telephone interview, that Twylia had confided in her that her father had raped her, undoubtedly her motivation for leaving

Figure 4.1 In 2006, researcher Micki Lavigne creatively used keywords in a Google search to find Twylia May Embrey, a woman who had lived under a false identity for more than 50 years. (Photo by author.)

home.[2] Assuming that Twylia had married but kept her first name, Kitt, Lavigne, and the author used every Internet people search engine at their fingertips to compile lists of hundreds of women in Twylia's projected age group, all with the first name of Twylia. For more than a year, Kitt and Lavigne telephoned most of the women, one by one, but none was Twylia May Embrey.

One day, in April 2006, Micki Lavigne creatively chose, as keywords (in quotes), *only* Twylia's mother's maiden name. Up popped an online obituary with both parents' correct first names (but "Enberey," an incorrect spelling of the family's last name of "Embrey"), as well as a correct date of birth. "It was a tedious daily play on words, over and over again," stated Lavigne in a subsequent interview. "I just kept using different combinations and misspellings, and it finally worked!"[3] Included in the online obituary was a photograph of the recently deceased woman. Her surviving sisters saw the family resemblance, even though Twylia's first name was "Theresa," and she also had different middle, maiden, and last names. Even more surprising to the family, who had always assumed that she had traveled to the West Coast, the obituary and the news accounts that followed revealed that Twylia/Theresa had spent the previous 50 years working as a typist and living near Boston, Massachusetts.[4] See Figure 4.2.

Twylia's Nebraska family had retained possession of her original Social Security card. A check with the Social Security Administration did not show any activity on her number, leading to the possibility that she was deceased; but no one during the search was aware that the young woman had applied for a second card with another number. After Micki Lavigne

Figure 4.2 Lavigne's discovery of Twylia was front-page news in *The North Platte Telegraph* on April 28, 2006. (Photo courtesy of *The North Platte Telegraph*.)

found Twylia's obituary, and the family was convinced that it was her, the author requested "Theresa's" application from the Social Security Administration. Twylia's secrets then began to come out of the past. (See Chapter 12 for more on Social Security records.) In 1955, three years after she left Nebraska, the young woman created a new identity with a false maiden name, as well as a false date and place of birth. At the time—long before computerized databases—changing one's identity was not difficult to do. In a box that asked if she had ever applied for, or had, a previous Social Security number, she simply marked the box labeled "No."[5]

During the search for the identity of Boulder Jane Doe, and the spin-off research on the missing Twylia May Embrey, a detective at the Boulder County Sheriff's Office in 2005, had essentially reported Twylia missing when he entered her name into the National Crime Information Center (NCIC) database. After Lavigne found "Theresa's" obituary, the detective contacted the obituary's informant, a close friend of the deceased in Massachusetts. The friend confirmed that "Theresa" had spoken of her parents and place of birth on her deathbed. Thanks to Google, and a researcher's creative use of keywords, generations of family members received the resolution they had sought for more than a half century. Twylia May Embrey's missing persons case was officially closed.[6] (For an example of a fugitive who changed his name and was found through the skills of a forensic sculptor, see Chapter 15.)

Case History: Find, Then Print, Sensitive Information

As with any information on the Internet, investigators and researchers have found that it is important to print and keep hard copies of sensitive or unusual search results. The reason is simple: the web page may suddenly disappear. It is also important to document what the printouts mean and when and why they were done. The importance of keeping a hard copy became evident several years ago when a fellow researcher of the author Googled serial killer Harvey M. Glatman, possible murderer, in 1954, of "Boulder Jane Doe."

"You won't believe this," the researcher wrote in the subject line of his e-mail, in 2005. He then explained that in a routine Google search of Glatman's name, he found a "Harvey M. Glatman Memorial Scholarship" at the University of Denver, in Denver, Colorado. On the day of the search and according to the private university's website, the endowed scholarship had been established with a bequest from Glatman's mother and it supported students of junior or senior standing who were majoring in accounting or business administration in the Daniels College of Business.[7] (See Chapter 12 for a discussion of Glatman's mother's probate records.)

Suspecting that Jane Doe might have been a University of Denver student in the business college, the author gave the school a call to see if its administrators knew of any missing female students in 1954. They did not have any missing-student records, but they certainly were surprised, and probably embarrassed as well, to learn that the school had a scholarship named for a serial killer! And, he was a very prominent serial killer, as he was the inspiration for Los Angeles Police Department Detective Pierce Brooks to create the Violent Criminal Apprehension Program (ViCAP). (For more on ViCAP, see Chapter 5.) Further research indicated that even though Glatman's mother had made the bequest, she died in 1968 (see Figure 4.3) and her nephew (Glatman's cousin) had made the final arrangements with the university in 1985. After the serial killer connection was made in 2005, all mention of the scholarship was immediately

Figure 4.3 Ophelia Glatman and her husband, Albert Glatman, are buried in the Mount Nebo Cemetery, in Aurora, Colorado. (Photo by author.)

removed from the website. Who knows what the students had been told when the scholarship money was handed out year after year?

Harvey Glatman was executed in the California State Prison at San Quentin in 1959, so in this instance, the existence of the scholarship was only of historical interest. But, without a hard copy (or a screen shot) of the Google search results, there would be no record of its existence in the author's files unless the webpage had been saved in the Internet Archive's Wayback Machine. Although the particular webpage that had listed the Glatman Scholarship had not been archived, the Wayback Machine is often worth checking, as it has archived more than 150 billion web pages from 1996 to the current day.[8]

Some Additional, and Helpful, People Search Options

The following people search websites contain free searching capabilities and can be helpful in various ways. As with TLO, ACCURINT® for Law Enforcement, and other law enforcement accessible sources, however, all should be tried on oneself in order to understand, firsthand, their strengths and limitations. For instance, a "possible relative" can often be a spouse's ex-spouse, and a "possible associate" can be a former renter or owner of one's current residence.

Veromi (People Search Option)

Veromi, www.veromi.net/Search/People/name.htm, is a free website that lists names, ages, cities and states, and possible relatives and asssociates. The information, all on one computer screen, is helpful in establishing family relationships. One technique is to plug names into veromi and other people search engines, then figure out how the people overlap. The results can help narrow the names of those who share the same residence, particularly when a woman with a specific first name is "related to" or "associated with" a woman with the same first name and a different last name.

For example, if all that is known about the name of a (married) woman is her maiden name ["Joanne Miller"], then entering that woman's maiden name ["Joanne Miller"] will often reveal her married name ["Joanne Duncan"] as well. The opposite also is true. Entering a married woman's name ["Joanne Duncan"] can reveal her maiden name ["Joanne Miller"], which can lead to parents and siblings with the same ["Miller"] name. Once names are sorted into family groups, they can be correlated into lists that may even include aliases. These names can then be plugged into TLO and other law enforcement search engines or traced through recorded documents. (See Chapter 12.)

Dexknows/White Pages (The Internet's Alternative to a Telephone Directory)

The Dexknows, http://dexknows.whitepages.com, website (and others that are similar) is good for reverse searches, confirming specific residences, and determining if a person has a current landline.

Pipl

Pipl, http://pipl.com, claims to be the "most comprehensive people search on the web." Although birth records may have errors, and addresses may be out of date, the website is a good starting point for public records, as well as personal profiles on social networking sites.

Next of Kin Registry

The Next of Kin Registry (NOKR), www.nokr.org, is a nonprofit humanitarian organization, established in 2004 as a central depository for rapid emergency contact information in the United States, plus 87 other countries. The information belongs to the registrants and is made available, securely, to registered emergency agencies during times of urgent need.

Social Security Death Index

Obviously, when searching for missing persons, witnesses, and even fugitives, the first piece of essential information is to determine if the person is dead or alive. Instead of, or to supplement, TLO, ACCURINT for Law Enforcement, and other law enforcement accessible websites, a good place to start is with the Social Security Death Index (SSDI). The index claims to have more than 90 million records and is available in several locations on the Internet. Some locations charge a fee; however, access is free on the website of The Church of Jesus Christ of Latter Day Saints. See www.familysearch.org/eng/Search/frameset_search.asp and go to "US Social Security Death Index."

In most instances, in addition to a deceased person's date of death, the results will provide a birth date, Social Security number, the person's last recorded address, and the state where the number was issued. The date of death and the address can be very helpful in tracking down an obituary which often will lead to the names, addresses, and relationships of family members. (See Chapter 11 for the section, "Understanding Obituaries.")

Anyone can try out the Social Security Death Index by typing in the name of a person already known to be deceased, such as one's parent or grandparent. There are some differences, however, between the generations.

In 2011, the Social Security Administration began issuing numbers at random.[9] In recent years, infants have been, and continue to be, issued their numbers shortly after birth. But, from 1936 (when the first nine-digit numbers were assigned) to 2011, the first three digits indicated the state where the individual first received their Social Security card. "Baby boomers," and others in their age range, however, normally received their numbers as teenagers, when they got their first paying jobs.

The Social Security Administration lists the three-digit numbers on its website under "Social Security Number Allocations" (www.socialsecurity.gov/employer/stateweb.htm), so it is easy to determine where a person applied for his card. For instance, numbers between 159 and 211 indicate that the cardholder was issued his or her number in Pennsylvania.[10] TLO and the other law enforcement websites that indicate the Social Security numbers of living people will also give the states in which the numbers were issued. Knowing that information can help in tracing a person's paper trail and also in determining family relationships.

Investigators can begin their searches on the SSDI by entering a name on the form. The name, however, has to match the SSDI records, and a search for "James T. Smith" could be under "James Smith," or "J. T. Smith," or even "Jim Smith." All combinations of proper versus informal names, and middle initials versus no middle initials, may need to be tried in a name-only search. However, if the date or place of death is known, or if the Social Security number is known, then just a last name and another piece of identifying information may be all that is needed to find the records of the deceased person. As with any search engine, it is sometimes necessary to manipulate the parameters.

In addition to the need to try variations in names, the SSDI has some other limitations. If a person is not found, that does not mean he or she is necessarily still living. For instance, few records are included for deaths that occurred prior to 1962. Names after that date can be missing too, if a funeral home or a relative failed to notify the Social Security Administration of a person's death, or if a spouse or dependents were, or are, not receiving survivor death benefits. Keep in mind, too, that the Index is of no use at all if the person one is searching for is deceased but no body has been found or, like Twylia May Embrey, the person changed his or her identity.

Ancestry.com

Ancestry.com can be found at http://ancestry.com. Family history research is not just for little old ladies looking for obscure facts about their great-grandfathers. Research is research, whether it is for one's own family or that of another, and family history (genealogy) websites provide an additional tool.

Obituaries—sometimes found on Ancestry.com—of victims, witnesses, or suspects can be invaluable in determining next of kin, as well as former or current names, relationships, and addresses. (For more on finding obituaries, see Chapter 11.) More advanced family history research includes digging into public records and can also be very helpful when searching for people and determining their relationships. (See Chapter 12.)

Some family history websites are free. One of these is FamilySearch.org, a service provided by The Church of Jesus Christ of Latter-Day Saints and mentioned in the section on the Social Security Death Index.[11] The most comprehensive, however, with seven billion historical records, is Ancestry.com. According to its own website, Ancestry's "Public Records Index" is gathered from telephone directory white pages, telephone directory assistance records, marketing lists, postal change-of-address forms, public record filings, and historical residential records that span the years 1950 through 1993.[12] Although a library version is accessible for free at most public libraries, the regular and more complete version requires either a monthly or annual subscription. These subscriptions may not be cost-effective for agencies to buy on their own, but agencies would be prudent to work with volunteers who already subscribe and are familiar with family history research.

The use of Ancestry.com in cold case research hit home when the author learned from a sheriff's office investigator that the trail of a suspect in a 1970 homicide had gone cold. A long turnover of detectives had compiled enough evidence to make an arrest. But, even with the latest search engines, investigative websites, and databases, no one could find the alleged murderer or even determine if he were dead or alive. In light of the man's criminal history, it was speculated that he may have been in a witness protection program. When the suspect's name and date of birth were plugged into Ancestry.com, however, data extracted from an Oregon death certificate popped up on the computer screen. This new information led to the suspect's alias, along with more questions, but it also led to the case being closed, "Exceptionally Cleared; Death of Offender."[13]

Fee-Based Law Enforcement Websites

ACCURINT for Law Enforcement

LexisNexis® owns ACCURINT for Law Enforcement and ACCURINT for LE Plus. As described on the company's website, these data aggregators "expedite the identification of people and their assets, addresses, relatives, and business associates by providing instant access to a comprehensive database of public records that would ordinarily take days to collect. Billions of records and thousands of independent data sources are searched in order to provide the broadest and most accurate information."[14]

And, as on TLO, investigators using ACCURINT for Law Enforcement can access subject information including:

- Names
- Addresses
- Telephone numbers (landlines and some cell phones)
- Dates of birth
- Ages
- Social Security numbers of living persons
- Others associated with the subjects' Social Security numbers
- Aliases
- Bankruptcies
- Liens and Judgments
- Uniform Commercial Code (UCC) filings
- Co-workers
- Driver's licenses
- Possible properties owned
- Motor vehicles registered
- Watercraft
- Federal Aviation Administration (FAA) certifications
- Federal Aviation Administration (FAA) aircraft
- Possible criminal records
- Sexual offenses
- Florida accidents
- Professional licenses
- Voter registrations
- Hunting and fishing permits
- Concealed weapons permits
- Possible associates
- Possible relatives
- Neighbors

Unlike TLO, however, ACCURINT for Law Enforcement (and the other law enforcement websites mentioned on the following pages) charges fees to law enforcement agency users. Included in ACCURINT for Law Enforcement's fees, though, is the LexisNexis Investigators Network, where law enforcement investigators can exchange professional experiences and also share expertise and insights with others in the field.

CLEAR: Consolidated Lead Evaluation and Reporting

On its website, CLEAR is advertised as "the next-generation public record data delivery platform available exclusively to law enforcement and other government investigators," adding that it is the only online investigative source that offers both a "vast collection of public and unique proprietary records" and "timesaving analytics that probe deep into the Web."

Locate Plus

Locate Plus's Police Investigation Database advertises a flat-rate plan that covers searches by name, address, Social Security number, license plate, and vehicle identification number (VIN), as well as landlines and some cell phone numbers. After the initial search, more detailed reporting options are available.

Summary

Resources in this chapter include:

- The use of Google in cold case research
- Other people searching options, in addition to Google and TLO (see Chapter 3.)

For effective people searching, investigators have found that it helps to become familiar with as many online tools as possible, find the ones that work best, and bookmark them to keep them handy.

- Google (one of several search engines) can be the easiest of searches or the most frustrating, depending upon how one goes about performing a search. Tips include putting search terms in quotes in order to keep a search focused.
- A researcher's creative use of keywords located a missing woman who had lived under a false identity for 50 years.
- Printing (or taking screen shots) of search results that contain sensitive data is recommended, as the web page may suddenly disappear.
- "Google Alerts" are helpful in keeping up to date on media coverage of an individual, a specific agency, a developing case, or even oneself.
- Various websites, such as veromi.net, have people search options that can help in determining family relationships.
- The Social Security Death Index has some limitations, but it can determine if a person is dead or alive.

- Ancestry.com requires a subscription, but this premier family history research tool provides additional people searching options.
- Several fee-based data aggregators are available to law enforcement.

Endnotes

1. Pettem, Silvia. *Someone's Daughter: In Search of Justice for Jane Doe* (Lanham, MD: Taylor Trade, 2009), 112.
2. Pettem, Silvia. *Someone's Daughter: In Search of Justice for Jane Doe* (Lanham, MD: Taylor Trade, 2009), 111.
3. Lavigne, Micki. E-mail correspondence with author, August 6, 2011.
4. Pettem, Silvia. *Someone's Daughter: In Search of Justice for Jane Doe* (Lanham, MD: Taylor Trade, 2009), 174–175.
5. Pettem, Silvia.*Someone's Daughter: In Search of Justice for Jane Doe* (Lanham, MD: Taylor Trade, 2009), 175.
6. Pettem, Silvia. *Someone's Daughter: In Search of Justice for Jane Doe* (Lanham, MD: Taylor Trade, 2009),176.
7. Pettem, Silvia. *Someone's Daughter: In Search of Justice for Jane Doe* (Lanham, MD: Taylor Trade, 2009),132–133.
8. Internet Archive Wayback Machine, www.archive.org/web/web.php (accessed December 26, 2011).
9. Social Security Administration, Randomization, www.socialsecurity.gov/employer/randomization.html (accessed December 26, 2011).
10. Social Security Administration, Number allocations, www.socialsecurity.gov/employer/stateweb.htm (accessed December 26, 2011).
11. Family Search, https://www.familysearch.org/ (accessed December 26, 2011).
12. Ancestry.com, www.ancestry.com/ (accessed December 26, 2011).
13. Pettem, Silvia. "Out of the Past: A Fresh Look at Cold Cases," *Evidence Technology Magazine* 8:2 (March–April 2010).
14. LexisNexis, www.lexisnexis.com/government/solutions/investigative/accurint-le-features.aspx (accessed December 26, 2011).

5 Dealing with Databases

Databases, loosely defined, are collections of computer data that are structured to make data digitally accessible. In addition to the Social Security Death Index and Ancestry.com, mentioned in Chapter 4, also see Chapters 6 through 8. This chapter is not all-inclusive, but it covers some of the other databases that may be helpful in cold case research.

Selected databases include:

- CODIS: Combined DNA and National DNA Index Systems, along with a discussion of the services of the University of North Texas Center for Human Identification (UNTCHI)
- IAFIS: Integrated Automated Fingerprint Identification System
- NamUs System (See Chapter 6, "NamUs: Connecting the Missing and Unidentified," and Chapter 7, "Entering and Searching in the NamUs System.")
- NCMEC: National Center for Missing and Exploited Children
- NCIC: National Crime Information Center (including its historical database)
- NIBIN: National Integrated Ballistic Information Network
- State clearinghouses, for example, CBI: Cold Case Files of the Colorado Bureau of Investigation
- The Doe Network: International Center for Unidentified and Missing Persons (and a sampling of other privately funded databases)
- ViCAP: Violent Criminal Apprehension Program
- Individual Agency Cold Case Websites (See Chapter 16, "Taking Advantage of the Media.")

Databases

Combined DNA Index System and National DNA Index System

CODIS, www.fbi.gov/about-us/lab/codis, was established by the Federal Bureau of Investigation in 1992, and links crimes to criminals by allowing law enforcement officials to enter profiles of DNA found at crime scenes into a national database of criminal offenders, the National DNA Index System

(NDIS). Computer software automatically searches across the following indices for potential matches.

The convicted offender index contains DNA profiles of individuals convicted of certain crimes ranging from misdemeanors to sexual assaults and murders. Each state has different "qualifying offenses" for which the convicted persons must submit a biological sample for inclusion in the DNA database.

The forensic index contains DNA profiles obtained from crime scene evidence, such as semen, saliva, or blood. As stated on the website of the DNA Initiative, a match made between profiles in the forensic index can link crime scenes to each other, possibly identifying serial offenders. Based on these "forensic hits," police in multiple jurisdictions or states can coordinate their respective investigations and share leads they have developed independently of each other. Matches made between the forensic and convicted offender indices can provide investigators with the identity of a suspect or suspects. Writers of the DNA Initiative added, "It is important to note that if an 'offender hit' is obtained, that information typically is used as probable cause to obtain a new DNA sample from that suspect so the match can be confirmed by the crime laboratory before an arrest is made."[1]

Although the National DNA Index System (NDIS) contains a national database of criminal offenders, it also includes data of additional and special interest to cold case researchers, specifically:

- DNA profiled from family reference samples of relatives of missing persons
- DNA profiled from unidentified remains

This missing persons/unidentified remains database is kept separate from the criminal system to encourage family members to contribute. Figuring prominently in the identification of human remains is the University of North Texas Center for Human Identification (UNTCHI). Its personnel work with medical examiners, coroners' offices, the National Center for Missing and Exploited Children (NCMEC), and law enforcement agencies throughout the United States with the submission, collection, and analyses of missing persons' samples.

Missing persons reports are filed with the law enforcement agency having jurisdiction where the individual was last seen or last resided. The law enforcement agency then determines if the missing person meets a "high risk" criterion. The agency may ask the person's family for a direct reference sample (DRS) obtained from articles belonging to the missing person. In addition, the agency may need to collect family reference samples (FRS). The collection and submission of FRS can only be collected and submitted by the law enforcement agency. Family reference collection kits (with buccal swabs) and the required paperwork are provided free of charge by the UNTCHI. After analyses, the profiles are entered into the Federal Bureau of Investigation's (FBI's) DNA databases.

Correspondence is mediated through the respective law enforcement agency. If a match occurs, the agency notifies the family, and the law enforcement agency and medical examiner/coroner may need to submit samples of the unidentified human remains (UHR). According to the UNTCHI's website, "Identifying remains through DNA can be a lengthy process. There may be cases where there is no usable DNA or not enough relatives available for testing; however, the UNTCHI's professional staff will pursue every avenue to obtain a profile."[2]

Integrated Automated Fingerprint Identification System

IAFIS, www.fbi.gov/about-us/cjis/fingerprints_biometrics/iafis/iafis, is the Integrated Automated Fingerprint Identification System, which houses fingerprints for more than 66 million subjects in its criminal master file, including more than 25 million civil prints of individuals who have served, or are serving, in the U.S. military or have been, or are, employed by the federal government. In addition, the system stores corresponding criminal histories, mug shots, aliases, and photos of scars and tattoos, as well as lists of physical characteristics such as height, weight, and hair and eye color.

The FBI, which launched IAFIS in 1999, has been the national repository for fingerprints and related criminal history data since 1924 (see Figures 5.1 and 5.2). At that time, more than 800,000 fingerprint records from the National Bureau of Criminal Identification (NBCI) and Leavenworth Penitentiary were consolidated with the Bureau's files. The first use of computers to search fingerprint files took place in October 1980. Currently, the IAFIS System processes an average of approximately 162,000 ten-print submissions per day, with electronic image storage, electronic exchange of fingerprints and responses, and capabilities for automated fingerprint and latent searches. IAFIS can now archive latent prints and, as with DNA profiles, run the archived latent prints against other latent prints, as well as against known offenders. The system also accepts palm prints. The storage capability of IAFIS on a federal level is currently limited, but the software is available to local jurisdictions.

One very important point for investigators to remember, however—for both IAFIS and NIBIN (see below)—is the limitations of the database, and to beware of false negatives if, for instance, there is a backlog, or if juveniles are not included in one's jurisdiction. If a known suspect does not produce a hit in the system, a request for a manual comparison can be made.

Figure 5.1 The Federal Bureau of Investigation (FBI) has been the national repository for fingerprints since 1924, when this photograph was taken of the "fingerprint division." (Photo courtesy of the National Photo Company Collection, Library of Congress.)

National Center for Missing and Exploited Children Search Site

The National Center for Missing and Exploited Children, (NCMEC, www.missingkids.com), allows for a search of its database with the following parameters:

- Name (or partial name)
- Date missing, or specify missing in the last months or years
- Last seen (country, state, city, or region)
- Possible location (state, country)
- Description (height, weight, current age, sex, race, as well as hair and eye color)
- Case type (including unidentified persons)

As noted on its website, the information on missing children who appear with NCMEC's logo has been certified, as shown below:

- The case has been entered into the Federal Bureau of Investigation's National Crime Information Center (NCIC).

Figure 5.2 In 1939, FBI Director J. Edgar Hoover personally fingerprinted John Nance Garner, first Vice President under U.S. President Franklin D. Roosevelt. Of the vice presidency, Garner stated that it "was not worth a bucket of warm spit." (Photo courtesy of the Harris and Ewing Collection, Library of Congress.)

- A waiver from a parent, guardian, or law-enforcement agency is on file at NCMEC giving permission to disseminate a photograph of the missing child.
- Posters containing photographs of abductors are included only if felony warrants have been issued for the abductors and the subjects have been entered into the NCIC Wanted Person File.[3]

(See Chapter 15 for other support services offered by NCMEC.)

National Crime Information Center

The National Crime Information Center (NCIC, www.fbi.gov/about-us/cjis/ncic/ncic), is an electronic clearinghouse of crime data that can be tapped into by virtually every criminal justice agency nationwide, 24 hours a day, 365 days a year. Launched in 1967 with 356,784 records, it now contains more than 15 million active records and averages 7½ million transactions per day. The NCIC helps law enforcement officers apprehend fugitives, locate missing persons, recover stolen property, and identify terrorists. Its files cover persons and properties, as follows:

- Supervised Release

- National Sex Offender Registry
- Foreign Fugitive
- Immigration Violator
- Missing Person (as follows)
  - A person of any age who is missing and who is under proven physical/mental disability or is senile, thereby subjecting that person or others to personal and immediate danger
  - A person of any age who is missing under circumstances indicating that the disappearance was not voluntary
  - A person of any age who is missing under circumstances indicating that person's physical safety may be in danger
  - A person of any age who is missing after a catastrophe
  - A person who is missing and declared unemancipated as defined by the laws of the person's state of residence and does not meet any of the entry criteria set forth in first 4 bullet items above
- Protection Order
- Unidentified Person (as follows)
  - Any unidentified deceased person
  - Any person who is living and unable to provide their identity (e.g., infant, amnesia victim)
  - Any unidentified catastrophe victim
  - Body parts when a body has been dismembered
- U.S. Secret Service Protective
- Gang
- Known or Appropriately Suspected Terrorist
- Wanted Person
- Identity Theft
- Stolen articles
- Stolen boats
- Stolen guns
- Stolen license plates
- Stolen parts
- Stolen securities
- Stolen vehicles[4]

Of particular help to cold case investigators is the NCIC's historical database of records that have been removed from the active database. As stated in a 1983 *FBI Law Enforcement Bulletin*, "An offline search is a special inquiry of NCIC for information which cannot be obtained through online inquiry and may be made against two sources of NCIC records—the NCIC data base of active records and the historical data which is maintained offline on magnetic tape."[5]

For instance, even though an online inquiry may produce a "no record" response, an offline search of purged records can determine when a former request was entered and, subsequently, removed. These offline searches include:

- Use of nonunique personal descriptors, such as sex, height, estimated age, and hair color (these descriptors can be used in online searches but only in conjunction with other identifiers such as a person's name and date of birth)
- Partial information searches in which an officer, for example, only has three or four characters of a license plate or only half of a vehicle identification number (VIN)
- Checks of purged records, that is, records that have been removed by law enforcement or as a result of varying retention schedules
- Searches of pawn shop receipts for identifiable property—such as a Rolex watch with a serial number—stolen from a homicide victim or in the possession of a missing person
- Searches of NCIC's transaction logs, which may uncover other queries on the same suspect made by another law enforcement agency and helpful in establishing a suspect's whereabouts[6]

The following example from a Louisville, Kentucky, agency is given in an FBI news story titled, "When Offline is Better: Another Way to Search Crime Records:"

> On September 26, 2009, a 13-year-old girl was reported missing from Daviess County, Kentucky, and her information—including details about the convicted sex offender she was last seen with—was entered into NCIC. That night, an agent from our Louisville office, working with local authorities, contacted CJIS and requested an off-line search of the suspect's license plate. Very quickly, we discovered that the Sheboygan County, Wisconsin, Sheriff's Office had run a check on the license plate earlier that day (before Kentucky officials had a chance to enter the suspect's plate number into NCIC). Officials in Wisconsin were notified, and the man was located by 4 a.m. the next day in a Wisconsin hotel. The girl was recovered safely.[7]

National Integrated Ballistic Information Network

The National Integrated Ballistic Information Network (NIBIN, www.nibin.gov) was established by the Bureau of Alcohol, Tobacco, and Firearms (ATF) in 1999. ATF administers automated ballistic imaging technology for NIBIN partners in the United States who have entered into a formal agreement with the ATF to enter their bullet or shell casing information. Partners use Integrated Ballistic Identification Systems (IBIS) to acquire digital images of the markings made on fired cartridge cases and bullets recovered from a crime scene or a crime gun test fire and then, in a matter of hours, compare those images against earlier NIBIN entries via electronic image comparison. If a high-confidence candidate for a match emerges, firearms examiners compare the original evidence using a microscope to confirm the match or NIBIN "hit." By searching in an automated environment either locally, regionally, or nationally, NIBIN partners are able to discover links between crimes more quickly, including links that would never have been identified without the technology.

State Clearinghouses: Example, Cold Case Files of the Colorado Bureau of Investigation (CBI)

In recent years, bills have been, and continue to be, passed to create cold case databases in individual states. The Colorado Cold Case Database (https://www.colorado.gov/apps/coldcase/index.html) is a good example. It was created in 2007, when House Bill 07-1272 was passed by the Colorado legislature, requiring all law enforcement agencies in the state to provide to the Colorado Bureau of Investigation (CBI) copies of all homicide investigation files—from 1970 to the present—that had been open for more than three years. The purpose of the database is to assist law enforcement agencies in the development of information leading to the identification and arrest of any person or persons who may have committed any of the depicted crimes. CBI's database went live in August 2010, at the same time as Colorado cold cases were entered into the NamUs System and ViCAP. (For more on NamUs, see Chapters 6 and 7.)

Colorado has also developed a statewide Cold Case Task Force, comprised of law enforcement, victims' advocates, and family members of murder victims, as well as others who work with the group. Some of the task force members are also on the Colorado Cold Case Review Team, which meets quarterly to hear and discuss cold cases presented by law enforcement agencies throughout the state. (For more on the Cold Case Task Force and Review Team, see Chapter 15.)

The Doe Network: International Center for Unidentified and Missing Persons (and a Sampling of Other Privately Funded Databases)

The Doe Network: International Center for Unidentified and Missing Persons (www.doenetwork.org) is a volunteer nonprofit organization founded in 2000. Its volunteers post information on the missing and unidentified, but they also draw from additional sources, including public records and newspaper reports. The Doe Network database, therefore, often contains cases not listed in the NamUs System, including those in Canada, Europe, Australia, Mexico, and the Caribbean. When searching for the missing and unidentified, it is important to check both NamUs and the Doe Network, as well as other privately funded databases.

In March 2011, during some downtime on the graveyard shift at the Marion Police Department, in Marion, Ohio, dispatcher Matt Cole decided to look into one of his department's cold missing person's cases, that of Chad Griffith. Griffith's mother had not heard from her son since 1998, but she waited until 2006 to report him missing. The detectives had little to go on. Cole chose potential matches based on general descriptions, as well as when and where unidentified bodies had been found. He compiled a list of five or six cases of interest and was cleared by his supervisor to enter Griffith's information into the Doe Network database. There, network volunteers constantly cross-reference their files looking for matches. Within one day, a regional director called Cole and told him that one of his potential matches—in Tampa, Florida—looked good.[8]

A Marion Police Department detective then contacted Tampa officials to exchange fingerprint and DNA information. As a result, the victim in Tampa, buried as a John Doe, was positively identified as Chad Griffith. The then-20-year-old had been shot and killed in 1998, by a 14-year-old boy during a drug deal. "This was it. It was the only one," Cole told a newspaper reporter. "I was just glad for the family that they could get some answers. And it gives detectives in both cities some peace of mind because that's what they want—to solve mysteries."[9]

On the Doe Network database, both missing persons and unidentified remains can be searched geographically (by location), as well as chronologically (by year). As stated on the organization's website, "It is our mission to give the nameless back their names and return the missing to their families. We hope to accomplish this mission in three ways: by giving the cases exposure on our website, by having our volunteers search for clues on these cases as well as making possible matches between missing and unidentified persons, and lastly through attempting to get media exposure for these cases that need and deserve it."[10]

One of the other privately funded databases for missing and unidentified persons is The Charley Project, www.charleyproject.org, an online database that serves as a publicity vehicle by profiling more than 9,000 cases alphabetically, geographically, and chronologically. The database began, in 2001, as the Missing Persons Cold Case Network (MPCCN). In 2004, the name was changed to The Charley Project in memory of the unsolved abduction of Charles Brewster Ross, a 4-year-old from Pennsylvania. The Charley Project links to many more privately run missing persons websites that profile multiple missing person cases.

Some additional databases and forums include, but are by no means limited to:

- 4 Military Families.com, www.4militaryfamilies.com/lostandfound.htm
- I Care—Missing Persons Cold Cases, icaremissingpersonscoldcases.yuku.com
- Families of Homicide Victims and Missing Persons, www.echelon-data.com/clients/FOVAMP/victims/victimList.php (for more on FOHVAMP, see Chapter 14.)
- JusticeQuest, www.justicequest.net/forums/index.php
- Missing-and-unidentified.org, www.missing-and-unidentified.org
- Mississippi Missing and Unidentified Persons, www.mmup.info
- Naval Criminal Investigative Service, www.ncis.navy.mil/ContactUs/Pages/MissingPersons.aspx
- Pennsylvania Missing Persons, http://pamissing.com
- Porchlight International, http://s10.invisionfree.com/usedtobedoe
- Websleuths, www.websleuths.com
- Wisconsin Center 4 Missing Children & Adults, www.wcmckids.org
- Yahoo Groups—Cold Cases, http://groups.yahoo.com/group/ColdCases/?tab=s

ViCAP: Violent Criminal Apprehension Program

The Behavioral Analysis Unit 4—Violent Criminal Apprehension Program (ViCAP; www.fbi.gov/wanted/vicap) is a unit of the National Center for the Analysis of Violent Crime (NCAVC) and is the largest national investigative repository of detailed information on major violent crime cases committed in the United States. The computerized linkage analysis system is managed by the Federal Bureau of Identification at Quantico, Virginia. State and local law enforcement agencies submit information on their cases into the program for nationwide confidential comparison. This aids them in identifying patterns in criminal behavior and activity, thus enabling investigators to uncover similarities in cases that previously seemed unrelated.

ViCAP is a law enforcement tool used to compile information on the following:

- Homicides (and attempts), both solved and unsolved, especially those that involve an abduction, are apparently random, motiveless, or sexually oriented, or are known or suspected to be part of a series
- Sexual assaults (and attempts), both solved and unsolved, especially those committed by a stranger, or those known or suspected to be part of a series

Figure 5.3 ViCAP's first director was former Los Angeles Detective Pierce Brooks, photographed in 1958, in the Anza Desert, San Diego County, California, at the site of the murder of Shirley Ann Bridgeford. (Photo from author's collection.)

- Missing person cases where the circumstances indicate a strong possibility of foul play and the victim is still missing
- Unidentified human remains where the manner of death is known or suspected to be a homicide[11]

The program was envisioned by the late Detective Pierce Brooks, a legend at the Los Angeles Police Department (LAPD), and shown in Figure 5.3. He joined the department in 1948 and served in the vice, narcotics, patrol, and homicide divisions, but his work as an expert on serial killers became his lasting legacy. In 1958, Brooks was tracing Shirley Ann Bridgeford, a missing young woman who, Brooks later learned, had been strangled by Harvey M. Glatman in the Anza Desert, in San Diego County, California. A California Highway Patrol Officer arrested Glatman in October 1958, while Glatman attempted to sexually assault (and stated that he intended to kill) yet another young woman.[12] According to the case summary on Glatman prepared by F. R. Dickson, warden of the California State Prison at San Quentin while Glatman was awaiting execution, the warden's description of Bridgeford's murder (as well as the murders of Judy Dull and Ruth Mercado) was as follows:

> The defendant placed the blanket upon the ground and tied the victim's hands and feet. He then placed her on the blanket, rolled her over on her stomach, and tied another rope to the rope binding her ankles. He took this rope, lifted the victim's head, and looped it twice around her neck and pulled tight. The victim made a "funny little noise," but quickly went limp. After holding the rope from five to ten minutes, Glatman released his hold and unwound the rope from her neck.[13]

Once Brooks learned of Glatman's modus operandi, and long before the Internet, the veteran detective spent hours in public libraries reading articles about murders in hardcopies of newspapers from all over the country. He looked for similarities and suggested that the LAPD track various types of murders on a computer, only to be told that computers—in the 1950s and 1960s—were too big and too expensive. Brooks retired from the LAPD in 1969. Later he became police chief at the Springfield Police Department in Springfield, Oregon; then at the Lakewood Police Department in Lakewood, Colorado; and finally at the Eugene Police Department in Eugene, Oregon. In 1983, Brooks testified before the United States Congress, discussing the possibility that unsolved murders around the country might be attributed to serial killers, and that entering their information into a computer could lead to their capture.

In 1985, when ViCAP was implemented, and Brooks was its first director, the program's initial focus was transient/serial killers who managed to cross jurisdictional boundaries without getting caught. At the time, data were confined to a mainframe computer in Quantico, accessible only to FBI personnel. Most users submitted their case information through the mail on forms that were long and cumbersome. Then, beginning in the mid-1990s, with software provided by the FBI, law enforcement agencies began to send their case information electronically, along with requests for analytical assistance. Today, authorized users are provided with direct, real-time access to the national violent crime database. Users can enter their own cases and retrieve information about similar cases using simple queries. In addition, law enforcement agencies can still request analyses of their cases. ViCAP analysts conduct very in-depth analyses of investigative data and provide the requestors with comprehensive Crime Analysis Reports, with detailed results.[14]

Detective Pierce Brooks died in Vida, Oregon, in 1998, at the age of 75. "He was the closest thing I ever saw to Sherlock Holmes," retired Los Angeles police Detective Dan Bowser told a newspaper reporter at the time. Bowser, who was Brooks's partner off and on for nearly 20 years, added, "With his precision and his dedication, there was nobody better at that type of work."[15]

As Brooks envisioned, ViCAP is valuable in identifying and tracking serial offenders and dealing with missing person and unidentified human remains cases. Searches can be as simple as looking up one data point, such as a victim's name, or as complex as entering any combination of collected data. The more specific the criteria are, the narrower the result set; conversely, the more general the search criteria are, the greater the number of cases returned. In addition to victim and suspect details, the database also houses information that includes modus operandi, signature aspects, crime scene descriptions, and photographs.

For instance, in the past an agency had no way to identify a victim if the following scenario occurred.

> A prisoner informs law enforcement that his cellmate told him about a murder he did 10 or 11 years ago. According to the informant, the cellmate abducted a prostitute, sexually assaulted her, beat her, and left her for dead in a motel room.

Today, that same agency can narrow down its search to a manageable number of possible victims by querying the database requesting any record:

- Where the victim was female
- Where the body recovered was in a motel
- Where the cause of death was blunt force trauma
- With a timeframe in which the incident might have occurred

Retired Metropolitan Police Department Detective James Trainum stated, "The real value of ViCAP is the ability to identify cases based on vague leads, and that is how investigators can use it on a day-to-day basis. If the database is not of daily use to investigators, then there would not be as much buy-in and the database would suffer—since it is the investigators who are relied on to provide the data in most agencies." Trainum is also a big believer in agencies entering all of their cold cases, even though the process requires a lot of resources. "But," he adds, "that's what makes ViCAP a good system."[16]

Law enforcement agencies that would like to have access to ViCAP Web need to take the following steps:

- Select an agency point of contact to serve as the link between FBI-ViCAP and the users within the agency
- Obtain individual Law Enforcement Online (LEO) accounts for all users (for more on LEO, www.leo.gov, see Chapter 15)
- Contact FBI-ViCAP via ViCAP@leo.gov to request access to the ViCAP Web[17]

ViCAP was found to be so effective that Canada implemented its own version called the Violent Crime Linkage System (ViCLAS.)[18] Canadian legislation mandates that law enforcement agencies in Canada use ViCLAS for each and every homicide throughout the country. The Canadians also utilize Criminal Geographic Targeting, which is a computerized spatial profiling model. By analyzing the spatial information associated with a series of linked crimes, the program attempts to determine the most probable areas in which an offender's residence might be located, operating on the assumption that a relationship exists between crime location and the offender's residence.[19]

Once a case is entered into ViCAP, it will never be deleted, with two exceptions:

- A case was entered in error.
- A missing person is found and was missing of his or her own volition.

Investigators working cold cases run into all types of obstacles from poorly documented case information to files that were destroyed. If the case is reopened by a cold case squad or unit, the investigators who worked the original case may have retired, cannot recall key details of the case, or they may have died. By entering the case in ViCAP, the case information will never grow cold because every time a query is made in the system, all of the cases in the system are compared.[20] (See Chapter 15, "Cold Case Review Teams and Information Sharing Resources" for ViCAP and its collaboration with NamUs.)

Individual Agency Cold Case Websites

In addition, many individual law enforcement agencies now post write-ups on their unsolved homicides, and coroners and medical examiners list their unidentified remains. (See Chapter 16.)

Summary

Resources in this chapter include a guide to some of the databases that may be helpful in cold case research. Investigators use many databases in cold case research. Among them are the following:

- CODIS: Combined DNA and National DNA Index Systems, along with a discussion of the services of the University of North Texas Center for Human Identification (UNTCHI).
- IAFIS: Integrated Automated Fingerprint Identification System.

- NamUs System. (See Chapter 6, "NamUs: Connecting the Missing and Unidentified," and Chapter 7, "Entering and Searching in the NamUs System.")
- NCMEC: National Center for Missing and Exploited Children.
- NCIC: National Crime Information Center (including its historical database).
- NIBIN: National Integrated Ballistic Information Network.
- State clearinghouses, for example, CBI: Cold Case Files of the Colorado Bureau of Investigation.
- The Doe Network: International Center for Unidentified and Missing Persons (and a sampling of other privately funded databases).
- ViCAP: Violent Criminal Apprehension Program.
- Individual agency cold case websites. (See Chapter 16, "Taking Advantage of the Media.")

Endnotes

1. CODIS, www.dna.gov/dna-databases/codis (accessed December 26, 2011).
2. UNTCHI, www.hsc.unt.edu/departments/pathology_anatomy/dna/Forensics/Initiative/Information.cfm (accessed December 26, 2011).
3. NCMEC www.missingkids.com (accessed December 26, 2011).
4. NCIC www.fas.org/irp/agency/doj/fbi/is/ncic.htm and www.fbi.gov/about-us/cjis/ncic/ncic (accessed December 26, 2011).
5. Lyford, G. and Wood, U. "National Crime Information Center: Your Silent Partner," *FBI Law Enforcement Bulletin* 52:3 (March 1983), 10–15.
6. "When Offline is Better: Another Way to Search Crime Records," www.fbi.gov/news/stories/2010/january/ncic_010410, January 4, 2010.
7. "When Offline is Better, Another Way to Search Crime Records," www.fbi.gov/news/stories/2010/january/ncic_010410, January 4, 2010.
8. Zachariah, Holly. "Families of missing can find answers through online networks," *The Columbus Dispatch* (March 21, 2011).
9. Zachariah, Holly. "Families of missing can find answers through online networks," *The Columbus Dispatch* (March 21, 2011).
10. The Doe Network, www.doenetwork.org (accessed December 26, 2011).
11. ViCAP, Violent Criminal Apprehension Program, www.fbi.gov/wanted/vicap and www.fbi.gov/about-us/cirg/investigations-and-operations-support/vicap-brochure-1 (accessed December 26, 2011).
12. Dickson, F.R. Warden. California State Prison at San Quentin, *Cumulative Case Summary on Condemned Inmate Harvey Murray Glatman* (February 25, 1959).
13. Dickson, F.R. Warden. California State Prison at San Quentin, *Cumulative Case Summary on Condemned Inmate Harvey Murray Glatman* (February 25, 1959).
14. Stiltner, Suzanne. E-mail correspondence with author, 28 November 2011.
15. Taylor, Michael. March 4, 1998, Obituary—Pierce Brooks. http://articles.sfgate.com/1998-03-04/news/17715701_1_serial-killers-mr-brooks-onion-field (accessed December 26, 2011).

16. Trainum, James. Detective. E-mail correspondence with author, September 8, 2011.
17. ViCAP, Violent Criminal Apprehension Program, www.fbi.gov/wanted/vicap and www.fbi.gov/about-us/cirg/investigations-and-operations-support/vicap-brochure-1 (accessed December 26, 2011).
18. Royal Canadian Mounted Police, ViCLAS, www.rcmp-grc.gc.ca/tops-opst/bs-sc/viclas-salvac-eng.htm (accessed December 26, 2011).
19. Mardigian, Special Agent Steve. E-mail correspondence with author, October 4, 2011.
20. ViCAP, Violent Criminal Apprehension Program, www.fbi.gov/wanted/vicap and www.fbi.gov/about-us/cirg/investigations-and-operations-support/vicap-brochure-1 (accessed December 26, 2011).

II

Missing, Murdered, and Unidentified

NamUs: Connecting the Missing and Unidentified

6

As shown in Chapter 5, "Dealing with Databases," investigators use many different databases in their investigations. The NamUs System, which was new in 2009, is already proving essential in research on missing and unidentified persons. The system's powerful database links NamUs-MP (data on missing persons) to NamUs-UP (data on unidentified persons). The following case of Paula Beverly Davis and Englewood Jane Doe (found in Montgomery County, Ohio) is one of the database's early success stories, but there are many others, leading to resolution for law enforcement, medical examiners/coroners, and family members.

Case History: Paula Beverly Davis and Englewood Jane Doe

PAULA BEVERLY DAVIS MISSING

On August 8, 1987, 21-year-old Paula Beverly Davis visited her parents' home in Kansas City, Missouri. She did her laundry, and then she and her 14-year-old sister Stephanie Beverly (now Stephanie Beverly Clack) went out for a pizza. They talked about getting tickets to a concert by the rock band, Bon Jovi. Nothing was out of the ordinary, and it never occurred to Stephanie that she would not see Paula again, or that she, Stephanie, would play a major role one day in restoring her sister's identity.

In a telephone interview with the author, Stephanie described Paula as "a pretty brunette" who was very outgoing and could make new friends instantly.[1] (See Figure 6.1.) Paula had married and moved out of her parents' home, but she had separated from her husband and at the time of her disappearance lived in the Kansas City area in an apartment with a female roommate. At three a.m. on the morning of August 9, 1987, Paula's roommate called the Beverly household saying that Paula had not come home as expected. The roommate had last seen her at a truck stop near the exit at Oak Grove, Missouri, on Interstate 70. Within hours, Paula's mother, Esther Beverly, took Stephanie and went to her local police department where she filed a missing person's report, even noting a bleached-out spot on the back pocket of Paula's blue jeans. And, of most importance many years later, Mrs. Beverly specified that her daughter had two tattoos: a unicorn on her right breast and a red rose with green leaves on her left breast.[2]

Figure 6.1 Paula Beverly Davis was reported missing from Kansas City, Missouri, on August 9, 1987. (Photo courtesy of the Beverly family.)

Because Paula was an adult, her family was told that she may have left willingly, although they were certain that Paula would not have taken off without telling anyone. All the police agreed to do was to give Mrs. Beverly a copy of the report, which she filed away. Although deeply worried and concerned, Paula's parents, Stephanie, and a middle sister, Alice Beverly, held out hope that she was alive. As the years went by, Paula's sisters grew up and family members tried to get on with their lives. A couple of years after Paula's disappearance, the extended family moved from Kansas City to a smaller town and eventually to rural Missouri, where they remained physically and emotionally close to one another. Esther Beverly died in 2005, never knowing what happened to her oldest child.[3]

JANE DOE FOUND IN OHIO

Meanwhile, nearly 600 miles to the east, near Englewood, Montgomery County, Ohio, an unidentified white female's semi-nude body was found near an eastbound ramp off Interstate 70. The date was August 10, 1987, the day after Esther Beverly reported Paula missing in Missouri.[4] The Montgomery County Coroner's Office, in Dayton, Ohio, examined Jane Doe and estimated that she was between 17 and 25 years of age, approximately five-foot-five-inches tall, and weighed 125 pounds. The cause of her death was "ligature strangulation." The unidentified Caucasian woman had brown eyes and brown hair, was wearing blue jeans and a blue headband, and she had a tattoo of a unicorn on her right breast and a red rose with green leaves on her left breast.[5]

Ohio authorities relegated their unidentified victim to an obscure gravesite in Westmont Cemetery, surrounded by forests, beyond a locked gate and down a mile-long gravel road off South Gettysburg Avenue, south of Dayton. This burial ground for the county's indigent and unknown had opened in 1943. It was owned and operated by the nearby Dayton Human Rehabilitation Center, whose inmates made the wooden caskets and buried the bodies. The last burial was in 2002 when the then-73-year-old jail closed its doors. Westmont Cemetery, now owned by the city of Dayton, is a classic "potters' field," a Biblical reference for the final resting place of the poor. When a reporter for the *Dayton Daily News* visited the cemetery in 1999, he called it a "no-frills burial ground for the penniless and forgotten."[6] (Today, to save on burial costs, the county's indigent are cremated and interred at the Woodlawn Cemetery in downtown Dayton.)

Many of the deceased had no friends, no family, and no assets. Veterans' tabs were picked up by the federal government, and the state of Ohio paid for Medicaid recipients. According to a newspaper article written in 2004, only three of the burials were of unidentified remains. In addition to Jane Doe, there were two males, one black and one Caucasian, both buried in 2001 and both estimated to have been born in the 1930s. Public access to the cemetery is only available on Memorial Day. Although a few wooden crosses and plastic flowers are left by the once-a-year visitors, only one of the 2,651 burials is marked with a gravestone. In 1992, however, the jail staff mounted a plaque on a large boulder easily visible to anyone who came to visit. On the plaque is the following inscription, a common, and poignant epitaph, and one of several variations of a verse that dates back to medieval England.

> Remember me as you walk by
> As you are now, so once was I
> As I am now, soon you must be
> So walk on by, but think of me.[7]

ENGLEWOOD JANE DOE IDENTIFIED AS PAULA BEVERLY DAVIS

As the number of burials at Westmont Cemetery continued to increase, Jane Doe was not entirely forgotten. Englewood Police Department Sergeant Mike Lang had started his law enforcement career as a dispatcher when he was still in college. Even then, he got teletypes with possible leads on the unknown victim. None of the tips, at the time, however, led to her identification. Lang started working as a detective in 2000 and remembers her case being passed from one detective to another. "We knew we had a woman who was savagely murdered," he told a reporter in 2010, "but we had no idea who she was."[8]

Unfortunately, the above scenario—a missing person in one state and unidentified remains in another—is still far too common. (See Chapter 16 for the John Doe/Joseph Coogan case that took two decades to solve.) For more than two decades, no one made the connection between Paula missing in Missouri and the unidentified remains in Englewood, Ohio. In the spring of 2009, however, former Chief Deputy Investigator Harry Brown, along with Ken Betz, director of both the Montgomery County coroner's office and its crime laboratory, entered descriptions of their handful of unidentified remains cases into NamUs-UP. This unidentified remains database is linked to the missing persons database, NamUs-MP, to form the National Missing and Unidentified Persons System of the National Institute of Justice (NIJ).

The Englewood Jane Doe case from 1987 was one of the first cases that the Montgomery County Coroner's Office entered into NamUs-UP, as UP-985. In a telephone interview with the author, James H. Davis, MD, (See Figure 6.2.) longtime coroner of Montgomery County (having been associated with the coroner's office since 1975), stated, "We learned of NamUs through the National Association of Medical Examiners (NAME), and we discussed its value—as far as everyone being able to investigate—at meetings of the National Institute of Justice." In praise of

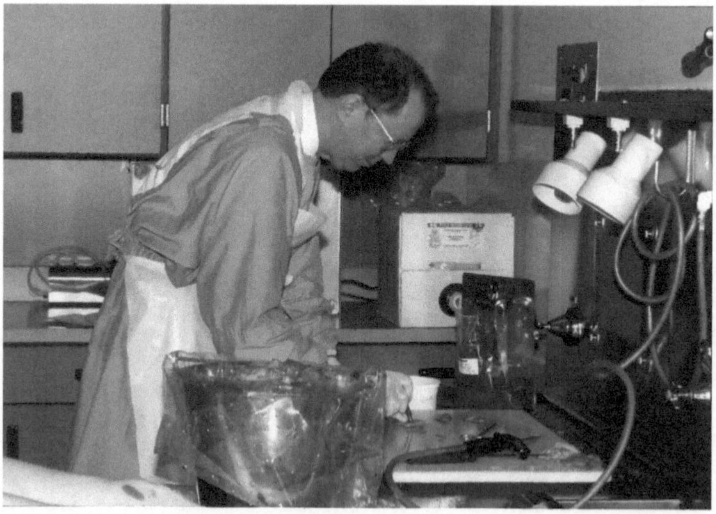

Figure 6.2 The day after Paula Beverly Davis disappeared from Missouri, Englewood Jane Doe was found in Montgomery County, Ohio. James H. Davis, MD, coroner of Montgomery County, Ohio (no relation to the victim) is shown performing an autopsy in the early 1980s. (Photo courtesy of the Montgomery County Coroner's Office.)

the well-organized structure of the NamUs System's interlocking databases Dr. Davis added, "We were hopeful that it would bring closure to families. You never get anything without asking for it. We were just rolling the dice. It's important to get the word out."[9]

A few months later, in October 2009, one of Stephanie Clack's family members told her about a public service announcement that had aired after a television episode of *The Forgotten*. The PSA gave a brief explanation of the NamUs searchable databases, the first government-sponsored databases of their kind to allow access not only to law enforcement and medical examiners/coroners, but also to the general public. Stephanie and her sister Alice decided to give it a try. The two women, now in their thirties, sat down at their computer with a copy of Paula's missing person report and started plugging Paula's basic identifying information into the NamUs-UP website. The first parameters the sisters entered were Paula's sex: female, age: 21, race: white, and Missouri, the state where she was last seen alive. But no cases came up as a result of their first search. They knew to manipulate the parameters, so they removed Missouri from the criteria and tried again.

The second attempt produced 10 search results. Stephanie and Alice quickly read through the first nine and ruled them all out. Then they got to the very last profile, which was a description of an unidentified female found in Montgomery County, Ohio, complete with a tattoo of a unicorn on her right breast and a red rose with green leaves on her left breast. "We knew, right away, it was Paula," said Stephanie. "The search only took about 30 minutes. Initially, we didn't believe that we would find her. We just started crying. We looked at each other and asked, 'Oh my God, what do we do now?'"[10]

Still in shock, Stephanie called the contact number listed on the NamUs-UP database, which was the Englewood Police Department. Her call, however, was on a weekend, so she had to wait until the next business day. As soon as she spoke with a detective, Stephanie emphatically told him that Englewood's Jane Doe was her sister. She explained about the tattoos and even mentioned the bleached-out spot on the back pocket of Paula's blue jeans. An incredulous man's voice on the other end of the line told Stephanie that he had examined the jeans in his evidence room, and, sure enough, the bleached-out spot was still there. On December 11, 2009, DNA comparison of saliva from inside the cheek of Paula's father, along with evidence that the Englewood Police Department had collected from the crime scene and the Montgomery County Coroner's Office had preserved from the autopsy positively identified the Ohio victim as Paula Beverly Davis.

FORENSICS, AND BRINGING PAULA HOME

As Stephanie Clack learned when she called the Englewood Police Department, the police had kept Paula's clothing, but tissue samples, rape kit contents, and anything on or about the body was, and is, preserved by the coroner's office. "We thought about new technology in the future and kept samples of our victims' DNA, long before DNA was even used in identifications," said Dr. Davis, who, incidentally, is not related to Paula. "Providing the information to solve this victim's identity is critical to the resolution of this case. NamUs is an extremely useful tool."[11]

Next for the Beverly family was the daunting task of bringing Paula home. Exhumation, cremation, and reburial fees would cost thousands of dollars, beyond their means. So, the family held fundraisers and accepted donations, including one from the cast of *The Forgotten*. In May 2010, Stephanie spoke at a hearing in the Montgomery County Probate Court. Then she and her family members went to Westmont Cemetery for Paula's exhumation, but authorities kept them away from the grave and blocked their view when it was being opened. Paula's plot had a number, but nothing to identify it on the ground. Numbered concrete markers, however, identified various sections. In order for groundsmen to locate Paula's grave, they had to use ropes to further define the cemetery's grid system. A local mortuary then cremated Paula's remains, which the family took with them back home to Missouri.

On a hot day in June 2010, family and friends gathered under an awning for a memorial service in the same cemetery that holds Esther Beverly's grave. Paula and her mother finally were together again after 22 years. Among the memorial's attendees was Marianne Asher-Chapman, mother of a missing young woman and one of the founders of the missing persons support group, Missouri Missing.[12] (See Chapter 14, "Contact with Co-Victims.") "I was honored to attend the service," said Marianne in a telephone interview. "I was in awe of Paula's family. I stood there with kindred spirits, people who fully understood the roller coaster I was on and am still on."[13] Stephanie, now a member of the group, spoke on behalf of her sister Alice and herself. Then came a recording of Jason Michael Carroll's song "Hurry Home," with its haunting chorus, in part: "It doesn't matter what you've done, I still love you. It doesn't matter where you've been, you can still come home."

Finally, the family placed Paula's cremated remains in a niche. On its cover, along with her name and dates, is an engraving of a unicorn and a rose. The young woman was found through her family's love and perseverance, a well-filled-out missing person's report, DNA technology, and a coroner's office that diligently entered all of the components of the unidentified remains into the NamUs-UP database.

NamUs: An Investigative Tool

The identification of Englewood's Jane Doe as Paula Beverly Davis is a NamUs success story. It is also a great example of how dual databases were able to tie together a coroner's office and a family, both of whom had direct and tangible data to share with each other. For 22 years, Paula's family had no information at all. In Ohio, the Montgomery County coroner's investigators and the Englewood police detectives were stumped, until Paula's sisters, members of the general public, sat in their own living room and accessed this free online system. NamUs is an investigative tool: a user-friendly electronic registry with two linked databases. NamUs-MP contains data on missing persons, whereas information on the remains of unidentified persons is located in NamUs-UP. Both components of the NamUs System are accessible from the NamUs home page www.namus.gov.

All that Paula's sisters did, in October 2009, was perform a simple search in NamUs-UP, the unidentified persons database. They typed in basic information on Paula, then deleted "Missouri" (where they had assumed her remains to be) when they initially did not get any results. The system was so new at the time, that Paula's missing person case had never been entered into NamUs-MP, the missing persons database. If Paula's missing person case had been in NamUs-MP, her identification with Englewood Jane Doe may have been discovered even earlier.

One of the advantages of access that members of law enforcement, coroners, and medical examiners (but not the public) enjoy are automatic matches. When Paula's sisters manipulated Paula's parameters in the NamUs-UP database, they narrowed their selection to 10 possible results. If Paula's case had been entered in the NamUs-MP database, those same 10 possible results would have automatically been viewable to the Montgomery County Coroner's Office, the Englewood Police Department, and even to the police who, 22 years earlier, had taken Paula's missing person's report. Luckily for Paula's family, an investigator in the coroner's office in Montgomery County, Ohio, had entered the Jane Doe case from Englewood, Ohio.

Although anyone can search the databases without registering, registration on the missing person website allows the user to enter missing persons into the database. A case manager then verifies the cases with law enforcement and obtains additional information, including an NCIC number, before the cases go live. Registered users can track cases they "own" or initiate, and they can follow their cases and those of others. When law enforcement, however, enters a case, sensitive case material (such as a photograph of a decomposed body) can be blocked from the general public.

An additional advantage of registering and using the system is that the NIJ funds free forensic services, including odontology, anthropology, and fingerprint and DNA analyses. The DNA testing is conducted at the University of North Texas Center for Human Identification (UNTCHI), which provides family reference-sample kits at no charge to any jurisdiction in the country. Other efforts include training law enforcement officers, medical examiners, judges, and attorneys on forensic DNA evidence. (See Chapter 15 for ViCAP and its collaboration with NamUs.)

How NamUs Evolved

In order to understand how NamUs came into existence, it is necessary to go back and explore the beginnings of a federal government program called the DNA Initiative. In August 2001, the U.S. attorney general directed the Office of Justice Program's (OJP) National Institute of Justice (NIJ) to assess criminal justice system delays in the analysis of DNA evidence and to develop recommendations to eliminate those delays. In response, the NIJ convened a working group that comprised a broad cross-section of federal, state, and local criminal justice and forensic science experts. The group met twice in 2002 to discuss the nature and causes of DNA backlogs and possible strategies for reducing the backlogs. Counseled by the findings of this working group, the NIJ submitted a report to the attorney general with a series of recommendations to eliminate the DNA testing backlog and to build the nation's capacity to use DNA evidence routinely as an investigative tool. The DNA Initiative's goal was to provide funding, training, and assistance to ensure that forensic DNA reaches its full potential to solve crimes, protect the innocent, and identify missing persons.

In 2003, the NIJ began funding major efforts to maximize the use of DNA technology in our criminal justice system. Much of the NIJ's work has focused on developing tools to investigate and solve the cases of missing persons and to identify unidentified remains. The impetus for the NamUs System really began that same year, 2003, when the International Homicide Investigators Association (IHIA) obtained grant funds from the Department of Justice's Office for Victims of Crime (OVC) to assemble a group to develop improved procedures for managing missing and unidentified persons. The group was developed as a public service with no funding and met numerous times between 2003 and 2006. Randy Hanzlick, MD, chief medical examiner, Fulton County, Georgia, was invited to attend because his office had a website listing unidentified cases, and he also represented the National Association of Medical Examiners. During those meetings, it became apparent that a web-based system such as NamUs was needed.[14]

Dr. Hanzlick contacted Dr. Steven C. Clark, a curriculum standards and systems developer who had directed research projects for the National Institute of Justice and the Centers for Disease Control (CDC) to see if he was interested in developing a pilot. Without funding to do so, Dr. Clark and his company, Occupational Research and Assessment, provided the computer program time, and Dr. Hanzlick became the expert on the subject matter. "We developed the Unidentified Decedent Reporting System (UDRS), and we had a pilot up and running in 2005," Dr. Hanzlick was quoted as stating in e-mail correspondence with Dr. Clark. "UDRS remained the online system until late 2007 when DOJ/NIJ then began to provide funding for system expansion. In late 2008, the UDRS merged into the system called NamUs-UP."[15]

Meanwhile, during the spring of 2005, the NIJ held a national strategy meeting in Philadelphia. Invited were federal, state, and local law enforcement officials, medical examiners and coroners, forensic scientists, key policymakers, victim advocates, and families from around the country. Called the Identifying the Missing Summit, the meeting defined major challenges in investigating and solving missing persons and unidentified decedent cases. As a result of that summit, the deputy attorney general created the National Missing Persons Task Force and charged the United States Department of Justice with identifying every available tool, and creating others, to solve these cases. One problem was a lack of reporting of adult missing persons. Those 18-years old and younger must be reported in NCIC, but getting missing persons over age 18 into databases is voluntary. When Paula Beverly Davis went missing, she was 21. The police told her family that she was an adult and, other than filing a report with information provided by her mother, there was nothing law enforcement officials could do. Now, with NamUs, there is.

NamUs was created to meet the need of improving access to databases by the people who can help. Initially the system was funded by the National Institute of Justice, in partnership with the National Forensic Science Technology Center in Largo, Florida, but, in November 2011, the partnership transitioned to the University of North Texas Center for Human Identification (UNTCHI).[16]

- Phase 1: The Unidentified Decedent Reporting System (UDRS), 2005–2007, was the pilot behind NamUs-UP, allowing searches based on characteristics including demographics, anthropological analysis, dental information, and distinct body features. Also, during this time, a functional and technical design was made of the national online missing persons database and nationwide resources which included a central access point for information on state clearinghouses, medical examiners' and coroners' offices, and victims' assistance resources, as well as legislation. A study was begun as well, to examine the legal ramifications of privacy laws and their impact on public access to information on missing persons.
- Phase 2: The Missing Persons System, an online national missing persons database, was created in 2007 and 2008.

- Phase 3: Finally, in 2009, NamUs-UP and NamUs-MP were integrated into the NamUs System to allow simultaneous searching of missing persons records with cases in the unidentified persons database.

Special Circumstances

As noted in Chapter 2, Detective Ron Lopez of the Missing Persons Unit of the Colorado Springs Police Department proactively uses NamUs to archive his solved missing persons cases in the event that those persons go missing again. Similarly, Hal G. Brown, Deputy Director of the Delaware Office of the Chief Medical Examiner (Delaware OCME) and Forensics Sciences Laboratory since 2005, (see Figure 6.3) proactively uses both NamUs databases to keep active his state's missing persons cases in which partially recovered, and forensically identified, remains have been found.

"Delaware is a coastal state, and thus we run into this scenario frequently—with skulls washing ashore on a Delaware beach many years postmortem," Brown stated in correspondence with the author.

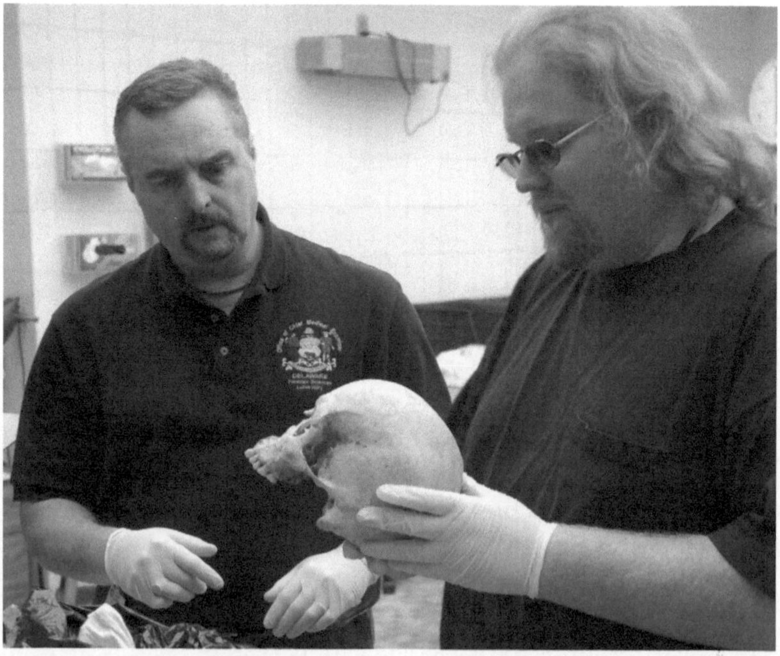

Figure 6.3 Deputy Director Hal G. Brown, left, and his assistant, Phillip Petty, examine the skull of an unidentified person in the morgue of the Delaware Office of the Chief Medical Examiner and Forensic Sciences Laboratory. (Photo courtesy of Hal G. Brown.)

Often, a serious problem is created when a missing person, following positive identification of partial remains, is completely removed from the NCIC and/or NamUs databases. Currently, neither of the databases recognizes the "partial remains" scenario as a separate category.

In NamUs, this results in the generation of many potential matches to unidentified persons when, in fact, the missing person has been identified. These situations are further compounded by regular staff turnover in law enforcement, as well as in coroners' and medical examiners' offices. In addition, case management and personal recollection of a potential missing person donor case may also be forgotten and compromised. The tragedy is finding ourselves in possession of someone's skull and absolutely no missing persons cases to serve as potential matches.[17]

Case History: Gary Mayo and Partial Remains

The no-match situation has been averted in the case of New Castle County, Delaware, drowning victim Gary Mayo. On November 22, 2007, Thanksgiving Day and the birthday of his wife, Regina Mayo, Gary and his cousin went out in a 20-foot motor boat to do a little fishing on the Christina River. In a telephone interview with the author, his widow, Regina, stated, "He'd often go out for an hour or so, and his going out that day was nothing out of the ordinary. He was a happy-go-lucky guy and lived life to the fullest, and he often said how much he was at peace on the water."[18] According to a newspaper article titled, "Weather and dark water hamper efforts by rescuers" in the following day's *News Journal*, Gary fell overboard while attempting to retrieve his hat. The water was dark, and his cousin could not see him. The cousin sounded the boat's air horn, summoning emergency personnel and divers, but a storm moved in, and repeated recovery attempts were unsuccessful.[19]

The next few years were very difficult for Regina and her children, as well as her parents and in-laws. Almost on a monthly basis, Regina was contacted by various people who claimed to have seen Gary. "Each time someone called," said Regina, "it was like a wound that kept being reopened. We were trying to get some closure, but we still had that glimmer of hope. Nothing was finalized." Instead of holding a memorial service, the family coped by placing roses in the water in memory of Gary every year on his birthday. Regina turned her birthday, the anniversary of Gary's death, into a celebration of his life.

As noted on the preceding pages, the NamUs Unidentified Persons and NamUs Missing Persons databases were integrated into the NamUs System that went "live" in 2009, and it would soon include Gary Mayo. Primarily on his own time, Hal G. Brown entered missing person data into the NamUs System, being careful to include as much information as possible about the cases. "A fully populated unidentified persons database in NamUs is of limited value, unless the missing persons database is also populated and every potential smidgen of forensic identification evidence has been tracked down and added, including fingerprints, DNA samples, and dental records," he stated.[20] Meanwhile, as part of Brown's endeavor to populate Delaware's NamUs missing persons database, he researched potential cases to add those involving the waterways around Wilmington, as well as Delaware's rivers, bay, and ocean coastline. Many of the missing persons cases that he added had not been listed in NCIC and had, essentially, been forgotten.

On April 23, 2010, Brown created a NamUs Missing Persons case file for Gary Mayo, then began the task of gathering additional data. More than eight months later, on January 4, 2011, a fisherman spotted a skull on a muddy tidal flat along the shoreline of the Delaware River (see Figure 6.4). The Christina River flows into the Delaware River, and the skull was located approximately 300 yards south of the port of Wilmington, seven miles downstream from where Gary was last seen. Medical–legal forensic investigator Jack Ingle of the Delaware Office of the Chief Medical Examiner Forensic Sciences Laboratory teamed with detectives of the Wilmington Police Department and took custody of the skull. The process set in motion the investigative process that became a model of multidisciplinary NamUs methodology, involving considerable collaborative and investigative tenacity.

Figure 6.4 Gary Mayo's skull was found on these tidal flats of the Delaware River, practically in the shadow of the Delaware Memorial Bridge. (Photo courtesy of Hal G. Brown.)

Deputy Director Hal G. Brown described three substantial breaks in establishing Gary Mayo's identity:

- First, there was a tip from Terri Sanginiti, a veteran reporter at the *News Journal* in Wilmington, Delaware. Sanginiti e-mailed Brown reminding him about the Gary Mayo case, asking if Mayo could be the potential donor of the skull.
- Second, Wilmington Police detectives, led by veteran Captain Nancy Dietz, were very proactive and maintained excellent working relationships with the Delaware Office of the Chief Medical Examiner.
- The third positive development was connecting with Detective Matthew Taylor of the Delaware State Police Troop 2. Brown described Taylor as "a consummate professional who cared greatly about this case and Mayo's grieving family."[21]

Brown also enlisted the assistance of additional forensic experts, sending Gary Mayo's skull to Pennsylvania, then Maine, and then to Alabama. Dr. Richard Scanlon, a forensic odontologist and a NamUs consultant in Lewiston, Pennsylvania, regularly assists Brown and many other agencies with dental examinations on human remains and missing persons cases. He compared a single tooth in the skull with dental radiographs of several possible donor decedents and reported, "The occlusal amalgam restoration in that tooth had a similar radiographic outline consistent with a match, but it was not sufficient to reach the level of positive dental identification." Dr. Scanlon did indicate that he was 95% sure the skull was that of Gary Mayo, but with only one degraded tooth, further forensic analysis was required before a positive identification could be established.[22]

Next, Brown sent the skull to forensic anthropologist Dr. Marcella Sorg of Oreno, Maine. She, with her assistant Jamie A. Wren, confirmed the initial assessment from the photographs as to age and sex, refining the age range from 35 to 46 and suggesting a postmortem interval of approximately three to five years. She could not exclude the skull as being Gary Mayo's. She also concluded that the skull exhibited primarily African American, Asian, and also Native American characteristics. Brown then interviewed Regina Mayo who revealed that her husband had Native American and also Asian ancestry in his maternal and paternal lines. Stated Brown, "This amazing revelation was entirely consistent with Dr. Sorg's assessment, but it still could not be forensically proven that the skull was that of Gary Mayo."[23]

Then, a search of Gary's medical records revealed that in the months prior to his disappearance, he had undergone a CT scan of his para-nasal sinuses. Next to examine the skull was Dr. Byron Gilliam Brogdon, of the University of South Alabama Medical Center. Meticulous positioning of the skull by Dr. Brogdon and his assistant Jamie Elifritz, enabled reconstruction of images to replicate the antemortem CT almost exactly, which produced many compelling matching features, particularly in the sphenoid sinuses and ultimately, an unequivocal positive identification. Stated Dr. Brogdon, "This may well be the first successful identification of an unknown body by comparison of the sphenoid sinuses on CT images of a skull when visualization of frontal sinus by conventional radiology was compromised."[24]

In February 2011, Brown, along with Corrie Schmitt of the Delaware State Police Victim Services Unit, personally visited Regina in her home to tell her the news. According to Regina, they were helpful and compassionate, took the time to explain the scientific findings, and explained that Gary Mayo's case will be kept active in both NCIC and NamUs. Finally, Regina and her family had the proof they needed to hold Gary's memorial service, a service that was attended by a standing-room-only gathering of friends and family. "The closure that we got helped a lot," said Regina. "I didn't realize how much grief I had."[25]

(For two additional stories of drowning victims, in very different circumstances, see the underwater sonar recovery of Scot Glover, under Ralston & Associates, in Chapter 14, as well as the identification of a John Doe as Joseph Coogan, in Chapter 16.)

Summary

Resources in this chapter include:

- An explanation of the NamUs System that connects a missing persons database with an unidentified persons database, along with a case study on its application
- Descriptions of free forensic services available to law enforcement and medical examiners/coroners
- A medical examiner/coroner example of how to handle a partial remains case

New in 2009, the NamUs System is a powerful investigative tool that links two databases: NamUs-MP, on missing persons, and NamUs-UP, on unidentified persons. A good example is the identification, 22-years later, of Paula Beverly Davis (who went missing from Kansas City, Missouri) as Englewood Jane Doe (found in Montgomery County, Ohio).

- NamUs was formed by combining the Unidentified Decedent Reporting System (UDRS) with the Missing Persons System (a missing persons database created in 2007 and 2008).
- NamUs provides (to law enforcement and medical examiner/coroners' office) free forensic services, including odontology, anthropology, and fingerprint and DNA analysis.
- Special circumstances include archiving solved missing persons' cases, as well as keeping those missing persons' cases active in which partial, and forensically identified, remains have been found. The discovery in Delaware of the skull belonging to drowning victim Gary Mayo is a good example of the handling of a partial remains case.

Endnotes

1. Clack, Stephanie. Telephone conversation with author, November 14, 2010.
2. Clack, Stephanie. Telephone conversation with author, November 14, 2010.
3. Clack, Stephanie. Telephone conversation with author, November 14, 2010.
4. Page, Doug. "Englewood 'Jane Doe' Pending Exhumation, Reburial," *Dayton Daily News* (May 5, 2010).
5. Davis, James H., MD. Telephone conversation with author, January 6, 2011.
6. Keilman, John. "Markers for the Nameless," *Dayton Daily News* (December 12, 1999), 1.
7. Keilman, John. "Markers for the Nameless," *Dayton Daily News* (December 12, 1999), 1.
8. Lohr, David. "TV Drama Helps Family Find Missing Loved One," *AOLNews* (February 9, 2010).
9. Davis, James H., MD. Telephone interview with author, January 6, 2011.
10. Clack, Stephanie. Telephone interview with author, November 14, 2010.
11. Davis, James H., MD. Telephone interview with author, January 6, 2011.
12. Missouri Missing, www.missourimissing.org
13. Asher-Chapman, Marianne. Telephone interview with author, December 21, 2010.
14. Hanzlick, Randy, MD. E-mail correspondence with author, January 10, 2011.
15. Clark, Dr. Steven. E-mail correspondence with author, January 13, 2011.
16. Russell, Dana Benton. "UNT Health Science Center Awarded NamUs Grant," *Wall Street Journal* (November 11, 2011).
17. Brown, Hal G. E-mail correspondence with author, October 24, 2011.
18. Mayo, Regina. Telephone interview with author, November 6, 2011.
19. Brown, Robin. "Weather and Dark Water Hamper Efforts by Rescuers," *The News Journal* (November 23, 2007).
20. Brown, Hal G. E-mail correspondence with author, November 14, 2011.
21. Brown, Hal G. E-mail correspondence with author, November 14, 2011.
22. Brown, Hal G. E-mail correspondence with author, November 14, 2011.
23. Brown, Hal G. E-mail correspondence with author, November 14, 2011.

24. Brown, Hal G. E-mail correspondence with author, November 14, 2011.
25. Mayo, Regina. Telephone interview with author, November 6, 2011.

7 Entering and Searching in the NamUs System

As shown in the previous chapter, the NamUs System is relatively new, but it is already proving to be invaluable in finding missing persons and identifying previously unidentified remains (see Figure 7.1). But, as Deputy Director Hal G. Brown of the Delaware Office of the Chief Medical Examiner stated in reference to populating both the Missing Persons and the Unidentified Persons databases, the system is only as good as the information that is provided. "While the record may reflect that there are no dental records, photographs, fingerprints, or DNA samples available, the reality is that a concerted effort to find such evidence may never have been completed," said Brown. "We never take 'not available' for an answer. For example, on a recent case, we were told crime scene images were nonexistent. Then, when my laboratory technician, Phillip Petty, conducted his own search, he found images from the 1960s—behind a refrigerator—where they had accidentally slipped into oblivion, perhaps decades before."[1]

Brown also advises that all previous forensic work and expert opinions on historic missing and unidentified persons cases be re-examined. He cites two 2011 case examples in which incorrect data were worse than no data at all. (For a similar case, see the case history of Surette Clark and Little Jane Doe in Chapter 1.)

- On November 2, 1991, a child found a human skull on the banks of the Delaware River in the town of New Castle, Delaware. Examinations at the time indicated that the remains were of a Caucasian female, and prior to 2011, potential missing persons cases were only compared to Caucasian females. As a result of the re-examination by the University of North Texas Center for Human Identification (UNTCHI), the sex and race of NamUs-UP, case number 6886, was changed to a Hispanic male.
- On October 18, 1995, a fisherman casting his net into a creek from the Buckam Bridge on County Road 418, ten miles east of Milford, Delaware, found a skull (absent the mandible) believed to have been that of a female Caucasian. As a result of Dr. Marcella Sorg's re-examination of NamUs UP-6276, she corrected the records to state that the skull was that of a male with mixed Caucasoid–Mongoloid (European and Asian or American Indian) ancestry.[2]

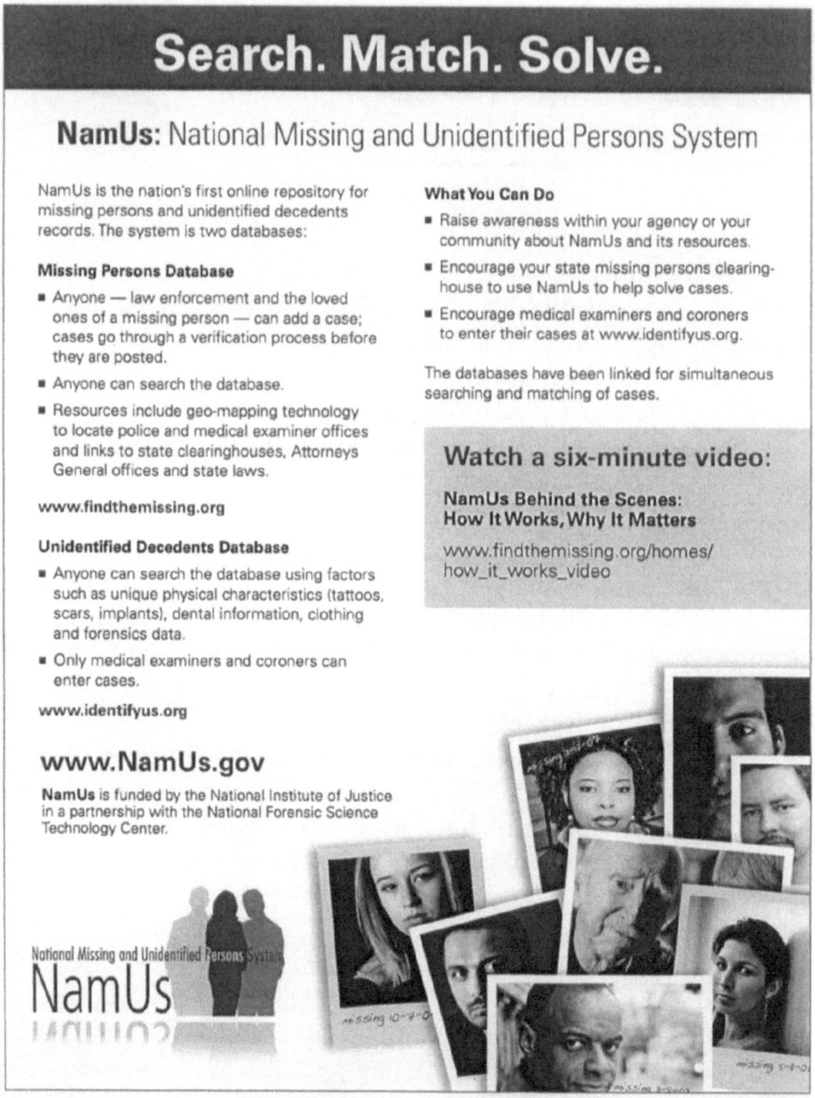

Figure 7.1 The NamUs system of linked databases on missing and unidentified persons advertises through public service announcements and encourages the public to search for missing family members. (Photo courtesy of the National Institute of Justice, U.S. Department of Justice.)

NamUs-MP: Creating a Missing Persons Case

Obviously, one's case file should be organized so that pertinent data from the missing person's report can be extracted and entered into the NamUs Missing Persons system. For long-time missing person cases, and in cases in which descriptive information such as eye color, scars, or tattoos was not recorded, additional information may need to be requested from family members. Data on missing persons cases can be entered by any registered user, but the data will not go live until they are vetted by the appropriate law enforcement agency. As soon as registration is complete, the "New Case" menu item is added to the standard menu bar. Clicking on this item loads a blank set of profile pages, although some (and parts of some) are not accessible by the general public. In entering data, it is important to include as much information as possible, but even a simple "unknown" is acceptable, as long as no required spaces are left blank. In order for the information on this and subsequent pages to make sense, go to www.namus.gov, click on the Missing Persons link, and follow along.[3]

Case Information Page: The following fields are marked with red asterisks and must be filled in (or stated "unknown"):

- First name
- Last name
- Date Last Known Alive (LKA)
- Age Last Known Alive (LKA): definite age or an age range
- Race
- Sex
- Height (in inches)
- Weight (in pounds)

The Case Information Page is also the section in which to add, if known, the missing person's middle and maiden names, nicknames, National Crime Information Center (NCIC) number, National Center for Missing and Exploited Children (NCMEC) number (if applicable), ethnicity, and blood type. (See Chapter 5 for more on NCIC and NCMEC.)

Additional required information (or "unknown"), also marked with red asterisks, is as follows:

- City (on Circumstances Page)
- State (on Circumstances Page)
- Circumstances (on Circumstances Page)
- Hair color (on Physical/ Medical Page)
- Eye color (on Physical/ Medical Page)
- Dental status (on Dental Page)
- DNA status (on DNA Page)
- Fingerprint status (on Fingerprint Page)
- Local contact's relationship (on Contact Page)

A Missing Persons (MP) case number is assigned when the "save" button is clicked once, but clicking after each page of new information is recommended, as the save mechanism reveals the case's profile strength (shown in yellow stars and described below). To ensure case validity, all new submissions are reviewed by case managers and assigned a local contact for specific case management purposes. The local contact is typically a law enforcement officer who has knowledge of and access to information about the case. All attempts are made to involve local law enforcement prior to publishing a case "live" to NamUs.

Circumstances Page: This section includes location information pertaining to the last-known address of the missing person, or in what city or state that person was last seen alive. It is also the place to enter details about the person's disappearance or any financial transactions that might be informative to the case. A default setting makes everything in this section viewable by the general public, unless a box indicating this option is unchecked.

Physical/ Medical Page: Hair and eye color (or "unknown") is required in this section. Other aspects of a missing person's physical description and medical condition, if known, are included here, as well. Medical conditions include implants, foreign objects, skeletal information, absent organs, prior surgery, medications, drugs of abuse, known allergies, and known illnesses, as well as medical disorders and other related information. This is also the place to include detailed information on amputations, deformities, scars and marks, tattoos, piercings, and prosthetics. As noted in the case of Englewood Jane Doe, her tattoos led directly to her identification as Paula Beverly Davis. Photographs of tattoos can be uploaded on the Images Page.

Clothing and Accessories Page: This section is used to inventory clothing and accessories on or associated with the person when last seen, as well as clothing the missing person habitually wore or used. If the information is unknown, the "clothing and accessories are unknown" button should be selected so that viewers know the page was not overlooked.

Electronic Communications Page: Any electronic data, that is, electronic footprint, that is helpful in locating a missing person is entered in this section. In addition to cell phone use and records, it can include social media, chat rooms, online nicknames, and frequented websites. This page is blocked to general public users.

Transportation Methods Page: Data about how a person traveled are listed in this section. In addition to personal transportation methods—car, truck, motorcycle, or bicycle, along with identifying information—it also covers public transportation used if an individual went missing while traveling.

Secondary Parties Page: This section is used to list persons who may have had contact with the missing person, and each individual is entered separately. These individuals can include relatives (i.e., husband, wife, father, mother, son, daughter, cousin, grandfather, grandmother, etc.) as well as a landlord, co-worker, or even someone the missing person may have met often for lunch.

Dental Page: Dental information is listed as shown below, but only its status (i.e., not the specifics) is viewable to general public users:

- Dental information/charting is currently not available. Explain in comments box below.
- Dental information/charting is available and will be entered later. Explain below.
- Dental information/charting is below. This option allows for detailed charting of each tooth.

DNA Page: Information on DNA testing and analysis is shown below, but only its status (i.e., not the specifics) is viewable to general public users:

- Sample is currently not available. Explain in comments box below.
- Initial inquiry underway.
- Sample available—Not yet submitted.
- Sample submitted—Tests not complete.
- Complete. This option opens up fields to indicate whether the DNA is a direct sample from the missing person, or if it is a family reference sample from a blood relative. Additional fields allow for the selection of either mitochondrial DNA (inherited only through a person's mother) or nuclear DNA, inherited from both of a person's parents, as well as the name of the testing laboratory.

Fingerprints Page: Fingerprint information is listed as shown below, but only its status (i.e., not the specifics) is viewable to general public users.

- Fingerprint information is currently not available. Explain in comments box below.
- Fingerprint information is available elsewhere. Explain below.
- Fingerprint information below. This option allows for the entering of fingerprint coding, as well as the uploading of an electronic fingerprint card.
- Images Page: Several different images—from facial and dental radiographs to clothing, jewelry, and tattoos—can be uploaded into this section. All images must be in JPEG format. A default setting makes everything in this section viewable by the general public, unless a box indicating this option is unchecked. However, the photographs will be reviewed for suitability for public viewing before they go live.

Documents Page: This section is similar to the Images Page, but it will accept electronic files in formats other than JPEG, such as PDF and

Word document files. Examples include a flyer for a missing person or a police report. A default setting makes everything in this section viewable by the general public, unless a box indicating this option is unchecked.

Police Information Page: Contact information for a specific agency or agencies goes in this section and is viewable by the general public. However, this is also the place for circumstances and case details of a sensitive nature that are not accessible to the public.

Reports Page: This section will generate the following reports:

- Case Report: A summary of information on the missing person's case profile
- Printable Poster: A PDF document that generally includes the person's facial image, basic demographic and case information, and any specific features that might lead to location and identification
- E-mail Poster: Allows the poster to be e-mailed to a specific address
- Case Chronology Report: Information from the missing person's Case Information Page, as well as changes made to the case
- Activities Log Report: A printer-friendly version of the Activities Log at the bottom of the screen

Contacts Page: The relationship of the local contact (often a family member, but it can also be an agency representative) to the case is required in this section. Additional contact information is provided for the case manager, regional administrator, and the person who entered the case.

Exclusion Page: This section provides the means by which investigators can submit to the NamUs case managers an exclusion for a missing person, added to a list of unidentified bodies already ruled out as the searched-for missing person.

Possible UP Matches Page: In this section, investigators and case managers can view possible side-by-side matches (including images) to unidentified persons that have been automatically generated by the NamUs system. If there are too many possible matches, click on "Adjust Sensitivity" to:

- Narrow down the matches by dental, DNA, or fingerprint availability
- Search a specific date range
- Sort the possible matches by state and even within a specified number of miles from the last known alive (LKA) location

If searching for skeletal remains, it is important to eliminate restrictions on weight. And, in addition to going through the possible matches for a missing person, one can join the coroners and medical examiners who are similarly searching from the NamUs Unidentified Persons (NamUs-UP) database.

Case Changes Page: Additions, changes, removals, and exclusions awaiting approval, denial, or being put on hold are included in this section.

An Activities Log is located at the bottom of every page in every case profile in the Missing Persons System (NamUs-MP). Case managers and those with law enforcement access can enter and build permanent records of tasks they undertake and interactions they have with others regarding specific cases. For instance, this is where Delaware's Hal G. Brown enters his information on the positive identification of partial remains.[4]

Missing Person Case Submission and Profile Strength

When all of the required fields have been completed, a "Submit to NamUs" button will appear on the screen. After it is clicked, NamUs administrators will begin their review. Even though the person who entered the case will be able to view the case online, others will not see it, nor will it be searchable, until the case is validated by a case manager and the case goes "live."

Even before missing persons cases go live, however, they are ranked in terms of the amount of their potentially useful information. NamUs-MP automatically assigns a star rating based on the data entered: that is, the number of stars increases as the case becomes more likely to be solved. Initially, all cases start with five uncolored star icons. As the amount of useful information increases, these images turn from five empty stars to five yellow stars. A minimum of one star is needed for posting. In general, the rating system is as follows:

- One Star: This missing person case includes a first name, last name, age, sex, race, height, weight, hair color, and eye color. Also there must be a date, city, and state where the person was last seen, as well as the circumstances of the disappearance. If information is unknown, then "unknown" can be inserted into the listing.
- Two Stars: This case includes all of the above plus a facial photo or law enforcement information with a case number.
- Three Stars: This case includes all of the above plus a facial photo and law enforcement information with a case number.
- Four Stars: This case meets the criteria for three stars and has, in addition, one of the following pieces of entered data:
  - Fingerprint information
  - A description of scars and marks along with a photo or photos
  - A description of tattoos with a photo or photos
  - Tooth-specific dental data
  - DNA profile information

- Five Stars: This case meets the criteria for three stars and has, in addition, two or more of the following pieces of entered data:
  - Fingerprint information
  - A description of scars and marks along with a photo or photos
  - A description of tattoos with a photo or photos
  - Tooth-specific dental data
  - DNA profile information[5]

Searching and Reviewing Missing Person Cases

There are three ways to search the NamUs-MP system. On the Home Page are both the Quick Search Feature and a Keyword Search Feature to the right of the menu bar. The Quick Search is the place to search by first name, last name, sex, or state by entering criteria into the appropriate input boxes. If using the Keyword Search, type in a name or case number, or even a street address or a year.

Also on the menu bar, under "Search," is an advanced "New Search" option. When performing this search, choose from several condensed categories that represent the various pages in the system, expand them into fields by clicking on the "+" next to the category's name, and click on "Search" at the bottom of the list. Items in lists and logs (such as date found and age range) can be sorted in ascending or descending order. Researchers can easily move from page to page, as well as from case to case.

The Search Results page displays cases that are based on the selected search criteria. They are presented in three formats: case log (by default), thumbnail photographs, and a map. From the map, individual and group markers open to display the missing persons' case profiles. This option can quickly reveal all missing persons, for example, named "Smith" in the United States, as well as all females in any particular state. Cases may be added to "Case Tracking" for future reference and shared with other users of the system.

The system also has several other distinctive features. In addition to the Quick Search, the Home Page also includes "Recent Cases," an "MP Case Breakdown," and a "State Case Breakdown." The Recent Cases section shows photos and links to two randomly selected cases, from the ten most recently entered into the system. The MP Case Breakdown gives statistics of total cases, open cases, closed cases, and NamUs-aided cases. Statistics for each state are available via a drop-down menu.

Although Search (with its resultant New Search) is an option on the drop-down menu, other resources are available through other drop-down menus. The menu titled "Resources" opens a generous listing of state-specific contact information with links to state clearinghouses, medical examiner and coroner offices, and law enforcement agencies. It also supplies articles, videos, and updates on DNA testing of unidentified remains, DNA reference

Figure 7.2 In 1938, the president of the Daughters of the American Revolution placed a wreath on the Tomb of the Unknown Soldier in Arlington National Cemetery, in Arlington, Virginia. The inscription on the tomb reads, "HERE RESTS IN HONORED GLORY AN AMERICAN SOLDIER KNOWN BUT TO GOD." (Photo courtesy of Harris and Ewing Collection, Library of Congress.)

kits, the DNA Initiative, and adult and child information from the National Criminal Justice Reference Service (NCJRS). The site can also generate missing persons posters and even map out possible travel routes that a missing person might have taken.

The News Room menu includes Media Resources, Public Service Announcements, NamUs in the News links, and contact information for media and congressional inquiries. The Help menu has several additional resources, including a User Guide and Frequently Asked Questions. And, to be proactive, like Detective Ron Lopez of the Colorado Springs Police Department, be sure to "Archive" (under "Dashboard") missing persons who are found, as they may become missing persons (or possible homicide victims) again.[6]

Remembering the unknown is a long-standing tradition (see Figure 7.2).

NamUs-UP: Creating an Unidentified Persons Case

Only medical examiners, coroners, or their authorized official designees (i.e., not law enforcement or the public) enter case information in the Unidentified

Persons Database. However, it is not necessary for them to be experts. To ensure accuracy, NamUs provides pro bono forensic specialists, including odontologists and anthropologists, who have the ability to edit specific data on all cases in their regions. The data entered into NamUs-UP include, but are not limited to, photographs, fingerprints, description of clothing and personal effects, scars, tattoos, dental and full-body x-rays/radiographs, and the availability of DNA or an already completed profile on file. The NamUs-UP website includes the following pages, depending upon user access:

Case Information: This section contains the unidentified person's basic information such as date found, case number, and current disposition.

Demographics: This section gives detailed biological information, including age, race, weight, and height.

Circumstances: This section shows the location where the body was found, as well as any circumstances surrounding the discovery.

Physical/Medical: Included in this section are data on the unidentified person's amputations, deformities, scars or marks, tattoos, piercings, medical implants, foreign objects, distinctive skeletal findings, absent organs during life, or evidence of prior surgery.

Fingerprints: This section shows the status of the unidentified person's fingerprint information, as well as the actual data, if available. Fingerprint coding can be entered into text boxes, and computer files of fingerprint data can be uploaded on the Images page.

Clothing and Accessories: This section is used to describe clothing on or with the body, as well as footwear, jewelry, and eyewear such as glasses or contact lenses.

Dental: A checklist is provided here to indicate general information about dental findings, as well as a box to code up to two features for each tooth using code letters (e.g., "CR" for crown, "RC" for root canal). National Crime Information Center dental coding can be converted to NamUs dental coding with a button click.

DNA: This section shows the unidentified person's DNA status as presented in five categories:

- Sample is currently not available.
- Sample available, not yet submitted.
- Sample available, tests not complete.
- Complete, insufficient DNA for profiling.
- Complete and entered below.

Images: This section allows the uploading and viewing of images (in JPEG format at least three inches by five inches and 96 dpi) of the unidentified person, as well as items found with the individual. A selection can be made as to whether each image should be viewable to the general public.

Documents: This section functions similarly to the Images Page and allows document files to be uploaded in both document and PDF file formats.

Police Information: This section is the place to enter the names and contact information for police officers, as well as sensitive information (not viewable to the general public) that should not be on the main Circumstances Page.

Reports: This section links to reports that can be generated based on the information in a case.

Contacts: Key NamUs contacts on a specific case are listed in this section. They include the local medical examiner/coroner, the case manager, and the regional administrator.

Exclusions: This section is used to list people who have been ruled out as being the unidentified person in the case being viewed. Fields are provided for details, such as "too old" or "visual check from family" that led to the exclusions.

Possible MP Matches: This section is one of the most important features of NamUs. It allows case managers, law enforcement, and forensic specialists (but not the general public) to view possible matches and images—in side-by-side displays—to missing persons that have been automatically generated by the NamUs System. There also is an option for moving cases to the Exclusions Page. As with Possible UP Matches, on the Missing Persons database, parameters can be changed with a click on "Adjust Sensitivity."

Case Changes: Any alternations to the existing case data are shown here.[7]

Unidentified Persons' Identification Potential

As shown above, the NamUs Missing Persons website uses a five-star scale for profile strength. Five stars are also used in the Unidentified Persons website to indicate identification potential. NamUs-UP automatically assigns a star rating based on the data entered: the number of stars increases as the case becomes more likely to be solved.

Initially, all cases start with five uncolored star icons. As the amount of useful information increases, these images turn from five empty stars to five yellow stars. A minimum of one star is needed for posting. In general, the rating system is as follows:

- One Star: This unidentified person's case includes a case number, the date the body or part was found, and the county and state where the body or part was found, as well as the condition of the remains. "Unsure" or "cannot estimate" may be entered into the following required fields: estimated age group, sex, weight, and height.

- Two Stars: This case has distinctive bodily features such as scars, marks, and tattoos, or there is distinctive clothing, footwear, eyewear, or jewelry.
- Three Stars: A fingerprint classification or card has been entered or uploaded, or information has been entered in a least one of the tooth boxes on the dental chart page, or the "Recognizable Face" option has been selected in the Body Condition section, and a facial photo or artist's rendering has been uploaded.
- Four Stars: This case meets the criteria for three stars and a mitochondrial or nuclear DNA profile has been established.
- Five Stars: The face is recognizable, a facial photo or rendering has been uploaded, fingerprint information has been entered or uploaded, a DNA profile has been established, and specific tooth information has been entered.[8]

NamUs-UP: Searching and Reviewing Unidentified Persons Cases

Once submitted, the unidentified persons case is reviewed before it can be viewable to other users. Other authorized users, however, can enter follow-up notes. And, as the sisters of Paula Beverly Davis did in their successful search for Paula's remains, the general public can view and search cases, without any registration, password, or user name at all.

The following are the types of users in the NamUs-UP System:

- General Public (Not Registered): Nonregistered public users can search the system and view cases. They only have access to limited data and some images.
- Public Users (Registered): Registered public users have the same abilities as the general public user except they can create a list of cases to track changes on and can leave messages on cases.
- Law Enforcement Officers: Law enforcement officers can view all data, images, and messages for each case in the system.
- Medicolegal Officers (Medical Examiner, Coroner, Medicolegal Death Investigators): Medicolegal officers have the same abilities as law enforcement officers except they can create cases.
- Forensic Specialists (Forensic Odontologists, Forensic Anthropologists): Forensic specialists have the ability to edit specific data on all cases in their regions. For example, a forensic odontologist registered for the state of Michigan is able to edit all dental information on cases in Michigan.
- Administrators (RSA, Case Manager): Administrators manage cases and users.

As on the NamUs-MP website, the NamUs-UP website also has Quick Search and Keyword Search features on its Home Page. Quick Search is the place to enter sex, race, ethnicity, date last known alive, age last known alive, and state last known alive. Additionally, these and other search criteria, such as a case number, can be entered as keywords to the right of the menu bar.

Similarly, an advanced "New Search" option is accessible under "Search" on the menu bar. Condensed categories represent the various pages (depending upon user status) in the system, and each expands into fields by clicking on the "+" next to the category's name, then clicking on "Search" at the bottom of the list. Items in lists and logs, such as date found and age range, can be sorted in ascending or descending order. Researchers can easily move from page to page, as well as from case to case. Exclusions are visible to all users on the Case Information Page.

Again, as on the NamUs-MP website, search results are displayed in three different views: the case log (by default), thumbnails, and a map. The map view displays the search results as plotted points based on the location where the unidentified persons were discovered. From the map, individual and group markers open up to display the unidentified persons' case profiles. Cases may be added to "Case Tracking" for future reference and shared with other users of the system.

The Unidentified Persons Home Page also includes "Recent Cases," a "UP Case Breakdown," and a "State Case Breakdown." The Recent Cases section shows photos and links to two randomly selected cases, from the 10 most recent entered into the system. The UP Case Breakdown gives statistics of total cases, open cases, closed cases, and NamUs-aided cases. Statistics for each state are available via a drop-down menu.[9]

Summary

Resources in this chapter include:

- Tips for law enforcement to enter cases in the NamUs Missing Persons database
- Tips for medical examiners/coroners to enter cases in the NamUs Unidentified Persons database
- How law enforcement, medical examiners/coroners, and also the public can enter and search

As valuable as the NamUs databases are, they are only as good as the information that is provided. Before entering data, it is recommended that all forensic work and expert opinions be re-examined. For best results, investigators need to search from both sides of the system by manipulating the parameters of both NamUs-MP, on missing persons, and NamUs-UP, on unidentified remains.

- To make the system effective, law enforcement agencies need to enter their cold missing person cases, and medical examiners/coroners are encouraged to input information on their unidentified remains.
- Data on missing persons cases can be entered by any registered user, including the public, but the data will not go live until they are vetted by the appropriate law-enforcement agency.
- In addition to investigators, the public is encouraged to search the site, as well as enter additional information such as jewelry regularly worn by the missing person.

Endnotes

1. Brown, Hal G. E-mail correspondence with author, November 14, 2011.
2. Brown, Hal G. E-mail correspondence with author, November 14, 2011.
3. U.S. Department of Justice, Office of Justice Programs, *NamUs: National Missing and Unidentified Persons System; A Guide for Users,* 2010.
4. U.S. Department of Justice, Office of Justice Programs, *NamUs: National Missing and Unidentified Persons System; A Guide for Users,* 2010.
5. U.S. Department of Justice, Office of Justice Programs, *NamUs: National Missing and Unidentified Persons System; A Guide for Users,* 2010.
6. U.S. Department of Justice, Office of Justice Programs, *NamUs: National Missing and Unidentified Persons System; A Guide for Users,* 2010.
7. U.S. Department of Justice, Office of Justice Programs, *NamUs: National Missing and Unidentified Persons System; A Guide for Users,* 2010.
8. U.S. Department of Justice, Office of Justice Programs, *NamUs: National Missing and Unidentified Persons System; A Guide for Users,* 2010.
9. U.S. Department of Justice, Office of Justice Programs, *NamUs: National Missing and Unidentified Persons System; A Guide for Users,* 2010.

PKU Cards Retain Overlooked DNA

8

In 1966, hospitals across the United States began routine screening of newborn babies for phenylketonuria (PKU).[1] The newborns are pricked on one of their heels, and a drop or two of blood is placed on a PKU/Guthrie card, then filed away. Parents may not even be aware of the procedure unless their babies cry. The test for this rare metabolic disorder affects very few newborns, so most parents do not give the PKU test a second thought.

It is important for cold case investigators to know that these direct DNA samples are retained in databases in each state and may provide accurate references for comparison to unidentified remains. All 50 states perform the test on every child, but the state health departments that maintain the records have vastly wide variations in the amount of time the dried blood samples are kept on file. For instance, the states of Kansas, Louisiana, and Missouri keep them for only 30 days, no help when tracking down a missing teenager. Others keep them for a specified number of months or years. The states that keep their samples indefinitely include California, Florida, Maine, Michigan, Minnesota, New York, and Vermont, although some other states keep their abnormal results indefinitely, as well. (See the section, "PKU/Guthrie Card Information, by State," at the end of this chapter.)

Case History: DNA from PKU Identified Ben Maurer

In June 2002, 17-year-old Ben Maurer, of Piscataway, New Jersey, vanished in the middle of the night. For the next seven years—unknown to his family or to the police—he lay in an unmarked grave in the New York City Cemetery, commonly called potter's field. The 101-acre graveyard, maintained by the New York Department of Corrections, lies on Hart Island, a part of the Bronx and east of Pelham Bay Park in Long Island Sound. Maurer's remains were among the more than 750,000 burials of the indigent and unidentified who have been interred on the island since 1869.[2] A mother's suggestion, followed by innovative investigators, resulted in the first known case in which a PKU test resulted in a direct sample used to solve a missing/unidentified person case.

INITIAL INVESTIGATION

At the time that the Maurer family reported Ben Mauer missing, Kevin Parmelee (see Figure 8.1) worked as an Identification Officer/Major Crime

Figure 8.1 When Detective Kevin Parmelee worked for the Piscataway Police Department, he used a direct DNA profile from a PKU card to solve the missing person case of Ben Mauer. Parmelee is shown here examining an automotive light fixture in his current position in the Forensic Unit of the Somerset County Prosecutor's Office, in Somerset, New Jersey. (Photo courtesy of Kevin Parmelee.)

Scene Detective for the Piscataway Police Department in the small town of Piscataway, New Jersey, approximately 50 miles southwest of New York City. Ben's family tacked up posters, ran announcements on a local access television channel, and created MySpace and Facebook social networking pages both to remember the high school junior and to keep his search alive.[3]

At the police department, Parmelee worked on Ben's case with lead detective David Carmen. Parmelee took a forensic science approach, and Carmen handled the behavioral investigation aspects of the case. The men entered the following identifying information into a missing person report on Ben in the National Crime Information Center (NCIC) database:

- Five-foot-eight-inches in height
- Weight: 135 pounds
- Thin, with crewcut hair style
- Contact lenses
- Wearing unknown clothing
- Multiple scars
- Partial x-rays available
- Dental records available

A background investigation revealed:

- Ben's parents were divorced
- Ben was an average student at Piscataway High School
- His family had a middle-income lifestyle
- Ben had an older brother
- Ben had a new girlfriend
- Ben had many friends and was well liked
- His family lived in a rural community
- Ben had no past history of running away, only staying out late

Detectives Parmelee and Carmen also determined that Ben had frequented a particular diner and had been seen in a convenience store. He also had been observed walking toward another town, Dunellen. There he was spotted at the local train station, where the New Jersey Transit shuttles passengers to New York City. An officer from another jurisdiction (who did not obtain witness information) was told by a juvenile that Ben did not appear upset or depressed and that he said he was going to New York.

Piscataway police then notified the New York Police Department's Missing Persons Unit, as well as MAGLOCLEN, the Middle Atlantic–Great Lakes Organized Crime Law Enforcement Network, one of the six regional centers of the Regional Information Sharing System (RISS) that aid in multijurisdictional, multistate, and, sometimes, international, investigations. (See Chapter 15 for more on RISS.) Somehow, though, Ben slipped through the cracks.

The very next day after Ben went missing, a young man with no identification committed suicide by jumping off a building in New York City. Seven years later—in 2009—the deceased was identified as Ben Maurer. Parmelee, now a cold case investigator at the Somerset County Prosecutor's Office Forensic Laboratory in Somerville, New Jersey, in e-mail correspondence with the author, stated, "Looking back, as with any such case by investigators, there were many descriptive and forensic opportunities that resulted in no connections or identification. Had there been a national standard protocol or nationwide database [such as the NamUs System that went live in 2009] at the onset of the investigation there may have been a better chance of an earlier identification."[4]

Continued Investigation

As Detectives Parmelee and Carmen continued their investigation, Ben's friends revealed some of the teenager's personal problems. The detectives sent updates to their county's missing juvenile persons bureau, as well as to the National Center for Missing and Exploited Children

(NCMEC). Then they uploaded Ben's dental records and blood type into the National Crime Information Center database. A check with the Social Security Administration revealed no activity, and several possible sightings of Ben turned out to be negative. Multiple reports of unidentified remains were not matches to Ben, either. One of these was an inconclusive report following the comparison of the John Doe in New York City with a mitochondrial DNA sample (half of Ben's profile) from his mother.

By 2005, all investigative leads had been exhausted. As a few additional sightings and reports of unidentified remains trickled in, they, too, proved not to be Ben. Detectives Parmelee and Carmen then asked family members to search for any items that could be used as a direct reference sample, anything that might contain Ben's DNA or fingerprints. Along with clothing, magazines, and schoolbooks (where one fingerprint was recovered), Ben's mother happened to mention his "newborn blood test." (See Figure 8.2.)

Getting the results of the PKU test took a grand jury subpoena. "This was necessary," stated Parmelee, "as a standard protocol of protection from legal complications since the New Jersey Department of Health is entrusted with safe keeping and confidentiality, and they needed to maintain their standards."[5] Fortunately, the New Jersey Department of Health stores its PKU records for 23 years, and the court order

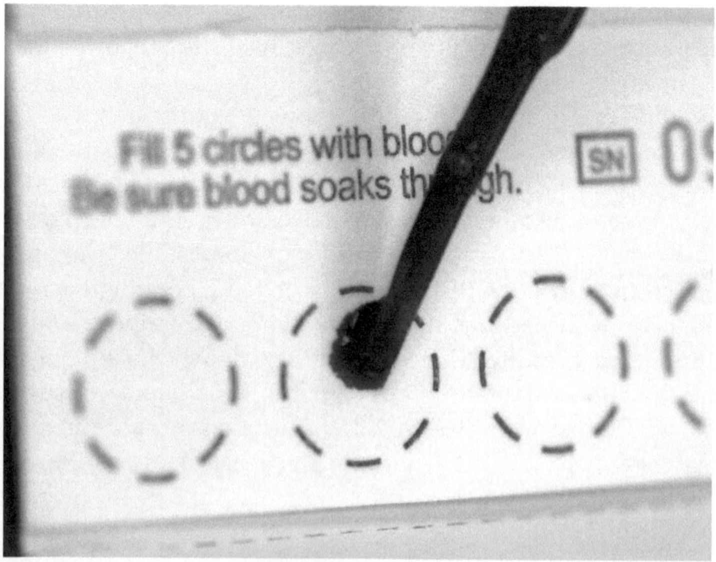

Figure 8.2 Drops of blood on PKU cards are often overlooked as accurate and direct DNA references for comparison to unidentified remains. (Photo courtesy of Kevin Parmelee.)

happened to occur in May 2008, which was a few weeks prior to the 23rd anniversary of Ben's birth on June 1, 1985.[6] After the Piscataway Police Department obtained the dried blood sample from its state's health department, detectives Parmelee and Carmen sent the sample to the University of North Texas Center for Human Identification (UNTCHI) for analysis and entry into both the Combined DNA Index System (CODIS) and the NamUs System.

On June 18, 2009, the New York City Office of the Chief Medical Examiner notified Detectives Parmelee and Carmen that Ben's PKU sample submitted to UNTCHI had been matched, after all, with the control samples of the young man who committed suicide on the day after Ben Mauer disappeared.[7] This positive identification provided resolution for his family, brought some answers to seven years of questions, but it undoubtedly raised some more. At his family's request, Ben's remains were exhumed from Hart Island and returned for burial in his hometown. In a tribute, following his online obituary, a friend wrote that Ben was "funny, friendly and so full of life."[8] Investigator Parmelee credits Ben's mother's recollection of the "newborn blood test" with solving her son's case.

PKU/Guthrie Card Information, by State

PKU/Guthrie cards provide excellent direct reference samples, especially for missing children who were adopted and no biological parents are known or available for collection. The PKU/Guthrie Card Contact Information listed on the following pages was compiled through a research project conducted by the National Center for Missing and Exploited Children under the direction of Cold Case Manager Pamela Reed. The state-by-state listings provide investigators with information on the retention policy for PKU/Guthrie cards, along with the points of contact and requirements for release in each state.[9]

Alabama

- Alabama Department of Public Health
- Cards kept since 1964, for three months
- No policy to release

Alaska

- Alaska Department of Health and Social Services, Division of Public Health
- Cards kept since 1967, for three years

- Released with parental and health care provider requests

Arizona

- Arizona Department of Health Services
- Cards kept since 1994, for three months
- No past experience in release

Arkansas

- Arkansas Department of Health
- Cards kept since 1967, for three to six months
- Released with court order, subpoena, or parental consent

California

- California Department of Health Services
- Cards kept since 1980, indefinitely
- Released with subpoena

Colorado

- Colorado Department of Public Health and Environment
- Cards kept since 1982, for six months
- Released to parents or by court order

Connecticut

- Connecticut Department of Public Health
- Cards kept since 1964, for six months
- Released to social worker or health care provider

Delaware

- Delaware Department of Health and Social Services
- Cards kept since 1972, for four months
- Release following review

District of Columbia

- District of Columbia Department of Health
- Cards kept since 1980, for one year
- Release requirements not specified

Florida

- Florida Department of Health
- Cards kept since 1965, indefinitely
- Released by law enforcement or medical examiners

Georgia

- Georgia Department of Human Resources, Division of Public Health
- Dates kept not specified
- Release requirements not specified

Hawaii

- Hawaii Department of Health
- Date of cards first kept not specified; cards kept for one year
- Released with court order or subpoena

Idaho

- Idaho Department of Health and Welfare
- Cards kept since the mid-1960s, for one year
- Released with custodial parental consent or court order

Illinois

- Illinois Department of Public Health
- Cards kept since 1965, for two months
- No past experience in release

Indiana

- Indiana Department of Health
- Cards kept since 1965, for 23 years
- Released with parental or legal guardian consent

Iowa

- Iowa Department of Public Health
- Cards kept since 1983, for five years
- Released with court order, subpoena, or by parental request

Kansas

- Kansas Department of Health and Environment
- Cards kept since 1967, for 30 days
- No past experience in release

Kentucky

- Kentucky Cabinet for Health and Family Services
- Cards kept since 1966, for 45 days (indefinitely, if abnormal)
- Released with court order

Louisiana

- Louisiana Department of Health and Hospitals
- Cards kept since 1963 or 1964, for 30 days (indefinitely, if abnormal)
- No past experience in release

Maine

- Maine Department of Health and Human Services
- Cards kept since 1999, indefinitely
- Released with parental request

Maryland

- Maryland Department of Health and Mental Hygiene
- Cards kept since 1965, for 24 years (beginning in 2004)
- Release requirements not specified

Massachusetts

- Massachusetts Department of Public Health
- Cards kept since 1990, for 10–18 years
- Released with court order or legal consultation

Michigan

- Michigan Department of Community Health
- Cards kept since 1984, indefinitely
- Released with parental consent

Minnesota

- Minnesota Department of Health
- Cards kept since 1965, indefinitely (subject to change in the future)
- Released with parental consent

Mississippi

- Mississippi Department of Health
- Cards kept since 1998, for three to four years
- No past experience in release

Missouri

- Missouri Department of Health and Senior Services
- Cards kept since 1964 or 1965, for 30 days
- Release requirements not specified

Montana

- Montana Department of Public Health and Human Services
- Cards kept since 1973, before 2008 for a few months (currently, indefinitely)
- Released with parental consent

Nebraska

- Nebraska Department of Health and Human Services
- Cards kept since 1967 (some hospitals, 1962), for 90 days
- Released with court order, subpoena, or parental consent

Nevada

- Nevada Department of Health and Human Services, Health Division
- Cards kept since 1978, for two years
- Released with parental consent

New Hampshire

- New Hampshire Department of Health and Human Services
- Cards kept since 1965, for six months
- Released with law enforcement request

New Jersey

- New Jersey Department of Health and Senior Services
- Cards kept since late 1970s, for 23 years
- Released with court order

New Mexico

- New Mexico Department of Health
- Cards kept since 1978, for one year
- Released with subpoena

New York

- New York Department of Health
- Cards kept since 1965, indefinitely
- Released with court order or request from medical examiner, physician, or parent

North Carolina

- North Carolina Department of Health, Human Services
- Cards kept since 1965, indefinitely since 2002 (subject to change in the future)
- Released with parental consent

North Dakota

- North Dakota Department of Health
- Cards kept since the 1960s, indefinitely since 2001
- Released with parental consent

Ohio

- Ohio Department of Health
- Cards kept since the 1960s, for two years
- Released with parental consent or court order

Oklahoma

- Oklahoma Department of Health
- Cards kept since 1963, for 30–42 days
- Released with parental consent

Oregon

- Oregon Public Health Division
- Cards kept since 1961, for one year
- Released with parental consent

Pennsylvania

- Pennsylvania Department of Health
- Cards kept since 1965, for eight months
- Released with parental consent

Rhode Island

- Rhode Island Department of Health
- Cards kept since 1976, for 23 years
- Released with parental request or subpoena

South Carolina

- South Carolina Department of Health and Environmental Control
- Cards kept since 1965, for two years
- Released with court order, subpoena, or parental consent

South Dakota

- South Dakota Department of Health
- Cards kept since 1973, for one month
- Release requirements not specified

Tennessee

- Tennessee Department of Health
- Cards kept since 1968, for one year (longer if abnormal)
- Released with parental consent

Texas

- Texas Department of State Health Services
- Cards kept since 1960s, for 25 years
- Released with parental consent

Utah

- Utah Department of Health
- Cards kept since 1979, for two years
- Released with parental consent

Vermont

- Vermont Department of Health
- Cards kept since 1964, indefinitely (due to flooding, only have samples since 2002)
- Release requirements not specified

Virginia

- Virginia Department of Health
- Cards kept since 1966 or 1967, for six months (if abnormal, for 10 years)
- Released with parental consent or medical examiner request

Washington

- Washington Department of Health
- Cards kept since 1976 (1960s in some locations), for 10–21 years
- Released with parental consent

West Virginia

- West Virginia Department of Health and Human Resources
- Cards kept since 1967, for three months
- Released with parental consent

Wisconsin

- Wisconsin Department of Health Services
- Cards kept since 1978, for one year
- Released with "request for information"

Wyoming

- Wyoming Department of Health
- Information not listed

Summary

Resources in this chapter include:

- An explanation of PKU/Guthrie cards as sources of direct reference DNA samples
- Retention of these samples listed by state

PKU/Guthrie cards have been on file since 1966, but their use in missing persons cases is a new tool for law enforcement agencies. The identification of Ben Maurer in New Jersey in 2009, may have been the first case in which DNA extracted from a drop of blood on a PKU card was used to find a missing person and make a positive identification of an unidentified person.

- These direct DNA samples are retained by all 50 states, but each health department varies, widely, in the amount of time the dried blood is kept on file.
- PKU/Guthrie cards may prove especially helpful for missing children who were adopted and no biological parents are known or available for family reference samples.

Endnotes

1. Parmelee, Kevin. Investigator. "PKU card: A new tool in the search for missing and unidentified individuals," *UNT Health Science Center, Forensic Services Unit Newsletter* 2:3 (May/June 2011), 5.
2. Correction Department, City of New York, City Cemetery, www.correctionhistory.org/html/chronicl/nycdoc/html/hart.html (accessed December 26, 2011).
3. Hutchins, Ryan. "DNA test leads family to missing teenager found dead in N.Y.C.," *The Star-Ledger* (Newark, NJ; July 15, 2009).
4. Parmelee, Kevin. Investigator. E-mail correspondence with author, August 30, 2011.
5. Parmelee, Kevin. Investigator. E-mail correspondence with author, August 30, 2011.
6. Ben Maurer Obituary: June 1, 1985–June 26, 2002, Piscataway, New Jersey. www.tributes.com/show/Ben-Maurer-86342216 (accessed December 26, 2011).
7. Parmelee, Kevin. Investigator. E-mail correspondence with author, August 30, 2011.
8. Ben Maurer Obituary: June 1, 1985–June 26, 2002, Piscataway, New Jersey. www.tributes.com/show/Ben-Maurer-86342216 (accessed December 26, 2011).
9. Reed, Pamela. "Direct DNA references for missing persons," *UNT Health Science Center, Forensic Services Unit Bulletin* (July 2010).

The Plight of the Missing and Unknown 9

On any given day, there are as many as 100,000 active missing persons cases in the United States. In addition, every year, tens of thousands of people vanish under suspicious circumstances. The facts are sobering and lead to what has often been referred to as "the nation's silent mass disaster."[1] Some of the missing are found or have chosen to go missing. Tragically, others either arrive home in a coffin, or they lie, unidentified, among the many thousands of sets of unidentified human remains throughout the country and the world. Some cold missing persons cases—with and even without bodies or skeletal remains—turn into homicides. Stories of the families waiting for word of their loved ones are heartbreaking, but, with the advancement of technology, there is hope.

Today, law enforcement agencies are encouraged to enter their data into state and federal databases. In addition, some parts of the country are experimenting with high-risk potential victims DNA databases for prostitutes and chronic runaways. The good news is that the University of North Texas Center for Human Identification (UNTCHI), with funding from the National Institute of Justice (NIJ), makes available two free DNA sample collection kits, one for family reference samples submitted by law enforcement, and another for unidentified human remains submitted by coroners and medical examiners.

Behind the files of cold missing persons cases are several reasons for the individuals' disappearances, including homicide, choosing to walk away, suicide, and natural and accidental death. Along with a discussion of the plight of the missing, this chapter gives an explanation of how police and prosecutors handle no-body homicides, and it concludes with suggestions for revisiting cases of the unidentified remains of John and Jane Does.

One Scenario: The Missing Person Is Presumed Dead

When a person is missing under suspicious circumstances, he or she may have been murdered. Twenty-one-year-old Paula Beverly Davis fits this example well. As shown in Chapter 6, "NamUs: Connecting the Missing and Unidentified," Paula's mother filled out an extensive missing person's report the day after the young woman disappeared in 1987. Because Paula was an adult, the police told the family that all they could do would be to keep her report in their files. Her family members, however, fearing the worst, insisted that it would have been out of character for Paula to leave her Kansas City, Missouri, home without contacting them. Twenty-two years later, and after their mother died, Paula's sisters located the young woman's remains by searching the NamUs System, the dual databases of missing persons and unidentified remains. The young woman had been strangled and dumped off an exit ramp on I-70 in Ohio, nearly 600 miles away from where she went missing. At the time of this writing, Paula's murderer still has not been found.

Marion Joan McDowell, another young woman, has been presumed dead for nearly six decades. In December 1953, she was abducted from a lovers' lane in a suburb of Toronto, Ontario. Her boyfriend—who was cleared—told police that while the couple was parked in his car, he was struck on the head. When the boyfriend regained consciousness, he saw a man stuff Marion's bloody body into the trunk of another car and drive away. Family and the police were unable to come up with any explanation. Marion's mother had a nervous breakdown, and her brother made law enforcement his career in hopes of finding his sister. Marion's case received international attention, but her remains are still missing, and her case is unsolved.

As indicated above, murder victim Paula Beverly Davis was a Jane Doe whose remains, finally, were identified. The remains of Marion Joan McDowell, however, presumably also murdered, have never been found. But what of other homicides, where—even without a body—the killer confessed, leading to a trial and conviction? This was the case in 1996, when Wayne Clifford Roberts was convicted for the murder of his stepdaughter, as described in the case history of "Surette Clark and Little Jane Doe." (See Chapter 1.) Although a search for the child's remains was part of Roberts's trial, "Little Jane Doe" was not identified as Surette Clark until after Roberts's conviction, even after his release from prison.

There also are cases where the killers are known, but there is not enough evidence to go to trial. Or, the victims' remains are missing, but their homicides are closed. An example of the latter is the murder of Michelle "Angie" Yarnell, mentioned in Chapter 14. In Angie's case, her husband was convicted of her murder, but, at the time of this writing, the woman's remains still have not been found. Family members in these situations yearn for resolution, and if there is little or no contact from law enforcement, they often feel abandoned. When done correctly, an occasional "We're-still-thinking-of-you" telephone call from law enforcement to a victim's family has been known to lift their spirits, without raising false hopes.

No-body murder cases are a challenge: for investigators, families, and prosecutors. Investigators have found that some agencies do not keep the same level of documentation on missing person cases as they do on homicides, so when the case "turns into" a homicide, they have a lot of catching up to do. Often, for the families, there is a powerful need to hang on to the hope that the person is still alive, even when there is overwhelming evidence, such as a large quantity of the missing person's blood in his or her car.

Marcey Rinker, a victim advocate for the Homicide Unit at the U.S. Attorney's Office in Washington, DC, believes that in these types of no-body homicides it is important to have the presumed-dead missing person legally declared dead. In addition to bringing resolution to the family, reasons include arranging for the custody of children and the settling of financial affairs, including life insurance. According to the *Social Security Handbook* of the Social Security Administration, a missing person is presumed dead, "If he or she has been missing from home and has not been heard from for seven years or more," adding that this can only be disputed if it can be proven that the person is alive or an explanation is provided that explains the individual's absence and continued life.[2] Statutes vary from state to state, but courts require that investigators lay the usual people-searching groundwork, including lack of contact with the person's family and work, as well as lack of activity on a Social Security number.

As discussed in Chapter 14, Howard Morton, director of Families of Homicide Victims and Missing Persons (FOHVAMP) wrote, "It is said that to murder a person is to murder that victim's whole family. The life of each person who felt close to the victim is abruptly and permanently changed."[3] In a telephone interview with the author, Rinker echoed Morton's words by stating, "The disappearance changes the family dynamics, with much of the focus on the missing (sadness, grief, longing, and often idealizing the person), and it prevents siblings from the normal upbringing they might otherwise have had."[4] When the sometimes lengthy court proceedings finally result in a judge's order to issue a death certificate for a still-missing person presumed dead, Rinker warns that even though the family members do have some resolution, they may undergo an emotional let-down. In one of her cases—of a woman whose remains still had not been found after 11 years—Rinker stated, "When the death certificate was finalized, the victim's mother and sister broke down sobbing."[5]

Prosecuting No-Body Homicides

Former Assistant United States Attorney Thomas A. "Tad" DiBiase (see Figure 9.1) has been interested in no-body cases since 2006, when he successfully prosecuted the second no-body murder case in Washington, DC. He calls himself the "no body guy" and offers suggestions as to what police and prosecutors can do once a person is missing and presumed dead. "All of these techniques are useful, even if the victim is merely missing and not actually dead," he stated in correspondence with the author. "Don't treat the case like

Figure 9.1 Former Assistant U.S. Attorney Thomas A. "Tad" DiBiase, the "no body guy," offers suggestions as to what police and prosecutors can do once a person is missing and presumed dead. (Photo © Copyright Judah Lifschitz/ JFotoArt.)

a missing person case; treat it like a homicide where the best evidence of the crime is missing—the body."[6]

The following recommendations are paraphrased from "How to Successfully Investigate and Prosecute a No Body Homicide Case," on DiBiase's "No Body Murder Cases" website.[7] During the early phase of an investigation, DiBiase recommends:

- That the police, often with the help of a subpoena issued by the prosecutor's office, get the records from the victim's telephone to see who the victim was calling, when the calls stopped, and who called after the outgoing calls stopped.
- Interviewing (on videotape) as many people as possible who knew the victim. Lock in testimony as quickly as possible before witnesses get cold feet.
- Pursuing consent searches or getting search warrants for the victim's home and place of work (including computers), as well as places such as a boyfriend's or girlfriend's residence where the victim was known to spend time. Note what is missing and what is not missing, and be sure to get any items that may contain the victim's DNA, including a towel, toothbrush, or hairbrush.
- Following the money and electronic trails by accessing credit card, bank, and employment records. Someone who fled and is not

missing or dead would not be likely to forgo a paycheck or Social Security benefits, welfare, food stamps, or child support payments. Also check the paths of surveillance cameras in places the victim was likely to have been.
- If there is an obvious suspect, pressuring him or her for a confession. The suspect should also be under surveillance in case he or she returns to the crime scene or leads to the body.
- Looking for a motive or possible "trigger" event such as a divorce being made final, or a court order to pay alimony or child support.[8]

In the later stage of the investigation, DiBiase recommends:

- Using the media to one's advantage, especially on anniversaries. "The more people who are aware of the case," he states, "the greater the chances of getting a breakthrough via a previously unknown witness, as well as keeping the pressure on the defendant."
- Reinterviewing witnesses and suspects.
- Asking questions about the suspect. How did he react to the fact of the missing person? Did he cooperate with the search, with the police? How did he react on the anniversary? Did he talk to the media? Does he contact the police to keep up on the status of the case? Did he move in with someone new "too soon" or dispose of victim's things "too early?" Was the suspect's residence remodeled or changed in a significant way?[9]

For trial preparation, DiBiase recommends:

- Creating a timeline.
- Being prepared to argue why someone else did not commit the murder.
- Using the thoroughness of the investigation as a shield against the possible attack that someone else may have murdered the victim.
- Acquiring statements by the victim, if they can be admitted.
- Asking the court to inform the jury that circumstantial evidence should be treated the same as direct evidence.[10]

DiBiase added that often in a no-body murder case, the defense will argue that a missing piece of evidence is a "link" that "breaks the chain." "In fact," stated DiBiase, "the prosecution should argue that its evidence is more like a rope; that is, even if one strand of evidence breaks there are other strands holding up the case. This effectively takes away the defense argument that if the jury has a reasonable doubt about one piece of evidence, then they have reasonable doubt about the entire case."[11] When asked if a declaration of death would help in a prosecution, DiBiase said, "For the most part, being declared dead is not much of a help to a case because rarely is any investigation done to make the declaration. Even with that 'legal declaration,' the prosecution must still must prove, beyond a reasonable doubt, that the missing person is deceased."[12]

In conclusion, DiBiase likes to use, in closing arguments, what he calls the "Puzzle Argument." He suggests that prosecutors modify the following to suit their own circumstances:

> I have an older sister and like every good little brother I tried to be as much of a pest as possible when we were little. My sister loved to do jigsaw puzzles and would do these huge 500–1,000 piece puzzles of beach scenes, a park, the U.S. Capitol, whatever. They would take like a week to complete. Because I was a pest I would always steal two–three pieces and hide them under my mattress. Thus, I was secure in the knowledge that she would never, ever completely finish the puzzle. But you know what? My sister never cared. She would finish the puzzle, minus the two–three pieces I had hidden and she could still tell what the scene was. She knew I had the pieces but didn't care. It was still a picture of the beach, the park, the U.S. Capitol. Now, here I wish I could tell you I have the missing puzzle pieces under my bed. But I don't. But you know what, ladies and gentlemen, you can still see the whole puzzle here . . . [then review each piece of evidence]."[13]

Other Scenarios: Cold Missing Persons Cases

- Missing persons may be alive if:
  - They had motives to disappear.
  - Their families believe they left on their own.
- The family believes its missing person committed suicide.
- The missing person died a natural or an accidental death.
- The missing person died a natural or an accidental death or may have walked away.

Missing Persons May Be Alive if They Had Motives to Disappear

In 1952, Nebraska runaway, Twylia May Embrey, told her family that the day after she graduated from high school, they would never see her again. An interview with one of Twylia's female high school friends uncovered allegations of sexual abuse by Twylia's father, the likely motive for the teenager to leave home. No missing person's report was filed at the time, as her family assumed she would return home, but she never did. Her mother and father traveled to California, where they thought she had relocated, but both parents died without ever knowing what happened to their daughter.

Figure 9.2 Twylia May Embrey chose to break away from her family. A researcher uncovered Embrey's secret after her death, but the woman had lived under a false identify for 50 years. (Photo courtesy of Jennifer Kitt.)

In later years, one of Twylia's sisters corresponded extensively with a private investigator who, as it turned out, had known Twylia as a teenager. A generation later, after the siblings' searches, a great-niece followed up with the author and fellow researcher, Micki Lavigne. As explained in Chapter 4, Lavigne located Twylia, with just the right keywords in a Google search, three weeks after the missing woman died at the age of 71. Twylia had changed her identity, lived out her life in another part of the country, and—true to her word—never had any contact with her family again.[14] See Figure 9.2.

Missing Persons May Be Alive, if Their Families Believe They Left on Their Own

Boulder Jane Doe may also have left home of her own free will, but, unlike Twylia, she did not live to see her old age. Instead, the young woman's battered and naked body was found near Boulder, Colorado, in 1954. Fifty years later, in a partnership among law enforcement, forensic specialists, and the author, Jane Doe's remains were exhumed and her DNA profiled. As in Twylia's case, a great-niece took up the search on behalf of the family. In 2009, Jane Doe was identified as 18-year-old Dorothy Gay Howard, missing from Phoenix, Arizona. No missing person report is known to have ever been filed, her murder is unsolved, and her reasons for leaving Phoenix will, most likely, remain unknown. One of Dorothy's cousins confided to the author that the young woman's parents and siblings had always believed she was alive, and they hoped she would eventually come home. "Her disappearance was an unspoken tragedy in the family," the cousin stated. "They dealt with anger, sadness, and then a hopelessness bordering on despair."[15]

The Family Believes Its Missing Person Committed Suicide

It is not unusual for the family of a suicidal missing person initially to file a missing person's report and then accept the fact that the family member, most likely, committed suicide. For law enforcement, the case remains open, even though the family may prefer not to reopen old wounds.

The Missing Person Died a Natural or an Accidental Death

Unfortunately, there are far too many cases of people without identification who die natural or accidental deaths, and no one knows who they are. Others who die from accidental deaths may be known to their families and to the agencies that search for them, but they are still missing, because their bodies have not been recovered. In this category are the remains of more than a dozen people hidden in Priest Lake, a spectacularly beautiful and very deep lake in northern Idaho (see Figure 9.3).

The earliest known missing in Priest Lake are four men from Spokane, Washington, along with their guide, who all presumably drowned on a fishing expedition in 1919. (Their boat, and the body of a fifth man, were recovered.) Additional Priest Lake boating accidents with people still known to be missing occurred in 1945, 1948, 1950, 1960, 1987, 1996, and 2004. Figure 9.4 shows a 1948 newspaper article regarding a drowning that year.

After the 2004 accident, Ralston & Associates, an underwater recovery team with a remotely operated vehicle, worked with the Bonner County Sheriff's Office to search for the most recent victim's body. They did not find the remains they were looking for, but—at a depth of 322 feet—they found an old rowboat. Near it, at first, appeared to be human remains. Publicity surrounding the discovery stirred the emotions of family members who have not forgotten and will not forget. Even generations later, these families want closure. According to the Sheriff's Office's press release, on September 28, 2010, "Scientists were unable to extract any human DNA from the three samples which were retrieved."[16] (For additional information on Ralston & Associates, see Chapter 13.)

Figure 9.3 Priest Lake, Idaho, holds the remains of more than a dozen people. (Photo by author.)

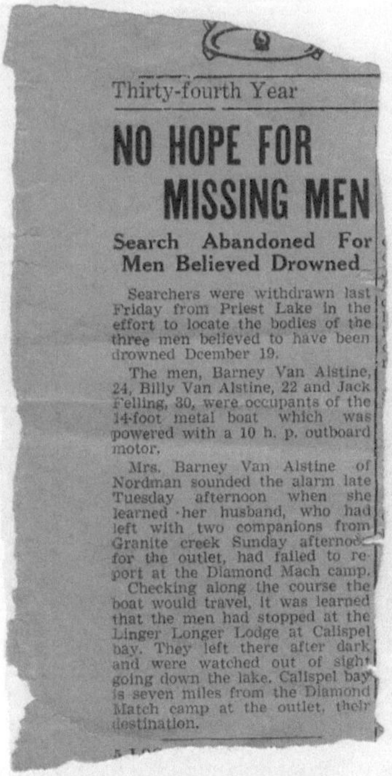

Thirty-fourth Year

NO HOPE FOR MISSING MEN

Search Abandoned For Men Believed Drowned

Searchers were withdrawn last Friday from Priest Lake in the effort to locate the bodies of the three men believed to have been drowned Dcember 19.

The men, Barney Van Alstine, 24, Billy Van Alstine, 22 and Jack Felling, 30, were occupants of the 14-foot metal boat which was powered with a 10 h. p. outboard motor.

Mrs. Barney Van Alstine of Nordman sounded the alarm late Tuesday afternoon when she learned her husband, who had left with two companions from Granite creek Sunday afternoon for the outlet, had failed to report at the Diamond Mach camp.

Checking along the course the boat would travel, it was learned that the men had stopped at the Linger Longer Lodge at Calispel bay. They left there after dark and were watched out of sight going down the lake. Calispel bay is seven miles from the Diamond Match camp at the outlet, their destination.

Figure 9.4 This newspaper article, from the *Priest River Times*, in late December 1948, was sent to the author by a descendant of one of the Priest Lake drowning victims. Even generations later, families want closure. (Author's collection.)

The Missing Person May Have Died a Natural or an Accidental Death or May Have Walked Away

Case History: Joseph Halpern Disappeared into Thin Air

As later generations of drowning victims continue to hope for the recovery of the remains of their family members at the bottom of Priest Lake, another family's search has taken its descendants to the mountaintops of Colorado. In the summer of 1933, 22-year-old Illinois resident Joseph Halpern (see Figure 9.5) was vacationing in Rocky Mountain National Park with his parents and Samuel Garrick, a college friend. The motorists had driven Joseph's Ford sedan and had stopped in the Black Hills and at Yellowstone National Park on their way west. Even though the country was in the midst of the Great Depression, the early 1930s was a good time for automobile tourism. As part of U.S. President Franklin D. Roosevelt's

Figure 9.5 Joseph Halpern's photograph was furnished to the FBI by the missing man's parents. The image accompanies the Rocky Mountain National Park Chief Ranger's "Report on the Disappearance of Joseph Laurence Halpern," found in the National Archives, decades after the man disappeared. (Photo courtesy of the National Archives, Rocky Mountain Region.)

promise of a New Deal, Roosevelt had put young men to work in the Civilian Conservation Corps (CCC). A year before Halpern's arrival in Colorado, CCC workers had completed the Trail Ridge Road from Estes Park to its intersection with the Fall River Road, crossing a high point of 12,183 feet. There was a lot for visitors from the Midwest to see.

On August 15, 1933, Joseph put on a white shirt with blue stripes, khaki trousers, and heavy shoes. He packed four or five sandwiches, one orange, two bananas, and a recent Rocky Mountain National Park Motorists Guide map into a small gray knapsack and left his parents at the Glacier Basin Campground. Joseph and Samuel drove to the Bear Lake parking area and set off on a day hike via the Flattop Mountain trail. By mid-afternoon, Samuel returned to the campsite saying that Joseph had headed off alone. Joseph, an inexperienced hiker who did not take a jacket, never returned, and no trace of him has ever been found. The young graduate student from the University of Chicago appeared to have disappeared into thin air.[17]

At the time, Joseph was employed at the Yerkes Observatory in Williams Bay, Wisconsin, and was working on his doctoral thesis on meteors and shooting stars. He was quite gifted, as correspondence from a family friend stated that Joseph "was singled out for the distinction of astronomically computing the precise moment for the opening of the [Chicago] World's Fair."[18] Before the Fair opened, on May 27, 1933 (less than three months before Joseph went missing), four large astronomical observatories, including Yerkes, had aimed their telescopes on the star Arcturus in order to capture the star's light rays on photoelectric cells. The light signals then were converted into energy, amplified, and used to turn on the machinery and lighting at the grounds of the Fair.[19]

Not knowing if Joseph was lost, injured, or had plunged to his death off a cliff, park rangers and at least 150 volunteer searchers, including CCC workers, combed the mountainous terrain by foot and on horseback. The park rangers questioned Samuel Garrick and fellow hikers and learned that Joseph had inquired about climbing Taylor Peak, but he may have, instead, headed toward Chief's Head Peak. At 13,579 feet, Chief's Head is the third-highest peak in the Park. Its northwest wall is a sheer granite cliff that plunges from its summit for more than 1,000 feet. Samuel also stated that it was possible that Joseph may have headed toward Andrews Glacier. According to the chief ranger's report—which contained the above conflicting statements—no one could really say which way the missing hiker had gone.[20] Midway into the search, Joseph's father, Solomon Halpern, wrote to his other son, Bernard Halpern (who had remained at the family's home in Chicago), "Four days of helpless agony and no end to it."[21]

For six days, park authorities searched drainages and followed all possible trails. They also checked the registers on Taylor and nearby peaks, but none showed Joseph's signature, a customary procedure for climbers once they reach a summit.[22] Perhaps trying to be encouraging, a writer for the Estes Park newspaper mentioned that during the previous year, a trail reconnaissance crew had stumbled upon the remains of a Texas theologian who had been missing for 17 years.[23] On September 18, 1933, the Park's superintendent wrote to Joseph's brother that he believed Joseph may have been killed in a fall or in a rock avalanche while attempting a shortcut.[24] In agreement was one of the park rangers who participated in the initial search, the late Jack C. Moomaw, author of *Recollections of a Rocky Mountain Ranger.* Of Joseph, Moomaw stated, "Some people, including the parents, are of the opinion that the missing boy may have lost his mind and wandered away, but I believe that, somewhere up there on the barrens, the wind is moaning through his bones."[25]

Others were not so sure. Four months after Joseph's disappearance, his father wrote to the Park's superintendent that he had filed a missing person report with the police, in the event that Joseph "wandered away due to some injury having affected his reason or memory, or for some other reason."[26] The possible other reason was hinted at in excerpts of Joseph's letters that the family reread after he vanished. In 1930, Joseph wrote, "And so I stare face out at a cruel harsh economically depressed world and am waiting for the day when I'll be a hobo." In another letter, written at Yerkes Observatory in 1933, he added the following, perhaps in relation to his work in capturing the rays of Arcturus prior to the opening of the Chicago World's Fair:

> The sun falls in the deep northwest, and soon again the stars will be free to shine on me as I harness their feeble rays for the benefit of science. Patiently, I will hold them, minute after minute, hours and hours, and their impression will be preserved for the perpetual future. Enormous volumes of imperfect observations for the use of imperfect observers. Happy is the life of an astronomer! Away, far away, from the banalities of men, detached in the beautiful soliloquies of comprehensiveness and unity. The mortal cares, worries, being, loves—vanish into insignificance before this formidability of nature.[27]

The Perseids meteor shower had reached a peak of 50 to 80 meteors per hour only two or three days before Joseph went missing.[28] Did he wait for the sun to go down and revel in the night sky, then linger too long on a mountaintop?

Three of Joseph's fingerprints (obtained from a postal savings account) were forwarded to the Federal Bureau of Investigation (FBI), but the federal agency told the family that it could not initiate an investigation because the young man's disappearance had not been in violation of any federal laws. In 1950, after continued correspondence that even included the private secretary of U.S. President Franklin D. Roosevelt, Joseph's parents went to probate court and filed notice of "legal presumption of death."[29]

Ten years later, in 1960, Joseph's brother Bernard wrote to the FBI:

> When I visited my parents recently, my father mentioned for the first time a circumstance that could possibly lead to some information concerning the disappearance of my brother. He [the father] stated that forest rangers were of the opinion that my brother's companion knew more about the disappearance than he would admit at that time. Since he was a friend of my brother's, my father asked the rangers to cease questioning him as he was obviously in an agitated state of mind.[30]

JOSEPH'S NEPHEW CONTINUES THE FAMILY'S SEARCH

After Joseph Halpern's parents died, Bernard was left in charge of the family's mystery. Then, after Bernard's death, his son Roland Halpern picked up the threads of the search. At first, Roland (who is Joseph's nephew) sent copies of his family's correspondence to the National Park Service and asked for any advice or assistance it could provide. In the summer of 2010, a few months before Joseph's 100th birthday, Roland took his then-11-year-old son on a hike of the Taylor Peak area, extending the search into the fourth generation (see Figure 9.6). Something else, in addition to Joseph, was still missing: the facts surrounding the mystery as to what had happened.

Roland had started his search by contacting the sheriffs' offices in the four counties that border Rocky Mountain National Park. He asked about unidentified remains that might be identifiable with DNA comparisons, but there were none (known at the time) from the time period. In 2009, when the NamUs System was inaugurated, Roland, as a member of the public, entered Joseph as Missing Person number 2797. The National Park Service is listed as the contacting agency, and Joseph's identifying information, as well as a profile of family DNA, is now on file to be matched to unidentified remains. (See Chapters 6 and 7.)

Joseph's nephew then pursued two federal sources of information: the Rocky Mountain Region of the National Archives and the FBI. The National Archives has an Accidents in National Parks file that contained, "A Report on the Disappearance of Joseph Laurence Halpern." It was written on August 23, 1933 by John S. McLaughlin, former chief ranger of the Rocky Mountain National Park, and contained information on the initial search, the photo of Joseph submitted by his parents, and a detailed colored map of six days of search routes.[31]

Figure 9.6 In the summer of 2010, Roland Halpern took his son, Koa Halpern, pictured, to the top of the Tyndall Glacier, in Rocky Mountain National Park, near the area where Joseph Halpern was last reported to have been seen. (Photo courtesy of Roland Halpern.)

The FBI mailed Joseph's missing person file to Roland after he filed a Freedom of Information Act (FOIA) request. The file included some, but not all, of his family's correspondence as well as some new and startling information that Joseph may actually have walked away from the park. The new information included a letter from an Iowa resident, in 1933, stating that Joseph had been part of a "rough crowd," as well as a statement from a family friend indicating that Joseph had been seen in Phoenix, Arizona, in 1934. Additional references tied Joseph to CCC and hobo camps, eerily echoing his own words of wanting to be a hobo. In 1935, Joseph reportedly worked for the Lewis Brothers Circus in Michigan. The FBI file also included his fingerprints from the postal savings account.[32]

"Advances in technology have made old and almost forgotten documents available with a few clicks of the mouse," stated Roland, in correspondence with the author. "I have been amazed at what we have been able to uncover and hope that with today's resources our family will finally get closure so that my son doesn't have to wonder what happened to Joe."[33] At the time of this writing, Roland is still trying to solve the mystery of Joseph's disappearance, but the information that Roland has learned—by doing his own research—has stirred up new questions. Did Joseph fall to his death in the Park, as the park rangers believed? If so, why has no shred of clothing or any of his remains been found? Or, did he choose to walk away? If that was the case, did he tell his (now-deceased) friend and hiking partner of his plan? If Joseph left on his own, where did he go, and why? What did he do with his life, and where did he spend his last days? These and other questions, for the families of the missing, do not go away.

Others Who Either Died Natural or Accidental Deaths or Walked Away

In addition to Joseph Halpern, questions surround other missing persons who may have died accidental deaths or walked away. Two of the oldest cases still debated today are those of Glen and Bessie Hyde. As depicted in Brad Dimock's book, *Sunk Without a Sound: The Tragic Colorado River Honeymoon of Glen and Bessie Hyde*, the couple left for their honeymoon on the Colorado River on October 20, 1928. A month later, they hiked to the rim of the Grand Canyon for supplies, then returned to their flat-bottomed boat on the river, deep within the canyon walls. The newlyweds never arrived at their destination, setting off an extensive search. Their boat was recovered in calm water, fully loaded, but no trace of Glen or Bessie has ever been found.

Another longtime missing person is Everett Ruess, now a legend in the Southwest. In November 1934, the then-20-year-old visual artist from California disappeared in canyon country near Escalante, in southern Utah. Like Joseph Halpern who was fascinated by the stars, Everett left behind letters, essays, and poems that showed that his passion was the ever-changing panoramas of the desert wilderness. His burros were found near his campsite, but the whereabouts of the young man or his remains has turned into a decades-long mystery. In 2009, however, Navajos in the area found skeletal remains and related them to a story, passed through generations, of the long-ago murder of a young white man. After the discovery, it appeared that the mystery of the missing Everett Ruess might, finally, be solved. But DNA comparisons ruled out the remains as being those of the young adventurer.[34]

The Unidentified Remains of John and Jane Does

As explained in Chapter 14, "Contact with Co-Victims," the pain of families with missing loved ones can be horrific. Similarly, unidentified remains haunt the most hardened of investigators as well as members of the public. These John and Jane Does need our help. When Boulder Jane Doe's battered and naked body was found along a mountain stream west of Boulder, Colorado, in 1954, the local community pitched in to give her a Christian burial. Among the cards sent with flowers to her funeral was one that poignantly stated, "To

Someone's Daughter." For 55 years, until 2009, when the young woman was identified as Dorothy Gay Howard, no one had a clue who she was.[35]

John and Jane Does Can Be Anywhere

A common misconception is that unidentified remains are an urban problem. Big cities, because of their large populations, have their share of them, but so, too, have many rural areas. Consider Leadville, a town of less than 3,000 people in Lake County, Colorado. In the Evergreen Cemetery alone, lie the remains of at least 41 unnamed individuals.[36] The cemetery was established in 1879, and some of the John and Jane Does date from the frontier era when Leadville's rough-and-tumble mining days put the town on the map. Notations in the old cemetery records give only brief information, such as "child without a name died at the poor house" and "found shot in Tennessee Park." Newspaper documentation has been located for only the two most recent burials of unidentified remains, and those are the only ones in marked graves: "Unidentified, October 1958" (see Figure 9.7) and "Unidentified Male, May 1970."

Various fraternal organizations, including the Benevolent and Protective Order of Elks and the Oro City Independent Order of the Odd Fellows, as well as the Hebrew, Protestant, and Catholic religious groups, have their own well-defined and looked-after sections of the cemetery. Most of the 41 unidentified burials, however, are spread throughout the 54 blocks of graves in the "Protestant Free" section. For many years, that part of the cemetery has not been formally maintained. Once in a while, a community member

Figure 9.7 The grave of "Unidentified: October 1958," in the Evergreen Cemetery in Leadville, Colorado, is indicated by a simple marker. (Photo by author.)

will cut down a tree or paint an iron railing, but the graves, both marked and unmarked, are being taken over by the surrounding forest and are fading into the past.

Siblings, and perhaps even parents or children, of the 1958 and 1970 John Does are likely still missing those family members. What can be done? For these and any John and Jane Doe cases, the appropriate law enforcement and coroner/medical examiner agencies need to compile their information and evidence. Then, to reconstruct or supplement case files, investigators would be prudent to search newspapers for articles from the time of the deaths. (See Chapter 11, "Newspaper Research: Online and Off.") Coroners and medical examiners can list their cases in the Unidentified Persons database on NamUs, and current article suggestions proposed to the media will give the cases new exposure. (See Chapters 7 and 16.)

Using the 1958 John Doe as an example, an article titled "Body of Unidentified Man Found Near Leadville" from the November 3, 1958, *Leadville Times* was found on microfilm at the Lake County Library in Leadville, Colorado:

> The body of a man found in Georgia Gulch south of Malta on Sunday has not yet been identified, according to County Coroner Andrew Cassidy. The badly decomposed body was discovered by Andy Schmidt, Safeway Store employee, who was seeking a land-marker for his own property in the area. According to Coroner Cassidy, an autopsy performed last night was inconclusive, and the cause of death has not been established. Cassidy said that the man was five-feet-seven-inches tall and weighed approximately 145 to 150 pounds. He had red hair and was approximately 45 years old, according to Cassidy. Cassidy said that he had probably been dead for about three or four months. His body was clothed only in a pair of trousers and a pair of socks. Efforts are being made to identify the body. Sheriff Clarence McMurrough has sent fingerprints to the FBI for positive identification.[37]

The above article provides the cold case investigator with specific names of people, as well as references to the sheriff, coroner, and the FBI, all of whom should have case files. The main points of the article are:

- The badly decomposed body was found in Georgia Gulch south of Malta.
- Property owner and Safeway employee Andy Schmidt found the body.
- Coroner Cassidy performed the autopsy and did not determine cause of death.
- Decedent's physical description and clothing were provided.
- Sheriff Clarence McMurrough sent fingerprints to the FBI.

Complicating the research, however, was the discovery of two more articles on the very same page, on the very same day, in the very same newspaper. One article was titled, "Man Found in Georgia Gulch Identified as Willard Yates," and the other stated, "Yates Denies He Identified Body Found Sunday." (Jess Yates who denied the identification was the brother of Willard Yates.) Historical research can be confusing, but contacting the people named in the articles (providing they are still alive) is a good place to start. (See Chapters 3 and 4.) Then, a spreadsheet of missing persons can be supplemented by:

- Searching for possible matches in NamUs; in the National Crime Information Center (NCIC), including its historical database; in the Violent Criminal Apprehension Program (ViCAP); and in the Doe Network and other missing person databases. (See Chapter 5, Dealing with Databases.)
- Searching for additional missing persons with Google News Archive and NewspaperArchive. (See Chapter 11, "Newspaper Research: Online and Off.")

Summary

Resources in this chapter include:

- One scenario: the missing person is presumed dead.
- Prosecuting no-body homicides.
- Examples of missing-person cases. In addition to missing under suspicious circumstances and presumed dead, other scenarios include a motive to disappear, walking away, committing suicide, and natural and accidental deaths.
- Suggestions for reconstructing case files of John and Jane Does, starting with newspaper articles, followed by database searches.

There are many reasons why individuals disappear. Some go missing under suspicious circumstances and are murdered. In some instances their bodies or skeletal remains are found, whereas other times they are not. The ones whose remains are not found present a particular challenge to investigators and prosecutors. If there are suspects and enough evidence, the cases can be tried as no-body homicides. As former Assistant U.S. Attorney, Thomas A. "Tad" DiBiase stated, "Don't treat the case like a missing person case; treat it like a homicide where the best evidence of the crime is missing—the body."

Missing persons with a motive to disappear or who chose to walk away may be alive and may not want to be found. Other missing persons may have committed suicide or died natural or accidental deaths. The case history, "Joseph Halpern Disappeared into Thin Air," illustrates a case in which the missing person may have died an accidental death or may have walked away. A nephew has taken up the search and has found a surprising amount of information in the National Archives and in FBI files. Readers interested in cold missing persons cases can join the ranks of those who follow the stories of Glen and Bessie Hyde (missing from the Grand Canyon in 1928) and Everett Ruess (missing from southern Utah in 1934).

Endnotes

1. Ritter, Nancy. "Missing persons and unidentified remains: The nation's silent mass disaster," *NIJ Journal*, 256 (January 2007).
2. *Social Security Handbook*, Chapter 17, "Evidence Required to Establish Rights to Benefits," 1721, "When Is a Missing Person Presumed Dead?"
3. Morton, Howard. *Forgotten Victims: What Cold Case Families Want From Law Enforcement*, (Fort Collins: Center for the Study of Crime and Justice, Department of Sociology, Colorado State University, 2009), Afterword.
4. Rinker, Marcey. Victim Advocate. Telephone interview with the author, December 18, 2011.
5. Rinker, Marcey. Victim Advocate. Telephone interview with the author, December 13, 2011.
6. DiBiase, Thomas A. "Tad." E-mail correspondence with the author, December 8, 2011.
7. No Body Murder Cases, http://nobodymurdercases.com/index.html (accessed December 26, 2011).
8. DiBiase, Thomas A. "Tad." "How to successfully investigate and prosecute a no-body homicide case," March 19, 2010. http://nobodymurdercases.com/tips.html (accessed December 26, 2011).
9. DiBiase, Thomas A. "Tad." "How to successfully investigate and prosecute a no-body homicide case," March 19, 2010. http://nobodymurdercases.com/tips.html (accessed December 26, 2011).
10. DiBiase, Thomas A. "Tad." "How to successfully investigate and prosecute a no-body homicide case," March 19, 2010. http://nobodymurdercases.com/tips.html (accessed December 26, 2011).
11. DiBiase, Thomas A. "Tad." "How to successfully investigate and prosecute a no-body homicide case," March 19, 2010. http://nobodymurdercases.com/tips.html (accessed December 26, 2011).
12. DiBiase, Thomas A. "Tad." E-mail correspondence with the author, December 14, 2011.
13. DiBiase, Thomas A. "Tad." "How to successfully investigate and prosecute a no-body homicide case," March 19, 2010. http://nobodymurdercases.com/tips.html (accessed December 26, 2011).
14. Pettem, Silvia. *Someone's Daughter: In Search of Justice for Jane Doe* (Lanham, MD: Taylor Trade, 2009), 174–175.

15. Pettem, Silvia. *Someone's Daughter: In Search of Justice for Jane Doe*, (Lanham, MD: Taylor Trade, 2009) Epilogue; www.silviapettem.com/JANE%20DOE%20 articles/Epilogue.html (accessed December 26, 2011).
16. Bonner County Sheriff's Office Press Release, September 28, 2010, www.bonnerso.org/pressreleases.html (accessed December 26, 2011).
17. McLaughlin, John S. "A Report on the Disappearance of Joseph Laurence Halpern," Rocky Mountain National Park Chief Ranger's Report, National Archives, August 23, 1933.
18. Greenfield, Samuel. Letter to J. Edgar Hoover, May 2, 1936. (FBI files, in possession of Roland Halpern.)
19. "The history of world expositions," www.expo2000.de/expo2000/geschichte/detail.php?wa_id=12&lang=1&s_typ=21 (accessed December 26, 2011).
20. McLaughlin, John S. "A report on the disappearance of Joseph Laurence Halpern," Rocky Mountain National Park Chief Ranger's Report, National Archives, August 23, 1933.
21. Halpern, Solomon. Postcard to Bernard Halpern, August 18, 1933. (In possession of Roland Halpern.)
22. McLaughlin, John S. "A report on the disappearance of Joseph Laurence Halpern," Rocky Mountain National Park Chief Ranger's Report, National Archives, August 23,1933.
23. Staff. "Hope Abandoned for Joe Halpern's Life," *The Estes Park Trail*, August 25, 1933.
24. Rogers, Edmund B. Letter to Bernard Halpern, September 18, 1933. (In possession of Roland Halpern.)
25. Moomaw, Jack C. *Recollections of a Rocky Mountain Ranger* (Estes Park, CO: YMCA of the Rockies, 1994), 111.
26. Halpern, Solomon. Letter to Edmund B. Rogers, December 13, 1933. (In possession of Roland Halpern.)
27. Miscellaneous documents, in possession of Roland Halpern.
28. Meteor showers online, http://meteorshowersonline.com/perseids.html (accessed December 26, 2011).
29. Halpern, Joseph L. Notice of Establishment of Legal Presumption of Death, Probate No. 23814, Dade County, Florida, August 9, 1950.
30. Halpern, Bernard. Letter to J. Edgar Hoover, November 1, 1960. (FBI files, in possession of Roland Halpern.)
31. McLaughlin, John S. "A report on the disappearance of Joseph Laurence Halpern," Rocky Mountain National Park Chief Ranger's Report, National Archives, August 23, 1933.
32. FBI to Roland Halpern, Freedom of Information Act request, August 29, 2011. (In possession of Roland Halpern.)
33. Halpern, Roland. E-mail correspondence with the author, October 19, 2011.
34. Meltzer, Erica. "CU-Boulder Prof Acknowledges DNA Mistake in Case of Poet Everett Ruess," Boulder *Daily Camera* (CO; October 21, 2009).
35. Anas, Brittany. "Mystery Solved: Boulder Sheriff IDs 'Jane Doe' as Dorothy Gay Howard," Boulder *Daily Camera* (CO; October 28, 2009).

36. Evergreen Cemetery Records, Lake County Library, www.lakecountypubliclibrary.org/Cemetery%20Records.htm (accessed December 26, 2011).
37. Staff. "Body of Unidentified Man Found Near Leadville, *Leadville Times* (November 3, 1958).

Resources for Expanded Research

III

Historical and Geographical Context 10

When investigators photograph a murder scene, they not only focus on the body, but they also take wide-angle shots to show the context of the crime. Historical context is the same thing. Investigators gain a clearer perspective of their cold case homicides, for instance, when they mentally travel back in time and place their victims in the eras in which they lived. Just as investigators on hot cases need to look at live crime scenes and "read" them, cold case investigators, and juries, too, have to be able to "feel" their crime scenes, long after the blood is cleaned up and the bodies are buried.

Similarly, geographical context involves physically revisiting the crime scenes, canvassing the neighborhoods, and taking a lot of photographs. Many of today's cold cases predate digital cameras. Because film cost money and camera-users often ran out of it, the photographs in older case files may not fully document the area. In the original photographs (if any survived), distances between important components may not be obvious. For instance, the house of a known drug dealer may look far away and unrelated, but perhaps the victim was headed that way or had come from the same direction. When the case was hot, the original investigators were rushed. Cold case investigators, however, can and should take their time. As shown in the following case study, a Connecticut resident did just that.

Case History: Different States, Same Highway

In the post-Great Depression years of the 1930s into the 1950s, young women often hitchhiked and considered it an acceptable means of transportation. College coeds and others without their own cars hitched rides to travel, visit friends, or go wherever they wanted to go. Although it is rare today to see a woman (or anyone) thumbing a ride at the side of the road, three young women from the Northeast—Katherine Hull, Paula Welden, and Connie Smith—all had one thing in common: they hitchhiked, and then they disappeared, on roads connecting to the same main thoroughfare. These three different cases, from three different states, appeared to be unrelated until news librarian and historical writer, Michael C. Dooling, investigated their historical and geographical contexts.

Katherine Hull's disappearance was the earliest, in April 1936. The 22-year-old stenographer, with her father, was visiting the young woman's grandmother in Lebanon Springs, New York, close to the Massachusetts border. On a cool spring day, Katherine threw on a green wool coat and told her family she was going for a walk. When she did not return that evening, her father called the New York State Police. Several witnesses claimed that they had seen a young woman matching Katherine's description hitchhiking along New York Route 22 and entering a car. According to a newspaper report, Katherine's grandmother told the police that the young woman "was fond of walking and frequently had gone on hitchhiking jaunts before."[1] However, her family said that on previous occasions, she had always left a note. During the following days and weeks, search teams were organized and reward posters were hung in bus stations and railroad terminals, but Katherine seemingly vanished without a trace.[2]

Then, in December 1943, deer hunters in the vicinity of Lebanon Springs stumbled upon human skeletal remains, including a lower jaw with teeth and some fillings. Local authorities sent the remains to the Massachusetts State Police Crime Laboratory in Boston. There they were examined by the state pathologist, a professor at Harvard University, who determined that the bones were consistent with Katherine's height. In addition, the young woman's dentist came forward with a description of a gold filling. A fragment of cloth found at the scene was believed to have been part of her green coat.[3]

By today's standards, this would not have been enough for a positive identification, but it satisfied the police and Katherine's family, as the case was then closed. No records of an autopsy or newspaper reports of how she might have died, or even a death certificate, have been found. Dooling speculates that the person who stopped to give Katherine a ride assaulted and murdered her. Her remains were found off a dirt road that connected Massachusetts with New York Route 22, the north–south road that parallels the eastern border of New York along Connecticut, Massachusetts, and Vermont.[4]

Thirty-eight miles north of Lebanon Springs, and east of the New York/Vermont state line, is Bennington, Vermont. Paula Welden, an 18-year-old art student at Bennington College, disappeared in 1946 after she, like Katherine, said she was going for a walk and was seen thumbing a ride along Vermont Route 9 that connects to the west to New York Route 22. Witnesses also observed Paula asking directions to Long Trail.[5] By accessing historical newspaper articles on his computer, Dooling was able to travel back in time more than 60 years. He learned about the details of the disappearances and the subsequent search efforts, but in Paula's case, he also was rewarded with a rare insight into her state of mind. In 1947, her mother told a newspaper reporter, "She [Paula] was completely naive. She was most innocent. Paula's character would never permit her to believe that anyone would do her harm. And for that reason, she would readily have taken a hitchhike ride with anyone who might have come along."[6]

Six years later, in Lakeville, Connecticut (nearly the same distance south of Lebanon Springs that Bennington, Vermont, is to the north, and just east of the New York/Connecticut state line) summer camp resident Connie Smith was also seen walking, asking directions, and thumbing a ride, before she, too, disappeared. She was last seen at Belgo Road, a country road that locals used (and still use) as a shortcut to drive to Route 22 in New York State. Connie, who went missing in 1952 and has never been found, came from a prominent and well-to-do family. Her grandfather was the former governor of Wyoming, and she was raised on her mother's expansive Wyoming ranch. Connie was in Connecticut to spend a month at Camp Sloane while her mother visited Connie's grandmother, also in Connecticut. Although Connie was only 10 years old, she was said to have looked older, was independent, and she loved the outdoors. She was spotted thumbing a ride toward Lakeville.[7] Hitchhiking may not have been at all out of character, either, for the ranch girl from the West.

Although there were, and are, other route options available, motorists who know the area often take the uncongested and scenic Route 22 that offers easy access from Lakeville to Lebanon Springs to Bennington. Dooling hypothesizes that a serial killer, preying on hitchhikers, was familiar with the roads in the area and may have used Route 22 as a convenient access in and out of the New England states to perpetrate his crimes. With communications between law enforcement agencies being poor across state lines in those days, the perpetrator may have used this to his advantage, abducting hitchhikers and quickly driving them out of state.

Dooling is a civilian, but he undoubtedly inherited the deductive reasoning skills of his father, a Connecticut State Police Detective Sergeant from 1935 to 1955 who became a private detective after retiring. Also, his maternal grandfather was head of the detective bureau and later chief of the Meriden Police Department, in Meriden, Connecticut. As Dooling grew up, famous and unsolved cases were a common topic of conversation in his household. In recent years, after reading a couple of articles, one on the Connie Smith case and another on geographical profiling, Dooling felt impelled to educate himself in the application of geographical profiling for cold case research and to try to figure out if other cases had similar characteristics.

With his experience in historical research, Dooling already had the skills he needed to access digital databases, newspaper archives, manuscript and map collections, public documents, and Freedom of Information requests. He began his research on Katherine, Paula, and Connie by poring over digitized historical newspaper accounts of missing persons in New England states, looking for combinations of keywords that included "girl," "woman," "disappeared," "missing," "murdered," and "hitchhiking." (See Chapter 11, "Newspaper Research: Online and

Off.") After compiling an impressive collection of newspaper references, he placed the disappearances into a geographical context by taking a hard look at the physical locations of the three cases. Then he studied historical United States Geological Survey (USGS) maps from the periods of the disappearances, as they offered views of the lay of the land as it appeared at the times of the crimes.

The older USGS maps show landmarks that may not exist anymore, such as roads, logging trails, houses, elevations, geographic features, and streams, as well as names of reference points that may have changed over the years. "These came in handy when I corresponded with one of the deer hunters who found Katherine Hull's body," stated Dooling, in e-mail correspondence with the author. See Figure 10.1.

> I was having difficulty identifying exactly where the remains were discovered. News accounts varied in accuracy and every article used a difference reference point. The hunter confidently placed an 'X' on the map where he made the discovery, using an old aircraft beacon tower on the old map as his reference point. The tower hasn't been there in years and doesn't appear on modern maps.[8]

In order to obtain a feel of the areas where the events occurred, Dooling drove and walked the roads and trails that the young women had walked, took new photographs, and examined old photographs of

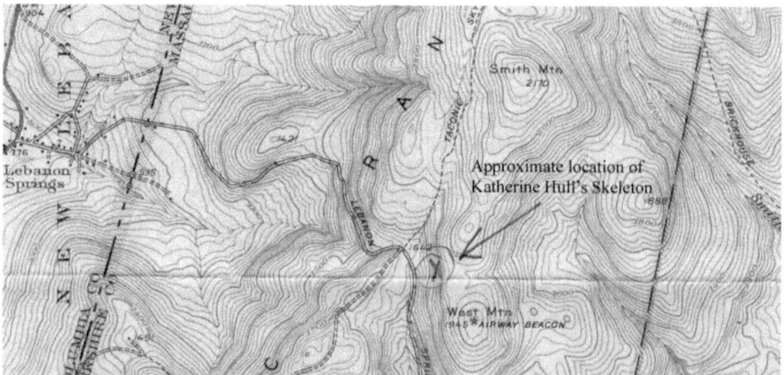

Figure 10.1 This portion of the 1947 USGS, Pittsfield West (Massachusetts) Quadrangle shows an aircraft beacon used as a reference point in determining the location of Katherine Hull's remains. (Modified USGS map courtesy of Michael C. Dooling.)

the areas that were found in historical societies and newspaper archives. He also calculated the average latitude and longitude coordinates of the points where the three young women were last seen. When he did this, he realized that the geographic midpoint (spatial mean) of the three cases was only a short distance from where Katherine Hull's skeletal remains were discovered (see Figure 10.2). Dooling plotted (on Google Earth) information about important locations that included paths traveled by the victims, points where they were seen by witnesses, where the victims were last seen, where Katherine's remains were found, and areas that had been searched. "When I looked at the crime scenes from satellite photos," stated Dooling, "I got a totally different perspective of the relationships between key landmarks, and I was able to view other potentially important landmarks not visible from ground level."[9]

In his book, *Clueless in New England*, Dooling speculates that Katherine, Paula, and Connie all may have been murdered by the same

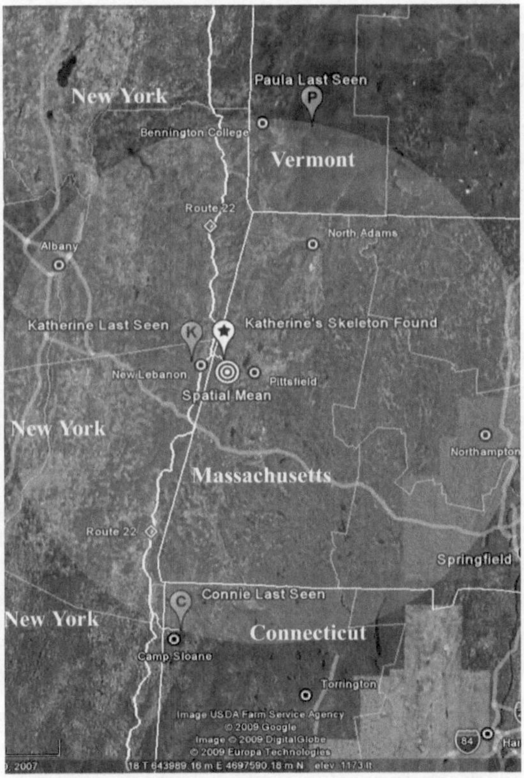

Figure 10.2 Michael C. Dooling determined that the geographic midpoint (the spatial mean) of the three New England cases was only a short distance from where Katherine Hull's skeletal remains had been found. (Modified Google Earth map courtesy of Michael C. Dooling.)

killer. Knowing that Katherine's skeletal remains were found off a dirt road connecting New York and Massachusetts (about five miles from where she was last seen), Dooling estimated where the other two bodies might have been disposed of, if the perpetrator were the same or used similar methods. At the time of this writing, neither Paula's nor Connie's remains have been found, but Dooling is the first person to take a serious look at the three disappearances as a whole and to speculate openly that the cases may be related.

Gaining Historical and Geographical Perspectives

The 1950s began with peace and prosperity. World War II veterans had completed their duties, many received college degrees with the assistance of the GI Bill, and even more were fulfilling the American dream of owning a home and starting a family. Gasoline was cheap, cars were big, and baby boomers were growing up with television shows that included "The Howdy Doody Show," "I Love Lucy," and "Leave It to Beaver." Viewers also watched Sergeant Joe Friday on "Dragnet," a crime drama based on true stories of the Los Angeles Police Department, a place where, on television, the criminals always were caught. Lurking in the background, in suburbia and elsewhere, however, were fears of nuclear war. Homeowners converted basements into fallout shelters, and cities planned for their civil defense.

Within a decade, a new social climate evolved. In 1964, United States President Lyndon B. Johnson announced major military commitments in Vietnam, and singer/songwriter Bob Dylan released his then-new hit song, "The Times They Are A-Changing." Anti-war protestors and others with "anti-establishment" views ushered in 1967's "Summer of Love," when illegal drugs and vulnerable young women freely changed hands, and the hippie counterculture came into public awareness. The use of lysergic acid diethylamide (LSD) was encouraged by Harvard professor Dr. Timothy Leary, who told his followers to "Turn on, tune in, and drop out." With the addition of heroin, methamphetamines, and similar hard-core drugs, the homicide rate started to climb, and the streets traveled on by many young people, both female and male, became increasingly dangerous.

As shown in Chapter 2, "Agency Organization: Cold Case Units," homicide cases spiraled out of control in the 1980s, leaving those that were not solved at the time to become the bulk of today's unsolved cases. Unlike in the earlier years when Katherine Hull, Paula Welden, and Connie Smith were reported missing, today's investigators can draw on the resources that cross jurisdictional lines, including CopLink, Law-Enforcement National Data Exchange (N-DEx), International Justice and Public Safety Information Sharing Network (formerly, the National Law Enforcement Telecommunications

System, NLETS), and the Regional Information Sharing System (RISS), specifically the RISS Cold Case Locater. (See Chapter 15, "Cold Case Review Teams and Information Sharing Resources.")

Working cold cases, however, involves more than a knowledge of the past along with the latest in technology and resources: it involves learning as much as possible about the time and location of the crimes. One of the places to start is with one's own agency. Who were the detectives on specific cases? Are those people available to interview? Do they have additional photographs or files? People searching will help to update witness lists and find family members who—when the time is appropriate—will also need to be contacted. (See Chapters 3, 4, and 14.)

To place a cold case in geographical context in an urban setting, investigators need to know if the buildings where the crimes took place have remained the same or been altered, replaced, or demolished. How has the neighborhood changed? Were the streets vacated or reconfigured? Are there additional maps and photographs from sources other than the case file that show the same location? In rural areas, country lanes may have become highways, and open fields may have developed into shopping centers. What is the same, and what has changed?

Also, when tracking the activities of victims, witnesses, or killers, it is helpful to place them in an historical context. Was a bus station, for instance, always in the same location? How and when did buses change their routes? What kinds of alternative transportation served the area? What about the weather? Some resources that may be helpful in placing crimes in historical and geographical contexts include the following:

- Historical United States Geological Survey Maps: The USGS Historical Quadrangle Scanning Project is in the process of scanning all scales and all editions of approximately 200,000 topographic maps published by the USGS since the inception of its topographic mapping program in 1884.[10]
- Google Earth (version 6.0) contains historical imagery. After zooming in on a specific location, look for the Clock icon that will indicate if previous satellite images are available. If so, move the slider on the timeline to view the same location in previous years.
- County road maps and city street maps from the year of the crime can be found in many local libraries and city or county transportation departments, or even from collectors of ephemera at out-of-print book stores and shows.
- Train and bus maps and timetables from the year of the crime may also be available from these same sources (e.g., see Figure 10.3).
- Road construction photographs may be filed in local libraries, city or county transportation departments, and newspaper archives.

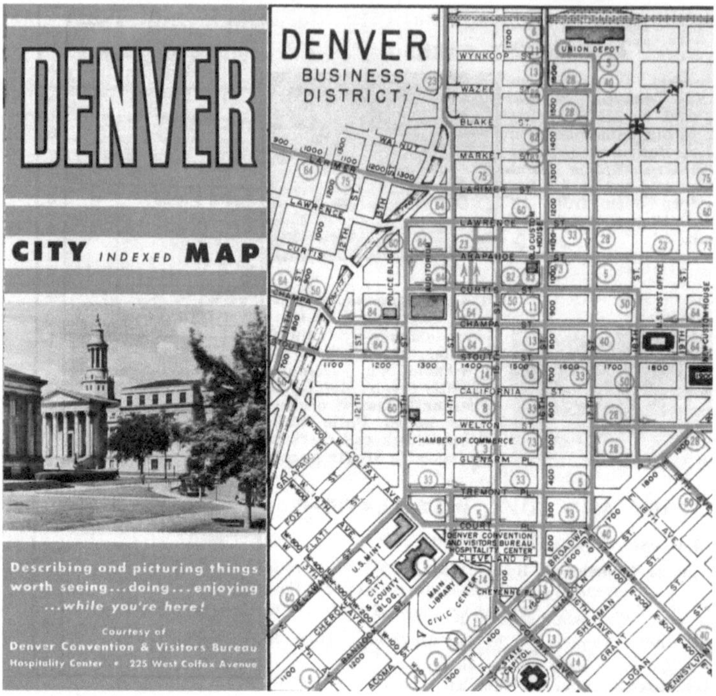

Figure 10.3 This 1954 Denver City Map of bus routes helped trace the activities of Harvey M. Glatman who, along with his female victims, boarded buses in downtown Denver. Glatman assaulted the women after he followed them off the buses in Denver's Capitol Hill neighborhood. (Photo courtesy of "Visit Denver.")

- Building photographs may be available from local libraries, assessors' offices, and newspaper files.
- Historical and genealogical societies often have historical photographs and maps, and they may even have members with specific and long-term knowledge of localities or events.
- Archaeological groups have members who do field surveys and are good at "reading the ground."
- Original newspaper photographs may be available from newspaper archives and libraries.
- City directories are shelved in the reference sections of many local libraries. (See Chapter 12, "Published and Public Records.")
- Weather conditions and forecasts can be found in newspapers, accessible on microfilm. Some historical weather data are also posted online, such as on the U.S. Department of Commerce's National Oceanic and Atmospheric Administration (NOAA) website. For instance, the following website lists minimum and maximum temperatures, snow cover, and precipitation amounts for Boulder, Colorado, from 1897 to the present day, www.esrl.noaa.gov/psd/boulder/getdata.html

Case History: Locating a Long-Forgotten Crime Scene

On April 8, 1954, two male college students discovered the naked and battered body of an unidentified young woman along the banks of Boulder Creek, west of Boulder, Colorado. When the author revisited this murder case in 2004, 50 years later, the file—along with all files from the same era—was missing from the Boulder County Sheriff's Office. The only available information had come from a few newspaper articles, published shortly after the students found the body. But, where, exactly, was the crime scene? None of the original players could provide any information. One of the former students was out of state and unavailable, and the other, who was in a nursing home, had had a stroke and suffered from Parkinson's disease. Only one former law-enforcement officer who had worked the case was still alive, but he was in his mid-nineties and was unable to remember the precise location.

A *Rocky Mountain News* photograph, found in a newspaper archive's clipping file and published on April 9, 1954, showed the two students at the edge of Boulder Creek, pointing to a small level area between two very distinctive rocks. A few days later, another newspaper article on the coroner's inquest stated that the young woman's body had been found "300 yards east of Boulder Falls [a popular tourist destination], twenty-nine feet below the roadway along the creek." In addition to the photograph of the young men, who had been following the creek at water level, another newspaper photograph (see Figure 10.4) showed a view from the Boulder Canyon road looking down to two detectives and a Douglas fir tree near the edge of Boulder Creek.[11]

The reopened case of Boulder Jane Doe is a good example of the results that can be achieved by studying and applying both historical and geographical context. The newspaper photograph of the students provided a visual image of the crime scene. Although the author knew the location of Boulder Falls and was aware that there were no buildings in the general vicinity, there still were questions to be researched on the area's historical context:

- In half a century, had the roadway been altered?
- If so, had construction moved or removed the distinctive rocks?
- If not, were the distinctive rocks still in place and still recognizable?

Questions on the area's geographical context included:

- Was the Douglas fir tree still in place?

Figure 10.4 A fir tree, now nothing more than a rotten stump, loomed over two Boulder police detectives when this newspaper photograph was taken on April 9, 1954, the day after an unidentified young woman's body was found along Boulder Creek. (Photo courtesy of the Boulder *Daily Camera*.)

- What was the significance of "twenty-nine feet below the roadway along the creek?"
- Could the body have been seen from the road? If not, why not?

To search for answers to the questions on historical context, the author started at the Carnegie Branch Library for Local History (a branch of the Boulder Public Library, in Boulder, Colorado) to see what documents were available on the canyon road that connected (and still connects) Boulder with the town of Nederland to the west. Most of the information was contained in newspaper articles, beginning in the nineteenth century when gold and tungsten ores were hauled to Boulder from the mountain mines. During the pre-World War I era, convicts from the Colorado State Penitentiary worked on the then-dirt one-lane road. The convicts were followed in the 1920s and 1930s by private contractors with steam-shovels and trucks who widened and regraded the road into a two-lane thoroughfare. In 1953, one year before the young woman's murder, yet another generation of road workers eliminated sharp curves, blasted rock cuts, bypassed many of the old bridges, bored a 340-foot tunnel, and raised the roadbed. After that, there were no major changes.[12] The good news was that the distinctive rocks might still be there.

With a digital camera and photocopies of the old newspaper photographs in hand, the author parked at the Boulder Falls turnout, then walked the estimated distance downstream, looking for the Douglas fir tree that had showed up in the photograph near the creek. The only tree in the general vicinity was too small to have been growing 50 years ago, but in the underbrush, there was a rotten stump where another tree had obviously once stood. Below the stump, at the edge of the creek, was a small level area.

The photograph of the students (see Figure 10.5) showed one of the distinctive rocks (see Figure 10.6), a large boulder with a dark "bear-claw-shaped" inclusion in the lighter-colored rock face. A half-century later, that same rock was still there. The newspaper photograph also showed another rock, about two or three feet long with a visible white quartz streak running along its top and side. That rock was still in place, too. Also recognizable from the old photograph was a third rock, a medium-sized horizontal boulder with a notchlike depression on the top. In addition, the 29-foot embankment was so steep that the level area where the students found the young woman's body was out of view of passing motorists on the canyon road. That explained how the naked and battered young woman's body could have remained unnoticed for a week to 10 days.[13]

Figure 10.5 University of Colorado college students James Andes, left, and Wayne Swanson, right, found the victim's body. They returned to the scene to point out the exact location to newspaper reporters. (Photo courtesy of E.W. Scripps Company.)

Figure 10.6 An arrow marks the dark inclusion on the large rock, right of center, that 50 years later still matched perfectly with the same rock shown in the photo of the students. Left of the large rock is the notched rock that was behind the head of Wayne Swanson. In the foreground, left of center, is the rock with the white quartz vein. (Photo by author.)

The discovery of the crime scene was a key element in revisiting the Boulder Jane Doe homicide case. Although her murder remains unsolved, circumstantial evidence points to Harvey M. Glatman, the convicted (and executed) serial killer whose California murders led Los Angeles Police Detective and Violent Criminal Apprehension Program (ViCAP) founder Pierce Brooks to look for patterns in criminal behavior and activity that would uncover similarities in cases that previously seemed unrelated. The Boulder County Sheriff's Office, with the assistance of the Vidocq Society, exhumed Jane Doe's remains in June 2004. (For more on the Vidocq Society, see Chapter 15). Five years later, after her DNA was profiled and several possible missing young women were excluded, a DNA match to a surviving sister positively identified the victim as Dorothy Gay Howard, of Phoenix, Arizona.[14]

Summary

Resources in this chapter include:

- An explanation of the importance of historical and geographical context and perspective

- A guide to finding maps, photographs, weather conditions at the time of the crime, and other historical resources helpful in reconstructing a case file
- Two case histories showing the applications of historical and geographical context

Investigators benefit from historical and geographical context. Historical context is mentally going back in time to place the victims in the eras in which they lived. Geographical context involves physically revisiting the crime scenes, canvassing the neighborhoods, and taking a lot of photographs.

- A Connecticut researcher and historian used both historical and geographical contexts to connect three previously unrelated missing persons cases in New England.
- Social changes from the 1950s to the present day contributed to a rise in homicide rates.
- Historical United States Geological Survey maps, Google Earth historical imagery maps, original newspaper photographs, weather reports from the day of the crime, and bus and train maps and timetables are just a few of the many resources available to researchers.
- Both historical and geographical contexts were used when the author located a long-forgotten crime scene by comparing the scene with historical photographs.

Endnotes

1. Staff. "Police Extend Hunt for Girl Missing 3 Days," *Albany Times Union* (NY; April 5, 1936), 2.
2. Dooling, Michael C. *Clueless in New England: The Unsolved Disappearances of Paula Welden, Connie Smith and Katherine Hull* (CT: Carrollton Press, 2010), 161.
3. Dooling, Michael C. *Clueless in New England: The Unsolved Disappearances of Paula Welden, Connie Smith and Katherine Hull* (CT: Carrollton Press, 2010), 167–170.
4. Dooling, Michael C. *Clueless in New England: The Unsolved Disappearances of Paula Welden, Connie Smith and Katherine Hull* (CT: Carrollton Press, 2010), 173–174.
5. Dooling, Michael C. *Clueless in New England: The Unsolved Disappearances of Paula Welden, Connie Smith and Katherine Hull* (CT: Carrollton Press, 2010), 33–36.
6. Staff. "Searchers Comb Vermont Region for Paula Welden," *Stamford Advocate* (CT; May 24, 1947), 1.
7. Dooling, Michael C. *Clueless in New England* (CT: Carrollton Press, 2010), 115–124.

8. Dooling, Michael C. E-mail correspondence with author, September 18, 2011.
9. Dooling, Michael C. E-mail correspondence with author, September 18, 2011.
10. Allord, G. J. and Carswell, W. J., Jr. "Scanning and georeferencing historical USGS quadrangles: U.S. Geological Survey Fact Sheet 2011–3009," http://pubs.usgs.gov/fs/2011/3009 (accessed December 26, 2011).
11. Pettem, Silvia. *Someone's Daughter: In Search of Justice for Jane Doe* (Lanham, MD: Taylor Trade, 2009), 66–68.
12. Pettem, Silvia. *Someone's Daughter: In Search of Justice for Jane Doe* (Lanham, MD: Taylor Trade, 2009), 66.
13. Pettem, Silvia. *Someone's Daughter: In Search of Justice for Jane Doe* (Lanham, MD: Taylor Trade, 2009), 68–69.
14. Anas, Brittany. "Mystery Solved: Boulder Sheriff IDs 'Jane Doe' as Dorothy Gay Howard," Boulder *Daily Camera* (CO; October 28, 2009).

Newspaper Research: Online and Off

11

Newspapers and their accompanying photographs play an important role in cold case research, especially when case files are incomplete or missing. As described in the previous chapter, when the Boulder Jane Doe case was revisited 50 years after the young woman's murder, the local sheriff's office no longer had the case file and a new one had to be reconstructed, starting with the original newspaper articles. Similarly, the same newspaper articles that led to the crime scene also led to the victim's autopsy report. The local coroner's office did not have the report, but the Boulder *Daily Camera* (in Boulder, Colorado) on April 9, 1954, the day after the woman's body was found, provided the name of the pathologist who had performed the autopsy.

The following is an excerpt from the article, "Body of Murdered, Unidentified Girl Found Near Boulder Creek":

> A pathologist who performed an autopsy said the girl definitely was alive, but probably unconscious, when she was thrown or rolled over an embankment from the Boulder Cañon highway about 300 yards below the Boulder Falls parking area. Sheriff Arthur T. Everson, Coroner George W. Howe, Deputy Attorney Joseph J. Dolan, and Dr. Freburn L. James, Sanitarium pathologist, concluded the badly fractured victim was beaten before she was dumped out of an automobile, although some of her broken bones could have resulted from the plunge down the embankment into jagged rocks.[1]

Fifty years later, the author located Dr. Freburn L. James with a Google search. On the telephone, the elderly then-retired pathologist said that he had always wondered about the woman he called "the mystery girl." He still had a copy of her original autopsy report filed in his living room, and he happily put it in the mail![2] (See Chapter 4 for more on Google.)

How Newspaper Research Can Help

Establishing contact with Dr. James and obtaining Boulder Jane Doe's autopsy report illustrates how valuable newspaper research can be in revealing the names of key players, which can lead to the discovery of formerly missing documents. The research can also help by:

- Bringing forward new witnesses
- Revealing lifestyles and opinions
- Putting crimes in historical context
- Providing new names for missing persons lists
- Aiding the prosecution

Newspapers Can Help by Bringing Forward New Witnesses

As discussed in Chapter 1, relationships between witnesses, or between suspects and their family members, may have changed. With new evidence, new witnesses come forward. Newspaper articles from the time of the crime may also provide the names of additional people to interview or reinterview, including former detectives and witnesses. Even the reporters may have new information to add. Like old cops, they like to reminisce, and they may remember rumors and information that they chose not to report on at the time.

Newspapers Can Help by Revealing Lifestyles and Opinions

Newspaper research can also reveal lifestyles and opinions. As Michael C. Dooling found in his research on the young women missing and presumably murdered in New England (see Chapter 10), one missing young woman's mother stated that her daughter would have climbed into the car "of anyone who might have come along."[3] Similarly, a newspaper article following the arrest of Harvey M. Glatman for the murders of two California women quoted then-Boulder County Sheriff Art Everson discussing the Boulder Jane Doe case. Everson told a reporter in October 1958 that he considered Glatman (who was executed in 1959) "a good suspect in the mystery slaying of 1954."[4] The original case file is missing, Everson is now deceased, and he did not confide his thoughts about the murder to his family, so the newspaper clipping is the only way to attempt to read his mind. In the revisited case 50 years later, Boulder County Sheriff officials independently reached the same conclusion.

Newspapers Can Help by Putting Crimes in Historical Context

What else was going on at the time of the crime? What was the weather? Perhaps there was a large music concert or a major snowstorm. Newspaper research does not have to be limited to specific articles on the crime, but it is helpful to include articles around the time of the crime as well.

Newspapers Can Help by Providing New Names for Missing Persons Lists

Searches of online newspapers—with keywords such as "missing woman" and a date range—are particularly helpful when putting together spreadsheets of missing persons. Often, their disappearances are mentioned but frustration comes when trying to chase down the details to find out if, and when, they returned home.

Newspapers Can Help by Aiding the Prosecution

Finding and cataloging newspaper articles from 10 or 20 years ago, or more, can also be critical in the prosecution of cold cases. When was information published, and when did witnesses learn specific details? It is not unusual for case files or interview notes to indicate that suspects or witnesses told their interrogators that they acquired particular items of information on a homicide, for instance, by reading about it in a newspaper. Cold case investigators use newspaper articles from the time of the crime to build timelines, with exact dates of the stories in which specific details were published, thereby either discrediting or corroborating the independent recollections of witnesses.

Newspaper Research Options

It is important to remember that as helpful as newspaper research can be, newspapers are a secondary source and facts should be independently verified. Today's newspaper researchers have several options though, each with its own advantages and limitations. The ones to use are the ones that provide the right answers, and that can take some experimentation.

- NewsBank: Online and free newspaper access with local library card
- ESBCO Host: Online journal and periodical aggregator includes free newspaper access with local library card
- Google News Newspapers: Online with both free and pay-per-view newspaper access
- Subscription-based online newspaper access: includes Newspaper ARCHIVE.com, ProQuest, and Ancestry.com
- Individual newspaper archives: most articles for a fee
- Microfilmed newspapers: usually free, through local public libraries and interlibrary loan
- Clipping files from newspapers: at public libraries and newspaper offices

Newsbank

NewsBank is funded by taxpayers, but it is free to users with a library card through most public libraries. The procedure is as follows:

- Access a local library's website.
- Click on "elibrary and research," or a similar listing.
- Find a list of databases.
- Click on "NewsBank for home use," or a similar remote access setting. At that point, most library websites will then request a name and library number.

On the "Locations" tab, the search can be narrowed to a specific locality. Although there are a few newspapers from Europe, Asia, and South America, most are from North America, primarily the United States. Opening the "United States" option under "Shortcuts" reveals the individual states, along with the District of Columbia and Puerto Rico. States can be selected separately or by region. The "Source Types" tab can be used to further narrow a search to the following:

- Blogs
- Journals
- Magazines
- Newspapers
- Newswires
- Transcripts
- Video
- Web-only sources

The "Source List" tab for "Newspapers" is the most comprehensive of the tabs and links to individual newspapers, specifying the dates for which the newspapers are online. The *Washington Post*, in Washington, DC, goes back the farthest. In NewsBank, the online articles extend from 1977 to the present day, even though the newspaper was digitized (and is available elsewhere) for the previous 100 years. But, the starting date (i.e., 1977) does not necessarily mean that a newsworthy event from an earlier time period is not included. Reporters often recall crimes at the times of their anniversaries, when new material surfaces, or simply to keep the story in the news. (See Chapter 16, "Taking Advantage of the Media.") For instance, consider a search for information on six murders which occurred in 1971 and 1972, by a serial killer known only as the Freeway Phantom. When "Freeway Phantom" is entered in quotation marks (to keep the search focused on the two words together), there are, at the time of this writing, 24 results listed by specific years.

Figure 11.1 On November 23, 1971, shortly after the Freeway Phantom had strangled his fifth victim, *Washington Daily News* reporter Judy Luce Mann handed Officer William Miscovic a representative sample of the scores of letters with tips received by the newspaper office. The *Washington Daily News* was purchased by the *Washington Star* in 1972. At the time of this writing, the young women's murders remain unsolved. (Photo reprinted with permission of the District of Columbia Public Library, Star collection ©Washington Post.)

One of the most complete articles, "'Freeway Phantom' Slayings Haunt Police, Families: Six Young D.C. Females Vanished in the '70s," was published in the *Washington Post* on June 26, 2006 (see Figure 11.1). The still-unidentified killer had strangled six black females, ages 10 through 18 before dumping their bodies on or near busy roads or highways in Maryland and in Washington, DC. Although from a researcher's point of view it would be better to read the day-to-day articles as the story unfolded in the early 1970s, a review of the crimes published at a later date is a good way for investigators new to these cases to get an overview of all of the murders and to see how the information was presented to the public. (Determined investigators can still access the day-to-day newspaper reports on microfilm, as discussed below.)

Ideally, the newspaper's librarian electronically archived the content and sent it to a vendor such as NewsBank, but with across-the-board budget cuts in recent years, the individuals who currently submit the stories may be editors or even reporters. Once the content is archived, the vendor then indexes and consolidates the data prior to making articles available on the Internet. Users can then enter different combinations of search terms, along with either a date range or a specific date. The advantages of the NewsBank service are that it is free to users and it is accessible online.

One of the disadvantages of NewsBank is that some content is not flagged to let the user know that it is paid, and not editorial, content. This includes obituaries and may soon include wedding, engagement, and anniversary announcements. Why does this matter? When librarians archived the contents, the stories were checked by a neutral party; there was quality control. As more and more newspapers are doing without librarians, the archiving has become automated. The articles are electronically submitted by editors or reporters; then they are sent to presentation editors who do the layout and design and who send them to NewsBank.

These automated articles, however, may have missing captions and bylines, and they may also be missing their "jumps" (i.e., continuing pages), for instance, from a front-page story. In addition, the date ranges of specific newspapers may not go far enough back in time, particularly if the dates one is searching are earlier than the mid-1980s. In some parts of the country, only a few newspapers are included in the database, and those newspapers may not be the ones that cover the person or topic being researched. NewsBank is well worth the effort, however, to obtain a local library card and try it out. Some libraries even accept online library card applications.

EBSCO Host

Another way to access newspaper articles online and with a local library card is through the online information resource EBSCO Host. Institutional and business subscribers have to log on, but, EBSCO, like NewsBank, is accessible for free to some local library users. Although the procedures are continually changing, look under "e-library and research," locate ESBCO, and then, under "General News Databases," go to "Newspaper Source." To get the best coverage, however, it may be necessary to overlap the services of both NewsBank and EBSCO. For example, the *Philadelphia Inquirer* is accessible on EBSCO from 1997 to the present, but it is not available, for any years, through NewsBank. Some newspapers are on both databases, but they do not necessarily cover the same years. As noted above, NewsBank has online articles from the *Washington Post* that go back decades, but those on EBSCO only date from 2003.

Google News—Newspapers

From 2008 to 2011, Google (http://news.google.com/newspapers) took on an ambitious newspaper scanning project, digitizing approximately 2,000 newspapers, some dating back 100 or more years. To the regret of longtime users, a former and very user-friendly search tool called the Google News

Archive Timeline is no longer available. However, the scanned historical newspapers can still be searched through "news.google.com/newspapers," and custom dates can be specified. Some of the newspaper articles are free, and some are pay-per-view.

Using the Freeway Phantom again as an example, and sorted by date with the oldest one first, brings up the November 30, 1971, article "Police Ask Help; Call 626-2145," in the *Washington Afro-American*. The article asks for any information that may aid police in their search. Issues of the newspaper, however, were scanned from 1916 to 1988, so a more thorough search—in that newspaper alone and with various keywords—might yield additional stories on the series of murders.

Subscription-Based Newspaper Access

- NewspaperARCHIVE, http://newspaperarchive.com, states that it is the world's largest online newspaper archive, with the bulk of its newspapers (some from large cities and some from small ones) from the 1950s through the 1980s. At the time of this writing, the website offers a three-month plan for approximately $10.
- ProQuest, www.proquest.com/en-US, is subscription-based but it can be remotely accessed for no charge through many colleges and universities. It has fewer newspapers than NewspaperARCHIVE, but the newspapers it covers are from several major cities and have longer runs. For instance, the *Washington Post* is searchable for 117 years: from 1877 to 1994.
- Ancestry.com, www.ancestry.com, is a genealogy site and, as shown in Chapter 4, it can be helpful in locating people. With the exception of some newspaper obituaries though, most of the website's extensive database of online newspapers are too far back in time to be of much use in cold case research. For instance, its searchable database of the *Washington Post* runs from 1904 to 1924, way before the time of the Freeway Phantom. The subscription-based website can be accessed (but not remotely) in some public libraries.

Individual Newspaper Archives

Using the *Washington Post* again as an example, it, like most newspapers, has a pay-per-article archive, and its available articles date back to 1987. At the time of this writing, purchase options vary from one article for a few dollars, up to 25 articles for slightly more than one dollar apiece. Because the *Post* was one of the major city newspapers to have been digitized by ProQuest, however, searching historical articles (from 1877 to 1986) is available on the *Post's* own website. A search in the historical article database for Freeway Phantom turned up 60 articles, the first from November 18, 1971, twelve days prior to the first article in the *Washington Afro-American*. The title, date, and a short abstract of the article are given, but to read it online in its entirety requires a fee. Although this information is continually changing, recent articles and obituaries (varies from newspaper to newspaper) are accessible online for free, but cold case researchers will find that the older ones require a fee.

In addition to the *Washington Afro-American*, other special-interest group newspapers also serve their communities. In Washington, DC, these include the *Washington Blade* for the gay community, as well as *The Hill Rag* that centers on activities on Capitol Hill. Campus newspapers at colleges and universities all over the country also report on crimes and topics of interest to students. These specialized newspapers may be out of print, and they should be contacted directly for access to their archives.

Digitized Newspaper Archives

Some states, including Colorado (with state funding administered by the Colorado State Library and the Colorado Historical Society) are digitizing some of their newspapers and making them available to the public to read online. However, as is the case with the Colorado Historic Newspaper Collection (currently covering 1859 through 1923), the newspapers that were archived first are the oldest ones.

Microfilmed Newspapers

Investigators today can go through life without ever accessing newspapers on microfilm, but if they do, they are limiting their research abilities. Instead, think of microfilm as a tool that can provide data that are unavailable anywhere else. Consider, for instance, a murder that occurred in 1980 and none of the online options above cover the date and location where the crime took place. Perhaps the case file has photocopies of some of the original newspaper articles, but detectives and prosecutors want to know if the collections of articles they have are complete. On microfilm, they can read day-by-day accounts as the story unfolds.

Fortunately, a cooperative national effort among the states and the federal government called the United States Newspaper Project is continuously locating, cataloging, and preserving hard copies of newspapers directly on microfilm. Funding is provided by the National Endowment for the Humanities, and technical assistance is furnished by the Library of Congress. Many newspapers, from the big-city dailies to small-town weeklies, can be read on microfilm. If a crime was local, even many years ago, chances are that microfilm of the local newspaper is on file at a local public library. If not, try state historical societies and large metropolitan public libraries with genealogical sections.

What if the crime, however, took place in another city or another state? All an investigator (or anyone) has to do is to go to one's public library and request, through interlibrary loan, a month or so of microfilmed newspapers that cover the specific place and time. Reference librarians know how to find the names of the appropriate newspapers and will track them down, if available. Most of the time this service is free. The wait for microfilm can take a couple of weeks, but it is worth the time when there is no alternative to reconstructing or supplementing a case file. Most libraries require that the microfilm be read in the libraries, but some of these research facilities provide twenty-first-century microfilm readers (see Figure 11.2) that allow the content to be scanned and even e-mailed to oneself or one's agency.

Another advantage of microfilm over specific copies of isolated articles is that the reader will get the entire newspaper, with all of its context, including the day's weather, other crimes, and ongoing events. Was the crime placed on the newspaper's front page, or tucked into an obscure section in the back? Funeral (death) notices for individuals without obituaries usually contain next-of-kin information and can easily be found on pages that contain classified advertising. Finally, the microfilmed articles, unlike those in NewsBank, can include photographs that can be invaluable in reconstructing case files and locating crime scenes. (See Chapter 10, "Historical and Geographical Context.")

Figure 11.2 This modern-day microfilm reader allows a library patron to zoom in on a specific article, then scan it to an adjoining computer to either print or e-mail. (Photo by author.)

Figure 11.3 For decades, newspaper librarians kept clipping files. Some newspapers still have the files in their archives, but others, if they have not been destroyed, may show up in research libraries. (Photo by author.)

Newspaper Clipping Files

Until the past few years, most newspaper offices' archives, or "morgues," had librarians who would research requested clipping and photograph files or allow researchers access on their own (see Figure 11.3). In small towns, this may still be possible. Some large-city collections, however, have been moved to public libraries, such as the files of Denver's former *Rocky Mountain News*, now housed at the Denver Public Library. Today's quickly changing media world is of great concern to historians, as, in some cases, hardcopies from newspaper archives may no longer be available at all. Clippings (filed under names and subjects) when they can be found, however, may contain actual hardcopies of the photographs that were used in the articles, a huge plus for cold case investigators.

Understanding Obituaries

When revisiting cold case homicides, investigators may want to update their witness lists to include the victims' extended family members. One of the best ways to determine family relationships is through obituaries. Currently, many recent obituaries are posted online by funeral homes and mortuaries (and also on individual newspaper websites). They can also be found through both online and offline newspaper research, as discussed on the previous pages. Yet another resource for obituaries is local public libraries where genealogical society members often compile collections of obituaries from their geographical areas. (As mentioned in Chapter 12, information in public libraries is as close as a telephone call or an e-mail to "Ask a Librarian.") It is important, however, to understand the changes that obituaries have undergone in recent years.

Traditional Newspaper Obituaries

Traditional newspaper obituaries written by a reporter followed a formula that usually covered the dates of the person's birth, marriage, and death, and brief facts on his or her occupation, church and fraternal organizations, funeral announcements, and survivors. The information was usually provided by a funeral home with factual data given by the family of the deceased. These obituaries were considered news content, and were entered into NewsBank and other information providers.

Paid Newspaper Obituaries

Paid obituaries, which generate revenue for newspaper companies, have in recent years taken the place of traditional obituaries in many newspapers. They are written by family members or friends of the deceased, can be quite lengthy, and are not edited or even spell-checked. They may be more likely than traditional obituaries to contain factual errors. If a descendant had a skeleton in his or her closet, the information provided may even be purposely inaccurate. Paid obituaries are classified by the newspapers as advertising, and may or may not be entered into NewsBank or other information providers. (See discussion under NewsBank.)

Summary

Resources in this chapter include:

- Information on locating historical newspaper articles online for context, to find new witnesses and missing persons, and to aid prosecutors
- How to find the same information when the newspaper articles are not online

Historical newspaper articles can be accessed both online and off. Either way, they can help to locate new witnesses, reveal lifestyles and opinions, put crimes in historical context, and provide new names for missing persons lists. Articles from the time of a crime can also aid the prosecution, for instance, in confirming whether a suspect or witness was telling the truth when he or she claimed to have acquired a particular item of information by reading about it in a newspaper.

Newspaper accounts, however, are secondary sources and the facts need to be independently verified. Obituaries are an excellent source for determining family relationships, but current-day obituaries are paid advertisements and may be less accurate than their traditional counterparts. The following newspaper resources are available to researchers and investigators:

- NewsBank
- ESBCO Host
- Google News Newspapers
- Subscription-based online newspaper access
- Individual newspaper archives
- Microfilmed newspapers
- Clipping files

Endnotes

1. Staff. "Body of Murdered, Unidentified Girl Found Near Boulder Creek," Boulder *Daily Camera* (CO; April 9, 1954).
2. Pettem, Silvia. *Someone's Daughter: In Search of Justice for Jane Doe* (Lanham, MD: Taylor Trade, 2009), 51.
3. Staff. "Searchers Comb Vermont Region for Paula Welden," *Stamford Advocate* (CT; May 24, 1947) 1.
4. Staff. "Slayer Once Abducted Boulder Mother; Also Suspected of Killing Mystery Girl Whose Body Was Found," Boulder *Daily Camera* (CO; October 31, 1958).

Published and Public Records 12

If the late Pierce Brooks and other highly skilled detectives from the pre-Internet days could see the research tools available to today's investigators, they would be astounded. Yet Brooks and his colleagues at the Los Angeles Police Department in the 1950s researched a lot of cases without the online access that we take for granted today. How did they do it? Our predecessors used what we now call "old-fashioned police work": they climbed the steps of county courthouses, where they searched public records, traced names, and determined relationships. Today, most—but not all—of this same investigative work can be done online.

As shown in Chapter 3, "TLO: The Latest Online Investigative System," and Chapter 4, "Additional Options for People Searches," placing an individual at a particular address during a specific time period is not difficult if the time period is after the mid-1980s. But, investigators searching for a current name, address, or telephone number, for instance, for a witness, suspect, or person of interest who shows up in a document, report, or newspaper article prior to the mid-1980s, will find the online information sketchy at best. Cold case researchers need to know how to access the past.

Even more challenging than pinpointing specific names and dates are changes in marital and family relationships. People-searching will reveal "relatives" and "associates," but which is the sister, the wife, or the ex-wife? An old document, report, or newspaper article may give the name of a female witness from 20 years ago, but when it comes time to reinterview her, all that an investigator may have is the woman's maiden, or a former married name. Similarly, a deceased person's daughter, "Carol Brown," may have been "Carol Jones" in a list of survivors in an obituary of 15 years ago. In recent years, the elusive female witness may have married and changed her name again, creating a challenge when it comes time to reopen the cold case file. The good news is that these name transitions show up in public records, by accessing the real courthouse records (see Figure 12.1), and they only take a little creativity to find.

This chapter addresses the following:

- What are published and public records?
- Where are these records found? (The listings in this chapter are not all-inclusive.)

Figure 12.1 Courthouses, such as this one in Prescott, Yavapai County, Arizona, hold thousands and thousands of public records. Today, much, but not all, courthouse research can be done online. (Photo by author.)

- How can the records help in cold case investigations? (See "Local Public Records" for tips on tracing name changes of women.)

In very loose terms, if a government entity receives public funds its documents are public records. But there are a lot of exceptions and variations, with drastic changes since the terrorist attacks on September 11, 2001. Because of identity theft concerns, many government offices have redacted Social Security numbers and other previously available data from their records. In situations where there has not been enough staff to remove the information, some "public records" (including many divorce records) are no longer available to the public at all, but these court records are still available to law enforcement. Public records, however, can be found on the federal, state, and local levels. Using Colorado as an example, the Colorado Open Records Act (CORA) defines public records in the Colorado Revised Statutes, 24-72-202 (6)(a) as all writings that are made, maintained, kept, or held by entities that are "for use in the exercise of functions required or authorized by law or administrative rule or involving the receipt or expenditure of public funds." Criminal records, however, are excluded. A "writing" is defined as "all books, papers, maps, photographs, cards, tapes, recordings, or other documentary materials, regardless of physical form or characteristics." Data that are stored digitally, including e-mail, are included in the definition.[1]

For the purpose of this book, the author defines published records as items such as telephone books and city directories, which are privately published but available to the public in public libraries.

Federal Public Records

The National Archives

The National Archives, www.archives.gov/research, divided into regions, preserves and makes available federal records and information, including files on court cases, employees, prisoners, and nearly everything imaginable that pertains to the federal government. For instance, the Rocky Mountain Region has a file on "Accidents in National Parks" that includes information on a hiker who went missing in Rocky Mountain National Park. (See Chapter 9, "The Plight of the Missing and Unknown.") Although the National Archives states on its website that only one to three percent of its holdings are so important for legal or historical reasons that they are kept forever, they claim that the sheets of paper in their holdings, laid end to end, would circle the earth more than 57 times. In addition to the paper, the archives has:

- More than 93,000 motion picture films
- More than 5.5 million maps, charts, and architectural drawings
- More than 207,000 sound and video recordings
- More than 18 million aerial photographs
- Nearly 35 million still pictures and posters
- More than 3.5 billion electronic records[2]

Freedom of Information Act (FOIA)/ Privacy Act

Requests for information from the federal government can be made through the Freedom of Information Act (FOIA) and the Privacy Act. When requests are made to the Federal Bureau of Investigation (FBI), the FOIA provides information about organizations, businesses, investigations, historical events, incidents, groups, and deceased persons, and the Privacy Act allows U.S. citizens and lawfully admitted aliens to request information on themselves or another living person.[3]

Social Security Applications for Deceased Individuals

Social Security application requests can be made on deceased individuals by accessing the website of the Social Security Administration. As shown in Chapter 4 in the case history of the woman who changed her identity, the author's receipt of Twylia May Embrey's fraudulent Social Security application provided long-sought answers to Twylia's aliases, as well as her fabricated date and place of birth.

State Public Records

Secretaries of states, departments of consumer affairs, and related statewide licensing boards and agencies (as well as locally recorded documents, see below) can be helpful when tracing witnesses with name variations or aliases so that investigators can compare signatures. Some states have searchable records with PDF files of signed documents viewable online. Some searches require a fee and others do not. Documents that can be searched include:

- Business licenses
- Trade name renewals
- Uniform Commercial Code (UCC) filings that include finance statements, security instruments, and tax liens

(See Chapter 16 for the use of the California Department of Consumer Affairs, Contractors State License Board, in a coroner's investigation.[4])

State Archives

State archive collections vary from Alabama to Wyoming, but their missions are similar; that is, they preserve and make available records and information created by state (and local) governments. These archives can be invaluable when researching district court cases from several years ago, or for penitentiary and reformatory records (see Figure 12.2). (Recent court data are often accessible under the judicial branches of individual states.) Using Colorado as an example, these older court files (varying by district) are housed in the state archives by case number, obtainable from the individual district courts. When researching Harvey M. Glatman, for instance, the author obtained Glatman's case file from 1945 through the early 1950s (see Figure 12.3). It contained legal correspondence and psychological assessments, as well as witnesses' names that led to an interview, in 2007, with one of Glatman's now-elderly assault victims.

Some state archives also house law enforcement files or microfilm. These may or may not be publicly viewable. If not, they are solely for preservation and backup, but can be checked out by the original agencies. Also publicly accessible, however, are penitentiary and reformatory records. Colorado has records of its state convicts from 1871 through 1973, with additional mug shots to 1992. The Records of Convicts includes:

- Name
- Date when convicted
- Date when received

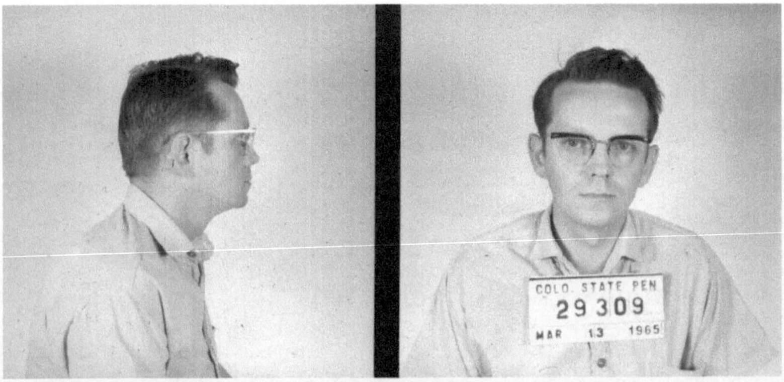

Figure 12.2 This mug shot is of Alvin Wesley Brooks, a taxi driver convicted of murdering a young woman in Denver, Colorado, in 1955. The photograph is part of the Records of Convicts collection at the Colorado State Archives. (Photo courtesy of the Colorado State Archives.)

Figure 12.3 The author reviews a case file in the Colorado State Archives. (Photo courtesy of Alan Cass.)

- Crime
- Sentence
- County
- Description (age, height, complexion, color of eyes, color of hair)
- Occupation
- Place of birth
- Next of kin (names of parents and residence, marital status, name of wife or husband and where living)
- Ability to read and write

- Signature
- Scars
- Additional remarks
- Mug shots

Local Public Records

Recorded Documents, Online (and Off)

Recorded documents tie individuals and businesses to dates and places. See the state-by-state list at the end of this chapter. A last name entered into the search field on a county recorder's website, for instance, can lead to new information on dates, addresses, family relationships, and even a woman's former name. Traditionally, the offices that housed recorded documents were located in courthouses, but where they are now and what they are called varies widely by locality. In some states, the offices use the name "register of deeds" or "clerk and recorder," but their functions are basically the same. Small rural communities may not have any online records at all, but access to their records can be obtained by telephoning, e-mailing, or walking in the door. Unless a previous courthouse building burned to the ground, the information, most likely, is still there.

Some local government websites are easy to navigate, whereas others leave plenty of room for improvement. One of the more user-friendly websites is the Maricopa County Recorder, in Arizona. Its recorded documents date all the way back to 1871. The county has more than 100 search types that include:

- Bankruptcy
- Child support
- Divorce
- Medical liens
- Power of attorney
- Property[5]

Name changes can be traced in the same way that title companies follow transfers of titles from grantors to grantees. For instance, entering a name in a document search can bring up all documents (depending upon the setting of parameters) that contain the same name. As indicated, above (in the section on Secretary of State records), in many cases a PDF file of the actual documents can be viewed online—complete with the names and signatures of both a husband and wife, or whoever signed the documents—as well as the names and dates of parties involved in related transactions. If "Delores H. and Gregory M. Abernathy," for example, owned property in joint tenancy, and then, a few years later, "Delores H. Manning" is the owner of the same property, chances are that Delores H. Abernathy changed her name to Delores H. Manning.

Many local-level recorded document offices also keep records of marriages (and even premarital agreements), which is the most obvious way to search for a woman's maiden, former, or married name. These online listings, however, vary by state and even county. Marriage records in some local governments can be searched online, whereas in other departments they have been removed. In Arizona, marriage records are kept by superior courts in the counties where the marriage licenses were obtained. Even if the records are not online though, the local-level governmental offices are the designated repositories for these records, and their records remain in their books. The process for obtaining the information can be initiated with a telephone call or an e-mail. See Figures 12.4 and 12.5.

Police Departments and Sheriffs' Offices

Law enforcement records are preserved in various formats, from accordion files and notebooks to microfiche and microfilm to historical data that can be searched via computer, whether through scanned images on

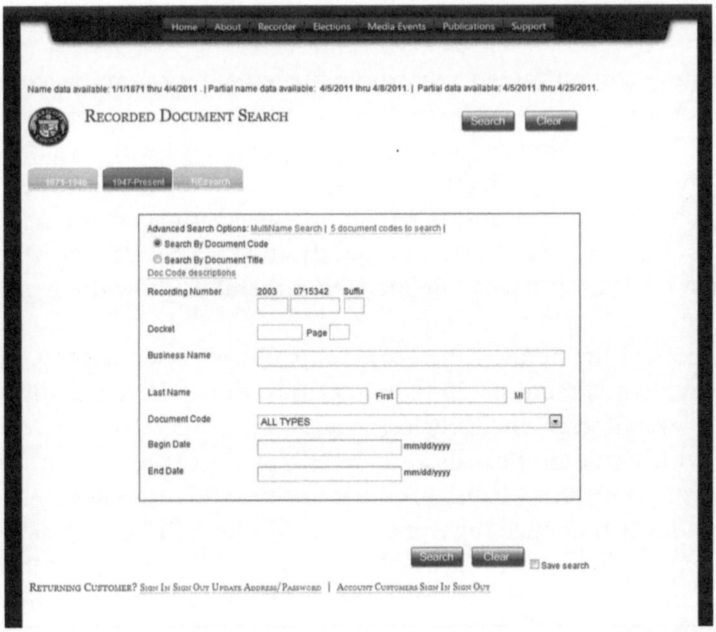

Figure 12.4 The Maricopa County Recorder's Office in Arizona is a good example of a user-friendly recorded document website. (Photo courtesy of Maricopa County Recorder, Helen Purcell.)

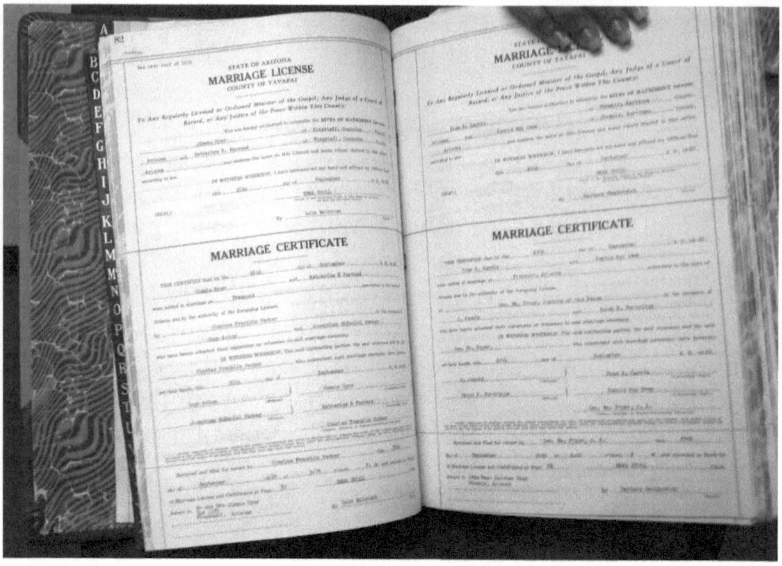

Figure 12.5 At the Yavapai County, Arizona, Superior Court, and in courthouses across the country, bound ledger books preserve marriage licenses and certificates. (Photo by author.)

DVD or new computerized records management systems. Separate copies of reports may even be in multiple locations, with different retention times. For instance, an original incident report may be filed in an agency's records division, a copy filed in the case file, another copy in the evidence technician's file, and yet another may be buried under other papers on a detective's desk. It never hurts to make friends with someone who knows the total system, as well as someone who remembers how the records were filed and stored "back in the day."

Members of the public can access some of the closed agency reports by filing open records requests; in ongoing cases, the files are usually available to outside law enforcement agencies. In addition, county jails often keep "jail jackets," with visitation records and "kites" (pieces of paper with, for example, requests to see the chaplain or obtain medical attention). A common practice today is that once reports are transferred to microfilm or DVD, the original reports are destroyed, unless they are of homicides or if they still have evidence and the case is within the statute of limitations. Agencies that maintain records on microfilm, microfiche, floppy disks, or other methods that are no longer in common use would do well to scan them into their records systems or keep their microfilm and microfiche readers, zip drives, and other outdated hardware in order to be able to read their old files.

District Attorneys' Offices and Court Records

If a grand jury was opened or subpoenas were issued, or an arrest was made, district attorney records most likely will contain case files, even if the original law enforcement files were purged or are missing from police departments' and sheriffs' offices. If the case was filed, some district attorney records may include PSIs (presentence investigation reports). Investigators have found that prosecutors' case files can be very helpful when reconstructing homicide case files, sometimes even leading to an original, and previously missing, file.

Court records of closed cases are also public records, and they can contain a wealth of information including copies of arrest warrants, search warrants, and even the name of the person who bailed a person out of jail. Court records can best be obtained by contacting the individual court where the original documents were filed, although the procedures vary by state. Some districts store their old files either as hardcopies or on microfilm, whereas others transfer them to their state archives, as noted in the section under State Public Records.

Coroners' and Medical Examiners' Offices

These offices maintain autopsy reports, death certificates, photographs, information on next of kin, and tissue samples and slides. In some states (Colorado is one of them) these records are open to the public, and in some states they are not. The Arapahoe County, Colorado, coroner keeps hard copies back to the 1950s and has electronic versions back to 2001. Coroners' and medical examiners' records are not protected by HIPPA (Health Insurance Portability and Accountability Act) privacy laws, as they would be if the records were in a hospital.

Probate Courts

Probate records can be helpful in determining a person's heirs, along with the last-known addresses of the heirs. As explained in Chapter 4, "Additional Options for People Searches," in a discussion of Google, the author was surprised to come across a reference to the Harvey M. Glatman Memorial Scholarship, at Denver University. The motivation for the bequest, named for a serial killer, was revealed in Glatman's mother's (Ophelia Glatman's) probate file, in Denver Probate Court (see Figure 12.6). Ophelia had died in 1968 and left most of her estate to "memorialize" her only son, Harvey M. Glatman. The mother was well aware of her son's criminal record, as she wrote her will in 1960, one year after Glatman was executed for murder at the California State Prison at San Quentin. The probate file also revealed that Ophelia Glatman's nephew, now deceased, was the executor of Ophelia's

"... and in so doing the Trustees shall in some manner or fashion call attention to the fact that the acts of said Trustees are being carried out to perpetuate the memory of my son, Harvey." ...

...

"... IN WITNESS WHEREOF, I have hereunto subscribed my name this 21st day of January, A.D. 1960."

Ophelia Glatman

Figure 12.6 Probate records, excerpted above, of Ophelia Glatman reveal that the woman established a trust fund to perpetuate the memory of her serial-killer son. (Author's collection.)

estate, and he was the person who actually carried out the mother's wishes and initiated the scholarship.[6]

Published Local Records

Public Libraries, Online (and Off)

A whole generation has grown up without telephone directories. Not long ago, the way to find a telephone number, or order a pizza, was to flip open a telephone book. Most people, today, look up current numbers on the Internet. But what if a case file included contact information from 25 or 30 years ago, and modern search engines show that the number either does not exist or has been assigned to an unrelated party? The place to begin is by opening a telephone book or city directory from the year being researched. Directories, like locally recorded documents, also place individuals and businesses in specific locations at specific times and can be useful in tracing name changes of women.

Reference sections of most public libraries have both telephone and city directories for their communities. Usually, these directories were issued annually and go back many decades. In addition to the telephone directories' "white pages" for residents and businesses, they include "yellow page" advertising, which aids in determining a business's location and whether it was open during a certain time period. When searching the "white pages," keep in mind that widows often kept the names of their late husbands, both for continuity—the wife may never have been listed in the first place—and for safety, so that it would appear that a man was living in the home.

Figure 12.7 City directories line the shelves of many public libraries and can be invaluable when searching for people prior to the mid-1980s. (Photo by author.)

Along with alphabetical listings of individuals, the entries often include occupations and places of employment. Individual and business names are cross-referenced by telephone numbers and street addresses showing, for instance, every address in sequence or in a city block or suburban subdivision. City directories provide the only way, prior to the beginning of the Internet era (mid-1980s), to figure out the names and addresses of everyone who lived in a particular neighborhood or on a specific street. See Figures 12.7 and 12.8. As shown in Chapter 10, additional public library resources include microfilmed (and sometimes bound) newspapers and copies of obituaries.

If a personal visit is inconvenient, or if the desired information is in another city or state, an online search for the website of a public library in the desired location will bring up a telephone number or an e-mail option titled, "Ask a Librarian." When calling (or e-mailing) a library, the answer to "What was Sally Smith's address in Kalamazoo, in 1982?" would, most likely, be given immediately, whereas a printout of all Smiths in the 1982 Kalamazoo directories probably would require scanning and e-mailing or photocopying and mailing. What is important to remember is that the information still exists and is easy to obtain.

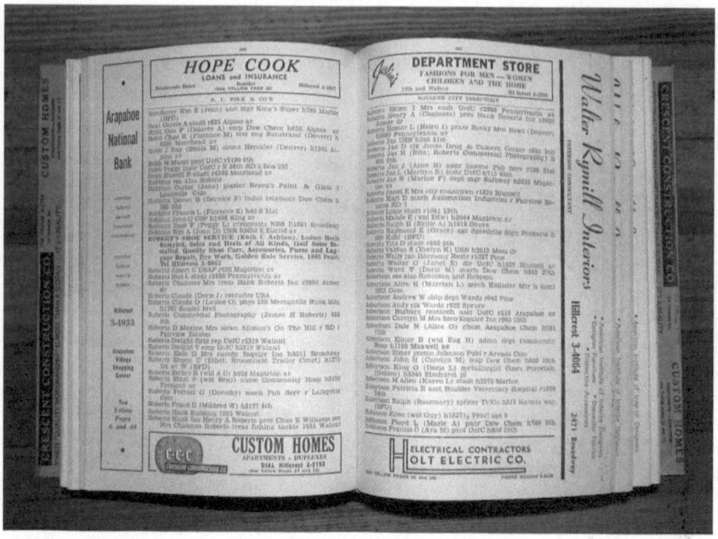

Figure 12.8 City directories list individuals and businesses alphabetically, and they also provide names of spouses, addresses, and places of employment. (Photo by author.)

When contacting librarians, it is important to:

- Make an appointment, if the library is local, to introduce oneself and to explain, firsthand, the information being sought. Some public libraries now offer "Book a Librarian" services for this very reason, to discuss research needs.
- Put as much information as possible into one's request, either in person, by e-mail, or on the telephone. For instance, if all that one gives is a name and there is a possibility that the name might be misspelled, then a cursory search would not find it. Give enough details to make the librarians feel invested in the request and to allow them to expand the request, if needed.
- Remember that libraries have other patrons and budgets are tight. Be patient and offer to pay for research time or photocopying and postage costs.
- Try again, if one's request does not provide the hoped-for results.
- Thank the librarians, as their help may be needed again in the future.

Public Records Can Be Missing

Sometimes public records can be missing. Records have been known to have been destroyed when courthouses (and other buildings) were damaged by fires and floods. A missing file is not the same as a file that did not exist.

Public Records Can Be Inaccurate

Sometimes public records have errors. This can happen with data aggregators because they get their data from public records, but it can also happen when searching directly from public records. Sorting fact from fiction became apparent to the author when researching Katharine Farrand Dyer. In the quest for the identity of Boulder Jane Doe, Dyer had risen to the top of the list of likely candidates on a spreadsheet of missing young women compiled from newspaper reports from 1954. In the process of following her paper trail, the author obtained a copy of both Dyer's marriage license and affidavit, by mail, from the clerk of a superior court in Arizona.

On the affidavit, the young woman had given her first name as "Katharine," and, "duly sworn upon her oath," told a long-ago clerk that she was born in San Antonio, Texas, in 1926. The author and a team of fellow researchers then searched census, birth, orphanage, school, and every kind of record obtainable, hoping to locate a sibling for a family DNA sample. Using the information that was in the public record, no family members were found, and for good reason. They did not exist!

The Boulder Jane Doe case took on a life of its own when a caregiver in Australia moved an elderly woman she knew as "Barbara" into a nursing home. In Barbara's belongings, the woman found an old and faded address book with the name Katharine Farrand Dyer. The caregiver Googled the name and ended up on the author's website where newspaper links had been posted, speculating that Katharine was Jane Doe. Because the woman turned up alive, she obviously was not the unidentified murder victim. (See Chapter 4 for more on Google.)

The woman's address book also revealed the name of her sister who, when contacted, explained that the name of "Barbara/Katharine" actually was "Emily." Instead of being born in Texas in 1926, she was born in Virginia, in 1925. Publicity on this new development moved the case forward, as it attracted the attention of the family of the real Jane Doe, Dorothy Gay Howard. In 2009, her identity was confirmed with DNA, by matching a direct reference sample from the victim's exhumed remains with a family reference sample from Dorothy's only surviving sister.

Recorded Document Offices

Because the names of the offices that house recorded documents vary by state, the following state-by-state list gives the names of each office, as well as individual links to the government websites of the counties that include each state's capitol. The website addresses are subject to change, but the names of the recorded document offices likely will not. When in doubt, an Internet search for the name of the state and "recorded documents," or an Internet search for the state and the specific name (such as "clerk and recorder") for the office that one is researching should get the requested results.[7]

Alabama: County Judge of Probate
Montgomery County, www.mc-ala.org

Alaska: District Recorder
Alaska Department of Natural Resources, Recorder's Office (statewide), http://dnr.alaska.gov

Arizona: County Recorder
Maricopa County, http://recorder.maricopa.gov (This is a good example of a user-friendly website.)

Arkansas: County Circuit Clerk
Pulaski County, www.pulaskiclerk.com

California: County Recorder
Sacramento County, www.erosi.saccounty.net

Colorado: County Clerk and Recorder
Denver County, www.denvergov.org

Connecticut: Town/City Clerk (All recording is done at the town/city level.)
Hartford City, www.hartford.gov

Delaware: County Recorder of Deeds
Kent County, http://de.uslandrecords.com

District of Columbia: Recorder of Deeds
District of Columbia, http://dc.gov/DC

Florida: Clerk of the Circuit Court
Leon County, www.clerk.leon.fl.us

Georgia: Clerk of Superior Court
Fulton County, www.fcclk.org

Hawaii: Bureau of Conveyances
Statewide, http://hawaii.gov/dlnr/boc

Idaho: County Clerk and Recorder
Boise County, www.boisecounty.us

Illinois: County Recorder; also Recorder of Deeds
Sangamon County, www.sangamoncountyrecorder.com

Indiana: County Recorder
Marion County, www.indy.gov

Iowa: County Recorder
Polk County, www.polkrecorder.com

Kansas: County Register of Deeds
Shawnee County, www.co.shawnee.ks.us/rd (This is a good example of a user-friendly website.)

Kentucky: County Clerk
Franklin County, http://franklincounty.ky.gov

Louisiana: Clerk of the Court
East Baton Rouge Parish, www.ebrclerkofcourt.org

Maine: County Register of Deeds
Kennebec County, http://gov.propertyinfo.com/me-kennebec

Maryland: Clerk of the Circuit Court
Anne Arundel County, www.clerkannearundel.org

Massachusetts: Register of Deeds
Suffolk County, www.suffolkdeeds.com

Michigan: County Register of Deeds
Ingham County, www.ingham.org/rd/rodindex.htm

Minnesota: County Recorder
Ramsey County, www.co.ramsey.mn.us/prr/recorder/index.htm

Mississippi: Chancery Clerk
Hinds County, www.co.hinds.ms.us/pgs/elected/chanceryclerk.asp

Missouri: Recorder of Deeds
Cole County, www.colecounty.org/cole1/cole/recorder/index.html

Montana: County Clerk and Recorder
Lewis and Clark County, www.co.lewis-clark.mt.us

Nebraska: County Clerk; also Register of Deeds
Lancaster County, http://lancaster.ne.gov/clerk/index.htm

Nevada: County Recorder
Carson City County, www.carson.org/Index.aspx?page=155

New Hampshire: Register of Deeds
Merrimack County, www.merrimackcounty.nh.us.landata.com

New Jersey: County Clerk, also Register of Deeds
Mercer County, http://nj.gov/counties/mercer/officials/clerk/index.html

New Mexico: County Clerk
Santa Fe County, www.santafecounty.org/clerk/publicrecordsrequest

New York: County Clerk; as well as the New York City Register for Bronx, Kings, New York, and Queens counties. (Staten Island is listed separately under Richmond County.)
Albany County, http://albanycounty.com/clerk

North Carolina: Register of Deeds
Wake County, http://web.co.wake.nc.us/rdeeds

North Dakota: County Recorder
Burleigh County, www.co.burleigh.nd.us/departments/rec

Ohio: County Recorder
Franklin County, www.franklincountyohio.gov/recorder

Oklahoma: County Clerk
Oklahoma County, http://countyclerk.oklahomacounty.org

Oregon: County Clerk
Marion County, www.co.marion.or.us/CO

Pennsylvania: Recorder of Deeds; also Prothonotary
Dauphin County, www.dauphinc.org/deeds

Rhode Island: Town/City Clerk (All recording is done at the town/city level.)
Providence County, http://cityof.providenceri.com/city-clerk

South Carolina: recorded document offices vary by county
Richland County, www.richlandonline.com/services/rodsearch.asp

South Dakota: Register of Deeds
Hughes County, www.hughescounty.org

Tennessee, Register of Deeds
Davidson County, www.nashville.gov/rod

Texas: County Clerk
Travis County, www.co.travis.tx.us/county_clerk

Utah: County Recorder; also Clerk of District Court
Salt Lake County, http://slcorecorder.siredocs.com/rechome/main.aspx

Vermont: Town/City Clerk (All recording is done at the town/city level.)
Washington Town, http://vermont-elections.org/elections1/town_clerks_guide.html

Virginia: Clerk of Circuit Court
Richmond County, www.courts.state.va.us/courts/circuit/Richmond_County/home.html

Washington: County Auditor
Thurston County, www.co.thurston.wa.us/auditor

West Virginia: County Clerk
Kanawha County, www.kanawha.us/countyclerk

Wisconsin: Register of Deeds; also Clerk of Court
Dane County, www.countyofdane.com/regdeeds

Wyoming: County Clerk
Laramie County, www.laramiecountyclerk.com

Summary

Resources in this chapter include:

- A description of public records and where to find them
- The use of public records in determining family relationships
- The use of public records in tracing name changes of women

The information on most online people searching resources, including investigative systems such as TLO, dates from the mid-1980s. Public records, however—and many are online—go back many decades. Whatever the time period, they can help investigators identify family relationships and trace name changes of women.

- Loosely defined, public records are records from government entities that receive public funds.
- Federal public records include the National Archives and Social Security applications for deceased individuals.
- State public records include statewide secretary of state offices and licensing boards, as well as state archives.
- Local public records include recorded documents offices (the names vary by state), police departments and sheriffs' offices, district attorneys' offices, coroners' and medical examiners' offices, and court records.
- Published records, such as telephone and city directories, are available in many local libraries.
- Public records can be missing and in rare cases they can also be inaccurate.

Endnotes

1. Colorado State Archives. Colorado Laws Concerning Public Records, www.colorado.gov/dpa/doit/archives/open/00openrec.htm; and Sunshine Review, Colorado Open Records Act, http://sunshinereview.org/index.php/Colorado_Open_Records_Act (accessed December 26, 2011).
2. National Archives. www.archives.gov/research (accessed December 26, 2011).
3. FBI Records, www.fbi.gov/foia/requesting-fbi-records (accessed December 26, 2011).
4. California Department of Consumer Affairs. Contractors State License Board, http://consumerwiki.dca.ca.gov/wiki/index.php/Contractors_State_License_Board (accessed December 26, 2011).

5. Maricopa County Recorder. http://recorder.maricopa.gov/recdocdata (accessed December 26, 2011).
6. Pettem, Silvia. *Someone's Daughter: In Search of Justice for Jane Doe* (Lanham, MD: Taylor Trade, 2009), 133.
7. Websites for state-by-state recorded documents accessed December 26, 2011.

Volunteers: How They Can Help

13

During frontier times, when a sheriff, for instance, had to chase a horse thief or track down an outlaw, he formed a posse. That was an innovative use of volunteers in time of need. Today, many agencies face budget cuts or are understaffed. At the same time, they have backlogs of cold cases that may only get looked at in an investigator's spare time (very rare) or the cases get passed on from one investigator to another. These situations call for a return to the same kind of action as in the "old days"—the use of volunteers.

Volunteers already assist law enforcement in many ways. In the specifics of cold case research:

- They come with different perspectives. After taking a cold case off the shelf, a volunteer with a fresh pair of eyes may uncover inconsistencies, discover gaps in the documentation, or even find telephone messages that were never returned.
- They have the time to do background work (such as chronologically arranging the contents of case files, making spreadsheets of family members, creating witness lists, and looking up current contacts) that allow detectives to focus on their jobs.
- They can offer specific skills, such as people searching, historical research, software expertise, or even web design.
- They are willing to work for free. Why? Some may be working toward a new career or following a specific interest, whereas others may simply want to make contributions to their communities.
- They have a passion for their work, otherwise they would not be there.

Volunteers in Cold Case Research

Some volunteers are retired professionals or interested civilians of all ages who work in the detective sections of individual agencies. An excellent example is Milli Knudsen, a civilian volunteer in the Cold Case Unit of the New Hampshire Department of Justice, Office of Attorney General (see the following profile). Others range from graduate student interns (see Chapter 2 on the discussion of the Metropolitan Police Department) and students in college groups, to retired law enforcement officers and FBI agents who have become bored with retirement and want to get back in the action. The students often follow a career path in criminal justice, and the retirees get a chance to continue doing the jobs they loved and are trained for, without putting in long hours. Volunteers can be recruited, too. Already vetted and interested persons may be as close as one's agency's citizens' academy.

The use of volunteers in cold case research varies by agency. Some agencies will only work with retired officers, whereas others welcome individuals they trust, providing the civilians have been vetted, undergone background checks, and sign confidentiality agreements. Obviously, agencies have legitimate concerns as to the protection of the integrity of their cases, but they can set mutually agreeable boundaries on activities such as access to case files or law-enforcement-only websites. With signed agreements, volunteers, as well as their supervisors, know where they stand. Also, it is beneficial to all for agencies to set up regular work schedules and let volunteers know they are part of the team. In the preparation of this book, the author did not find any agency that disclosed problems with cold case volunteers. In fact, the consensus was that there should be more of them, and that a mix of volunteers is ideal because they ensure a variety of backgrounds and experiences.[1]

As noted in the article, "Law Enforcement Volunteers: An Essential Tool in the Investigation of Cold Case Homicides" by Derek Regensburger (legal studies instructor at Everest College, in Thornton, Colorado), agencies planning to use volunteers in their cold case units should:

- Keep an open mind with respect to using civilian volunteers, particularly professionals.
- Make use of the talents and strengths of each volunteer. (Look for those who are detail-oriented and possess good organizational skills.)
- Develop a set schedule for the volunteer.
- Allow the volunteer access to case files in return for signing a confidentiality agreement.
- Develop clearly identifiable tasks for the volunteer to perform.
- Make the volunteer feel he or she is part of the team.[2]

The Volunteers in Police Service (VIPS) program is a resource for law enforcement agencies who do not have well-developed volunteer programs or who would like to start their own. The program was developed in 2002 by the International Association of Chiefs of Police (IACP), in partnership with the White House Office of the U.S. Freedom Corps and the Bureau of Justice Assistance, Office of Justice Programs, U.S. Department of Justice. VIPS publishes a newsletter addressing the issues related to law enforcement volunteer programs and also provides lists of policies and procedures, including drafts of confidentiality agreement forms.[3] Here, according to the VIPS website, is a summary of the program's resources:

- An online directory of law enforcement volunteer programs
- A resource library of sample documents, forms, and materials from law enforcement
- Volunteer programs and other sources
- A resource guide, "Volunteer Programs: Enhancing Public Safety by Leveraging Resources," to assist in the implementation or enhancement of an agency's volunteer program
- A model policy on volunteers
- Training and educational seminars for law enforcement
- No-cost technical assistance and mentoring for law enforcement agencies
- Educational videos
- VIPS in Focus, a publication series addressing specific elements and issues related to law enforcement volunteer programs
- VIPS Info, a monthly newsletter about resources and services for law enforcement[4]

Student Volunteers Tackle Tough Cases

Sheryl McCollum, a cold case analyst for the Pine Lake Police Department in a suburb of Atlanta, Georgia, created the Cold Case Investigative Research Institute (CCIRI) at Bauder College in 2005. At the time, McCollum had read a newspaper article about a homicide victim, Mary Shotwell Little, an Atlanta newlywed, and Mary became the group's first case. Approximately 100 Bauder College students participate in the Cold Case Institute to work with detectives and meet with victims' families to help solve cold cases. The students do not get class credit or receive grades for their work, and they use only public documents—court filings, historical accounts, and other information—for their research. They do not have access to confidential investigative police documents, and they always get permission from the victims' families before starting on a case.

The Institute has worked on the killing of rapper Tupac Shakur, the disappearance of teenager Natalee Holloway in Aruba, a series of Atlanta child murders from 1979 to 1981, and the now-solved Chandra Levy case. Chandra's mother credited the Institute for helping keep the case alive.[5] As Sheryl McCollum told a CNN reporter at the time of the Levy case, "The students became completely dedicated once they met the family members of the victims. The victims are real people, the cases are real cases, and the research is real investigative work."[6] (See Chapter 2 to see how student interns worked with the Metropolitan Police Department, in Washington, DC.)

Retired Law Enforcement Officers Come Back to Work

In December 2002, the administrators of the Douglas County Sheriff's Office in Roseburg, Oregon, came up with the idea of "hiring" retired law enforcement officers to volunteer their time to work on cold cases. The Sheriff's Office put an advertisement in the local newspaper, and of the 100 or so who responded, four were chosen: Al Olson, Syd Boyle, Tom Hall, and Thomas Schultz (see Figure 13.1). The result was a Cold Case Squad that wrote its own operating procedures and set a precedent as the first cold case squad of volunteer sworn officers in the country.

"Our reception was very positive, and we had the support of the whole department and the District Attorney's Office," stated Tom Hall, one of the original four, in a telephone interview with the author. "We had an advantage that no other detective unit had: we could work one case at a time, on our own time and with no distraction."[7] The men started work in January 2003. Four months later, they had solved the 28-year-old murder of Benny King, whose remains had been found only a few years earlier by mushroom pickers in a nearby forest. With their guns and badges, the men wore cowboy boots and hats, and the media began to refer to them as the Cold Case Cowboys (see Figure 13.2). After solving two more cases and appearing on the front page of the *Los Angeles Times*, the squad was featured on NBC's *Dateline*, A&E's *Cold Case Files*, and in a number of national and even international media outlets.

Figure 13.1 Left to right, Al Olson, Syd Boyle, Tom Hall, and Thomas Schultz, the first cold case squad of volunteer sworn officers in the country, were photographed in 2004 in the Callahan Mountains near where mushroom pickers found the remains of Benny King. (Photo courtesy of Tom Hall.)

Figure 13.2 Dressed in their Western attire as the Cold Case Cowboys, Syd Boyle, Tom Hall, Al Olson, and Lee Tyler currently offer their services to help other law enforcement agencies start volunteer cold case squads. (Photo courtesy of Tom Hall.)

The notoriety from the national and local press brought about several changes. Although there is still a cold case squad at the Douglas County Sheriff's Office (with some of the original members), the Cold Case Cowboys are now a separate entity and see their current role primarily as assisting other law enforcement agencies in starting their own cold case units. Meanwhile, the group added a new member, Lee Tyler, who replaced Thomas Schultz who moved away. "Volunteerism is needed," stated Hall. "The publicity we received has helped to get other cold case squads started. Every law enforcement agency in the country could use the resources of retired officers."[8] The Cold Case Cowboys can be contacted at www.thecoldcasecowboys.com.

Charlotte-Mecklenburg Police Department's Cold Case Unit Is a Model for the Country

As noted in Chapter 2, the Charlotte-Mecklenburg Police Department in Charlotte, North Carolina, has two volunteers who work two days per week, for several hours each day, directly for the agency's Cold Case Unit. At the time of this writing, one of these volunteers is a retired engineer from Duke Energy and the other is a retired police lieutenant from New York State. The unit's volunteers conduct initial reviews of case files, and they also search for and collect any available documentation related to the case that is not in the case file, including crime scene photographs and laboratory reports.

Then they copy the supplemented case files for review by each member of the Civilian Review Team, also volunteers. Stated Cold Case Unit Detective Stephen Furr, in e-mail correspondence with the author, "In addition, they perform other clerical and statistical work that frees time up for us to conduct investigative work."[9]

The Civilian Review Team members review each case file at their own speed. Added Detective Furr,

> Once they have completed the Homicide Case Review summary, they disseminate the review to the Cold Case Detectives, other members of the Cold Case Review Team, and the Cold Case volunteers prior to our monthly review team meeting. Each member can then read over the review and be prepared to discuss the case at the meeting which is attended by all members of the Review Team, the two Cold Case Detectives, the two Cold Case Squad volunteers and a member of the Crime Lab DNA section.[10]

The team then extensively discusses the month's case, asks questions, and makes suggestions. They also prioritize the case—with a number from one to five—according to the presence and existence of physical evidence conducive to modern technology, the availability of witnesses, and an identifiable and living suspect.

According to the Charlotte-Mecklenburg Police Department's website, the agency has approximately 500 homicide cases dating back to 1970. Since the Cold Case Unit (or Squad, the words seem to be used interchangeably) was established in 2003, its members have reviewed 131 cases and cleared 33.[11] The volunteers have won numerous awards, including the Department of Justice Citizen Volunteer Service Award, presented May 30, 2008, by U.S. Attorney General Michael B. Mukasey, in Washington, DC.[12] A year after inaugurating the unit, team member Vivian Lord wrote that the key to its success is "combining volunteer resources with experienced investigative expertise."[13] "Other agencies want to adopt what we're doing," stated Detective Furr. "We've become a model for the rest of the country."[14]

Profile: New Hampshire's Milli Knudsen in Win–Win Situation

Milli Knudsen is forging new ground as a civilian volunteer in the Cold Case Unit of the New Hampshire Department of Justice, Office of Attorney General (see Figure 13.3). What is in it for her is an apprenticeship, on-the-job experience, that she will take with her one day to a paying job as a paralegal. But Knudsen is far from a recent college graduate or an intern. Approaching what many people would consider retirement age, the former schoolteacher and author of seven books on New England history, contributes decades of work experience, most recently

Figure 13.3 Milli Knudsen works as a civilian volunteer in the Cold Case Unit of the New Hampshire Department of Justice, Office of Attorney General. (Photo courtesy of Detective Robert Freitas.)

as a volunteer archivist who meticulously sorted and cataloged thousands of court records at the New Hampshire State Archives.

In December 2009, while working at the archives, Knudsen read of the then newly formed Cold Case Unit and was amazed to learn that, since 1970, approximately 120 murders in her state had remained unsolved. With resume in hand, but no law enforcement experience, she contacted Senior Assistant Attorney General Will Delker who headed, and still heads, the unit. "I explained that what I thought he needed was a detailed index to each case," said Knudsen in e-mail correspondence with the author. After careful vetting that included reference and background checks and the signing of a confidentiality agreement, Knudsen joined Delker and three detectives to become part of the team. Knudsen found a void, filled it with energy and enthusiasm, and is committed to turning the tables on perpetrators who think they have committed the perfect crimes. Her review of case files and entry of decades-old data into spreadsheets has become a win–win situation for everyone.[15] See Figure 13.4.

In New Hampshire, the state's attorney general is the chief law enforcement officer and has exclusive jurisdiction over homicide cases. Most of these homicides are investigated by the New Hampshire State Police Major Crime Unit, but larger cities such Concord, Dover, Keene, Manchester, Nashua, and Portsmouth investigate homicides occurring within their jurisdictions. The Cold Case Unit was organized with federal stimulus funding to combine the experience of the attorney general's

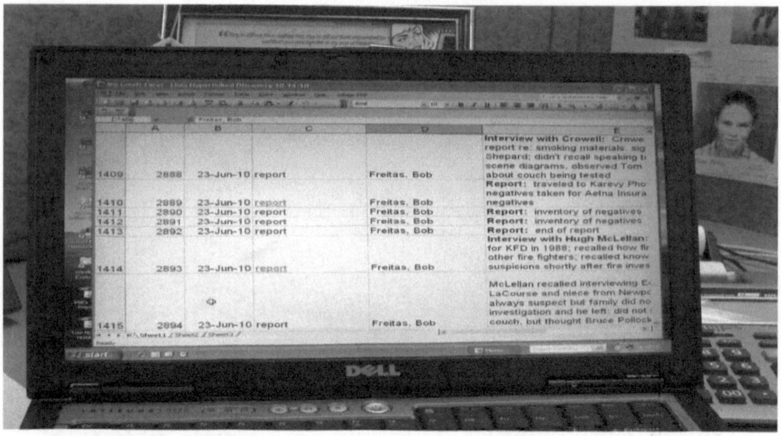

Figure 13.4 On Excel spreadsheets, Knudsen catalogs every page of each case file, as well as the names and contact information of all possible witnesses. (Photo courtesy of Detective Robert Freitas.)

office, the major crime unit, and a city detective. The unit focuses on unsolved homicides, unresolved suspicious deaths, and missing person cases in which foul play is suspected in a person's disappearance.

A driving force behind the unit's formation (House Bill 690, signed into law in July 2009 by Governor John Lynch), was the dedication of family members of murder victim, Kathy Lynn Gloddy. Ever since 1971, when the 13-year-old was raped and strangled in Franklin, New Hampshire, her three sisters—Janet Gloddy Young, Karen Beaudoin, and Ann Ring—have kept the case in front of the media. When the bill was introduced, all three sisters testified in front of the New Hampshire Senate Judiciary Committee, and all were passionate about finding Kathy's killer. A reporter for *The Citizen of Laconia* was in the hearing room when HB 690 was under consideration. The reporter quoted Young and described the beginning of her testimony by stating: " 'I'm the middle child,' she [Young] began softly, almost unable to talk about the 1971 murder of her youngest sister and the effects the unsolved crime has had on her and her family. 'We need this bill. We've had no answers.' "[16]

Private investigator and former police chief of Spencer, Massachusetts, Thomas Shamshak, also spoke in favor of the bill and addressed Gloddy's case, as well as others. "The ingredients for success are there," he told the legislators, adding that it would take some shoe leather, records research, and interviews. "We will leave no stone unturned."[17]

Knudsen, a native of Maine makes the hour-long drive from her rural home in Milford to a sprawling office complex in Concord every day, Monday through Friday, except for Monday afternoons when she runs a reading discussion group at an assisted-living facility in Peterborough.

Her only compensation is reimbursement for work-related mileage. She says she "keeps the home fires burning," while the detectives are out in the field. She is on call if her co-workers need some information or if tips come in, and she edits transcripts of their interviews for consistency. By being the anchor in the office, Knudsen frees up the detectives' time so they can concentrate on interviewing, following leads, uncovering new material, and tracking down additional material. And, she adds, they are patient in answering her many questions.

Her main contribution, however, is in indexing and organizing, specifically her comprehensive and interactive databases of cold case files. "I catalog every page of an old investigation on Sheet 1 of an Excel spreadsheet," Knudsen explained. "That's followed, on Sheet 2, with an alphabetical listing of every involved person in the case, including victims, suspects, families, neighbors, and friends—all the people who could be interviewed as potential witnesses—with updates, provided by the investigators, on current contact information. Sheet 3 is an alphabetical listing of every authority figure and business, that is, those who would be compelled to testify who have nothing at stake in the crime."[18]

With this careful scrutiny, Knudsen knows, for instance, if a detective, 20 years ago, did not return a phone call. Similarly, she has found mention of witnesses who told investigators that they learned their information from a newspaper, but the story containing those details was published days later. As anyone who's researched a cold case knows, most archived online newspapers start in the mid-1980s to early 1990s, and often later. To access the earlier newspapers, researchers need to go back to old-fashioned "gumshoe" techniques and read them on microfilm. (See Chapter 11, "Newspaper Research: Online and Off.") "I do a two-part collection," said Knudsen, who conducts her microfilm research at the New Hampshire State Library, a depository for all of the state's major and minor newspapers. "After finding the initial page where the story broke, I take an overview shot, in which the text is so small it is unreadable. Then I zoom in on the article and blow it up as far as I can."[19]

The purpose of the two-part system is to track the sizing and position of the articles as the story becomes old in the media. According to Knudsen, witnesses and suspects always pay close attention to the news initially, hoping to see, or not see, themselves mentioned. As soon as the news slips into the back pages of the newspaper, tension seems to lessen. "It's interesting to read the police reports and the signed statements from witnesses, then compare them to what the media is saying," she said. "People often speak freely to a journalist, even when they are reluctant to speak to authorities."[20]

Knudsen continues to look for and note other inconsistencies that could hold clues to the solving of the unit's cold cases. A true crime fan, she is excited that she is now an active participant in actually helping to solve these crimes. And, she is an integral part of the unit's monthly staff meetings where the investigative team prioritizes its cases according to whether they have a defined suspect, unexplored leads, and forensic evidence, as well as the likelihood of achieving a prosecution. As a result, she knows the cases better than the detectives currently working them. In return, she puts every detail at their fingertips.

Another aspect of cold cases that Knudsen finds fascinating is that in decades-old cases there sometimes are parallel investigations that have gone on with other law enforcement agencies, probate courts, insurance companies, utility companies, or unrelated crimes. An untimely death, no matter what the reason, generates paper of all kinds. "In a cold case, the dust has settled somewhat and the new investigators benefit from all the related activity that has gone on after the fact," said Knudsen. "A new homicide is more immediate, works under a strict time constraint, whereas in cold cases you have a great deal more patience to slowly pick away at an alibi, look at relationships between people, and see how they react long after the traumatic events."[21]

With knowledge, skills, and insight, Knudsen distills each document into a summary, with links back to the full and recently scanned document, making the system relevant and accessible for Will Delker to use in trial preparations. Together, they work on the cutting edge of cold case investigations. "She's invaluable," Delker told a *Boston Globe* reporter in an April 26, 2010, article titled, "Retired teacher's contribution to Cold Case Unit is priceless." He added, "I frankly don't know where we'd be without her assistance."[22]

Specialized and Independent Volunteers

The volunteers discussed on the previous pages of this chapter work primarily at their desks. Others, out in the field, have different missions, but they too are important cold case resources, volunteering to assist law enforcement agencies that search for missing persons or recover missing remains. The following is a small sample of the many specialized and independent volunteers.

Texas EquuSearch Mounted Search and Recovery Team

The Texas EquuSearch (TES) Mounted Search and Recovery Team was founded in August 2000 in order to provide volunteer horse-mounted search and recovery for lost and missing persons. It is now among the few specialized volunteer teams that offer law enforcement assistance in undertaking searches for missing persons presumed to be dead. The team initially formed in the North Galveston County area and is dedicated to the memory of Laura Miller, the daughter of its founding director, Tim Miller.

In 1984, Laura, a pretty 16-year-old with shoulder-length brown hair, was abducted when talking on the telephone at a convenience store. One-and-one-half years later, the teenager's skeletal remains (along with those of another young woman) were found in a dumping ground. In the 1990s, there were several more murders of young women in the area, and Miller would go to the spots where they had been found to see if he could find similarities with Laura's murder. Then he started meeting with several of the families. Before long, someone suggested that because he was a horseman, he should start a mounted search-and-rescue operation, which he did.

Unlike other search-and-rescue organizations, TES not only utilizes the skills and abilities of horseback riders, but the group can quickly marshal a large force of volunteers, and they are flexible enough to accept assistance from a variety of disciplines. According to "The Beginning of Equusearch," by Bonnie M. Wells, TES is funded solely by donations. "They sometimes operate at a deficit, but they keep going," Wells wrote, "because Tim Miller can not imagine telling a family in need that he does not have the resources to assist."[23]

Members of the team include business owners, medics, firefighters, housewives, electricians, students, former FBI and law enforcement, current law enforcement, former and current U.S. Marshals, and all walks of the military. In addition to using horses, they also search on foot, with ATVs, with dogs, on boats, and in the air. To date, the organization has been involved in more than 1,100 searches in 42 states and several foreign countries, has returned more than 300 missing people to their families, and has found the remains of 103 missing persons.[24]

NecroSearch

Colorado-based NecroSearch is a volunteer multidisciplinary team dedicated to assist law enforcement in the location of clandestine graves and the recovery of evidence (including human remains) from those graves. According to the organization's website, field investigations typically start with a sequence of nonintrusive methodologies such as Forward Looking Infrared (FLIR) and Ground Penetrating Radar (GPR) and may progress to actual excavation. Since 1987, the organization has participated in more than 300 cases in 39 states and in six foreign countries.[25] One of the team's well-known cases is that of Diane Keidel, murdered by her husband in 1966 and buried under concrete in the backyard of the family's Phoenix, Arizona, home. In 1994, Phoenix Police Department Detective Ed Reynolds solved the case at the same time that he was working on the murder of the little Navajo girl, Surette Clark.[26] (See "Case History: Surette Clark and Little Jane Doe" in Chapter 1.)

Ralston & Associates

Consider, too, the underwater search and recovery missions of Gene and Sandy Ralston, founders of Ralston & Associates, an environmental consulting firm specializing in water-related services in Boise, Idaho. For nearly three decades, the couple (see Figures 13.5 and 13.6) has traveled, and continues to travel, throughout the United States and Canada—without pay—in order to search for and recover the bodies of drowning victims. All the Ralstons ask in return is reimbursement of the expenses of pulling, behind their motor home, their boat and side-scan sonar equipment. Since 1983, they have located the remains of more than 70 people.[27] They also use a Remote Operated Vehicle (ROV), and, in most cases, recover remains as well.

The Ralstons' first experience in water search and rescue came when they manufactured whitewater river boats and donated a boat for rescue work, then recovered a drowning victim from the Boise River. "The gratitude expressed by the family and the tremendous feeling of satisfaction inspired us to continue to volunteer our time and equipment to assist in water search, rescue, and recovery," wrote Gene Ralston in a 2010 article in the *Journal of Ocean Technology*.[28] In 2002, on a case the Ralstons worked on with the Federal Bureau of Investigation (FBI), they located four heavily weighted homicide victims in New Melones Reservoir near Sonora, California. Because of the couple's assistance, the victims' perpetrators were convicted and sentenced variously to death or to life without parole.[29]

In their many years of searching for and recovering drowning victims, the Ralstons have learned that some families want their loved ones to rest in peace where they are, whereas other families are unable to go through the grieving process fully until they have physical remains to bury. The recoveries are numerous and are only made at the request of the families and with the cooperation of law enforcement. When Gene Ralston was asked for an example, he related the recovery, in February 2002, of the body of Scot Glover. After more than three years, the Ralstons were able to bring resolution and some measure of comfort to the man's young widow and three children.[30]

In October 1998, Scot had been fishing on Beardsley Reservoir, a small but deep lake near Yosemite National Park in California. He was last seen, by an eyewitness on the shore, standing in his boat, which was going full-throttle in a circle. When the witness looked back, Scot was gone. The local sheriff's office was unable to recover him. The following summer, his widow called the California Rescue Dog Association (CRDA). Handlers took three dogs who were trained to "alert" to human remains. All of the dogs identified the same area, but divers, sent down afterwards, were unable to find Scot's body.[31]

Ironically, in the summer of 2001, while Scot's body still lay deep underwater, the Tuolumne County Sheriff's Office invited the Ralstons to Beardsley Reservoir to provide training for its marine division. "While

Figure 13.5 Gene and Sandy Ralston, on the port side of their boat, observe the bottom of Flathead Lake, in Montana, through crystal-clear water. (Photo courtesy of Gene and Sandy Ralston.)

Figure 13.6 Gene Ralston operates the controls of the Ralstons' remote operated vehicle (ROV) to inspect an object underwater. (Photo courtesy of Gene and Sandy Ralston.)

there, we identified an object of interest, but it was too deep for the divers," stated Gene Ralston in e-mail correspondence with the author. "They told us to go home and they would try to do a training dive on it when the water went down later in the year, but they were never able to find the 'object.'" Follow-up communication among the Ralstons, the dog handlers, the family, and the sheriff's office prompted the Ralstons to return to the reservoir in February 2002 and search specifically for the body of Scot Glover.[32]

The Tuolumne County Sheriff's Office combined resources with the Calaveras County and Stanislaus County sheriffs' offices to bring in divers, support teams, and law enforcement personnel. Meanwhile, the Ralstons rigged their boat for work and confirmed that the "object" was in the same location as previously sighted. Then they placed their acoustical target (a four-foot box of copper tubing used as a reference point) 18 feet from the image. (Initially, the divers could not find the body, so the Ralstons moved the target to within two feet for the next day's dive.) When the divers then followed the cable from the target, they saw the body exactly where the sonar image had shown it. Scot's widow and mother were on the scene when his body, fragile after more than three years underwater, was brought to the surface.[33] "It gave us a good feeling," stated Gene Ralston, "to bring Scot home to his family, years after they had given up hope of ever having him home."[34]

When asked what drives the Ralstons and what it is like to bring closure to others, Gene Ralston explained to a *Blue Line Magazine* reporter,

> Perhaps it is best described as the result of having seen the anguish families go through waiting for their loved ones to be found, when the official search has been ended, and not knowing if they will ever be found. It is a long, agonizing and wearisome time for a family to go through. The feeling is likewise hard to describe. We are very elated we can bring some measure of resolution. I don't like the word "closure" [since] there is never a "close" to incidents like this—to a family's grief—but it is a bittersweet feeling. Many families we have helped stay in contact with us to let us know how they are doing and continue to express their appreciation for our efforts.[35]

(For two additional stories of drowning victims, in very different circumstances, see "Special Circumstances," on the recovery of the partial remains of Gary Mayo in Chapter 6, as well as the identification of a John Doe as Joseph Coogan in Chapter 16.)

Summary

Resources in this chapter include:

- A description of the Volunteers in Police Service (VIPS) Program that aids law enforcement agencies in their use of volunteers
- Profiles of volunteers and how they can help in cold case research

Volunteers include individuals, students, and retired law enforcement officers, and they all bring different skills and perspectives to cold case investigations. They may also have time to do background research, they work for free, and most are passionate about their work or they would not be doing it.

- The Volunteers in Police Service (VIPS) Program is a resource for law enforcement agencies that want to use volunteers.
- In its Cold Case Unit, the Charlotte-Mecklenburg Police Department in Charlotte, North Carolina, combines volunteers with experienced investigators and is a model for the country.
- Milli Knudsen's work in the Cold Case Unit of the New Hampshire Department of Justice, Office of Attorney General is an outstanding example of the use of a volunteer in law enforcement.
- Specialized and independent volunteers aid in cold case research too. Examples include Texas EquuSearch, NecroSearch, and Ralston & Associates.

Endnotes

1. Regensburger, Derek. "Law Enforcement Volunteers: An Essential Tool in the Investigation of Cold Case Homicides," *Sheriff Magazine* (May/June 2011).
2. Regensburger, Derek. "Law Enforcement Volunteers: An Essential Tool in the Investigation of Cold Case Homicides," *Sheriff Magazine* (May/June 2011).
3. Volunteers in Police Service, www.policevolunteers.org/resources (accessed December 26, 2011).
4. Volunteers in Police Service. www.policevolunteers.org/resources (accessed December 26, 2011).
5. National Sheriffs' Association, Justice Solutions, and National Organization of Parents of Murdered Children. *A Compilation of Cold Case Resources: Literature Review and Survey of Cold Case Units; Summary Report*, April 6, 2010.
6. O'Neill, Ann. "Students narrow suspects in Levy case to one," *CNN Justice* (February 27, 2009), http://articles.cnn.com/2009-02-27/justice/levy.campus.crime.club_1_ingmar-guandique-chandra-levy-susan-levy?_s=PM:CRIME (accessed December 26, 2011).
7. Hall, Tom. Telephone interview with author, December 14, 2011.

8. Hall, Tom. Telephone interview with author, December 14, 2011.
9. Furr, Stephen. Detective. E-mail correspondence with author, October 17, 2011.
10. Furr, Stephen. Detective. E-mail correspondence with author, October 17, 2011.
11. Furr, Stephen. Detective. E-mail correspondence with author, October 17, 2011.
12. Charlotte-Mecklenburg Police Department, Homicide Cold Case Unit. http://charmeck.org/city/charlotte/CMPD/organization/investigative/ViolentCrimes/Homicide/ColdCase/Pages/home.aspx (accessed December 26, 2011).
13. Lord, Vivian B. "Implementing a cold case homicide unit: A challenging task," *FBI Law Enforcement Bulletin*, 74: 2 (February, 2005).
14. Furr, Stephen. Detective. Telephone interview with author, April 7, 2011. Also, Lord, Vivian B. "Implementing a cold case homicide unit: A challenging task," *FBI Law Enforcement Bulletin* 74: 2 (February 2005).
15. Knudsen, Milli. E-mail correspondence with author, March 2, 2011.
16. Ober, Gail. "Gloddys plea for cold case unit," *The Citizen of Laconia* (NH; May 1, 2009).
17. Ober, Gail. "Gloddys plea for cold case unit," *The Citizen of Laconia* (NH; May 1, 2009).
18. Knudsen, Milli. E-mail correspondence with author, March 2, 2011.
19. Knudsen, Milli. E-mail correspondence with author, March 2, 2011.
20. Knudsen, Milli. E-mail correspondence with author, March 2, 2011.
21. Knudsen, Milli. E-mail correspondence with author, March 2, 2011.
22. Globe Wire Services. "Retired teacher's contribution to Cold Case Unit is priceless," *Boston Globe* (April 26, 2010).
23. Wells, Bonnie M. "The Beginning of EquuSearch," posted 2007, http://starlight-innerprizes.com/TheBeginningOfEquusearch.htm (accessed December 26, 2011).
24. Texas EquuSearch Mounted Search and Recovery Team. http://texasequusearch.org/ (accessed December 26, 2011).
25. NecroSearch. www.necrosearch.com/index.html (accessed December 26, 2011).
26. Jackson, Steve. *No Stone Unturned: The True Story of NecroSearch International, the World's Premier Forenisc Investigators* (Kensington Books: New York, 2002), 205, 223.
27. Ralston & Associates. http://gralston1.home.mindspring.com/Sidescan.html Also, Ralston, Gene and Pinksen, Junior. "Underwater technology used to bring closure to families of drowning victims," *Journal of Ocean Technology 2010* 5: 3 (2010).
28. Ralston, Gene and Pinksen, Junior. "Underwater technology used to bring closure to families of drowning victims," *Journal of Ocean Technology 2010*, 5: 3 (2010).
29. Dooley, Danette. "Volunteers travel North America finding the dead," *Blue Line Magazine* (December 2007).
30. Ralston, Gene. E-mail correspondence with author, October 19, 2011.
31. Ralston, Gene. E-mail correspondence with author, October 19, 2011.
32. Ralston, Gene. E-mail correspondence with author, October 19, 2011.

33. Gunn, Charlotte. "Drowning victim recovered from Beardsley Reservoir after 3 years; side-scan sonar mission, February 27–March 1, 2002," *Rescue: Idaho Mountain Search and Rescue Unit, Inc.*, 35: 2 (March 2002). Also, Ralston, Gene. E-mail correspondence with author, November 2, 2011.
34. Ralston, Gene. E-mail correspondence with author, November 2, 2011.
35. Dooley, Danette. "Volunteers travel North America finding the dead," *Blue Line Magazine* (December 2007).

Contact with Co-Victims

14

In 1979, in Denver, Colorado, Bonita Raye Morgan's murderer strangled the petite 27-year-old, threw her out of a hotel window into an alley, and then set her body on fire. The alleged killer (now deceased) was arrested, then freed by a district attorney for lack of evidence. At the time, Bonita's sister, Sharron Bullis, and other family members were informed of the suspect's bloody shoelaces and additional evidence collected by police at the scene. Three decades later, in 2009, Bullis contacted the Denver Police Department to ask if new technology, specifically DNA, could finally identify her sister's killer.

When Bonita's case was pulled and a member of the police department returned Bullis's call, he had the difficult task of telling her that the crime-scene evidence was noted as "missing" when his predecessor reviewed the case in 1990. That was long before 2004, when the department formed its cold case unit and began to review thousands of unsolved criminal cases, looking for those that contained DNA evidence that could be re-examined with new technology. Bullis is a co-victim who sees no justice for her sister, and the police are left with a case they are unable to solve or clear.

Profile: Victim Advocate Is Integral Member of Denver's Cold Case Unit

Straddling the middle in the above situation is Sarah Chaikin (see Figure 14.1), the cold case program coordinator of the Victim Assistance Unit at the Denver Police Department (see Figure 14.2). From her work with co-victims, she knows firsthand that even if a case is cold, it is part of the affected families' everyday lives. In a recent interview, Chaikin stated that as unfortunate as the situation is in Bonita Raye Morgan's case, the police department has an obligation to tell the truth to family members and to explain to them if a case cannot be solved.

Chaikin's job is unusual, if not unique, in a law enforcement agency. Along with eight dedicated detectives and their sergeant, she is an integral member of her agency's cold case unit. Hired in 2008 for a position that had been created in 2005 during the unit's ongoing evaluation, she came with a solid background in mediation and various victim services capacities. She is the primary point of contact for victims, co-victims, and other family members identified in unsolved sexual assaults and unresolved homicides. She empathizes with their anger and grief and provides

Figure 14.1 Sarah Chaikin, cold case program coordinator of the Victim Assistance Unit at the Denver Police Department, updates a family member on a cold case. (Photo by author.)

Figure 14.2 An image of the Denver Police Department's badge is engraved on the agency's Memorial to Fallen Officers. (Photo by author.)

updates and information to those who request it for as long as their cases remain unsolved or unresolved. Stated Chaikin, "Bonita's case has solidified, for me, the importance of what we're doing."[1]

Part of Chaikin's job is administrative. She keeps track of 700 unsolved homicides and updates all of the agency's cold cases, since 1970, on the department's website. For the older cases or ones with little information, she asks family members to provide personal statements which help the families feel connected and, sometimes, bring in new leads. Chaikin also reaches out to victims' families on the one-year anniversary of every murder that occurs in Denver, in compliance with Colorado Senate Bill 06-177 that took effect on July 1, 2006. In her letters, she lets the family members know that they can opt in to receive annual written updates on the status of their case. She also explains that she understands that receiving the letter can be difficult and may bring up questions, so she urges family members to call her if they want to talk with her. When they do, she listens, and she tries to help them understand why their family member's homicide remains unsolved. "I walk a fine line between being a voice for the victims," said Chaikin, "while still protecting the integrity of their cases."[2]

Whenever possible, Chaikin takes a proactive approach to her work. "When the family members receive the letters, approximately 50% of them want to meet with me," she said. "Some of them ask me where I was six months ago."[3] She hopes to be able to make her written contacts with co-victims earlier, rather than waiting for the one-year anniversary. She has also found that if she sets up a family meeting with a detective, the relationship with that family in the future is smoother than if there had been no interaction. In an interview with The National Center for the Victims of Crime, Chaikin stated that her work is important to victims and co-victims because it gives them a way to move forward. "Our work shows respect for victims where they are, and we help victims feel that they matter, that they are being heard," she stated. "Telling the truth, owning up to the limitations of the department, [and] owning up to the limitations of the case are ways to be responsible to victims."[4]

Case History: Justice Denied for Bonita Raye Morgan

On April 3, 1979, Bonita's father was home alone when the telephone rang at the family's home in North Carolina. A caller from a coroner's office asked if he had a daughter named Bonita, then wanted to know when someone would claim her body, as it had been in the morgue for a week. "No one even bothered to notify us of her death," said Bonita's younger sister Sharron Bullis, in a 2011 telephone interview. "My father had muscular dystrophy. After the phone call, a neighbor found him distraught and wobbling on crutches in the middle of the road."[5]

Gradually, many of the details of Bonita's brutal murder became known to Bullis, her parents, and another sister. They brought Bonita's body home and buried her, and they filed away every piece of documentation the detectives would share. Bullis remembers Bonita, who was four-feet-nine-inches tall, as "a little bitty stick of dynamite" and does not sugar-coat her lifestyle. Bonita worked at Kitty's, an adult theater, where her husband was a projectionist. "She was a proverbial flower child, had made some wrong choices, and couldn't learn from her mistakes," said Bullis. "Things were not getting better for her."[6]

At the time, Bonita was recently divorced, and Bullis believes the ex-husband, who reportedly had deep scratches on his face and arms immediately after the murder, was never questioned. The prime suspect in Bonita's murder was a man she was arguing and drinking with, a possible boyfriend. In the pre-DNA era, he was arrested and released. In 1980, when he was arrested again for another offense, Bullis traveled from North Carolina to Denver, but the suspect did not show up in court. In Denver, Bullis learned that Bonita's personal belongings were initially released to the boyfriend and, in addition to the bloody shoelaces (used as a ligature), the crime scene evidence included fingernail scrapings, hair, towels, and even plywood from the hotel room's windowsill. When the evidence mysteriously disappeared within a decade or so of the murder, no one told the family, who, according to Bullis, had continued to call and write to the police department throughout the years.

Both the ex-husband and the boyfriend are now deceased. Bonita's father has also died, leaving the rest of the family to deal with a heartache that has not gone away. Co-victims, including Bonita's family, have no expectations of closure, only of resolution. But, this young woman's family held out hope that, one day, justice would be done.

In 2009, after being told by the Denver Police Department that they no longer had any evidence, Bullis again traveled to Colorado and met with members of the cold case unit, including Sarah Chaikin. While there, she gave them two crime scene photographs that she had copies of in her files. When asked by the author how she felt at the time, she called the family's situation "another blow, albeit not truly unexpected, in a long list of ineptness and lack of compassion. It was like one 'n'er-do-well' doing away with another, and the family was far away, so who cares?"[7]

Bullis's advice for cold case investigators? "No matter what the police may think, people mean something to their families," she said. "It's very rare when you have someone who has no one to care for them. No matter how bad their lifestyle is, they are important to someone. If you can't use compassion in your position, if you can't empathize with that family, you need to get out of that line of work." She was quick to point out, however, that the current Denver Police Department administration is not responsible for mistakes made in the past. "This makes it extremely difficult for me to focus my frustration," she added. "When you hear my anger, please remember that it is meant for the previous regime, not the current. Today's police department is left with a travesty."[8]

Co-Victims and Law Enforcement

Families of homicide victims see the world going on as usual, but their own worlds have crashed. Between August 2008 and June 2009, Paul B. Stretesky, a sociology professor (at the time) from the Center for the Study of Crime and Justice at Colorado State University, interviewed 36 of these family members from 10 different law-enforcement jurisdictions. Most of those interviewed were parents, but they also included siblings, friends, adult children, an aunt, and a granddaughter. The most important indicator of a co-victim's satisfaction with law enforcement was acknowledgment that his or her loved one's case was still being actively investigated. According to Stretesky's report,"Forgotten Victims: What Cold Case Families Want From Law Enforcement," the biggest complaint was the need for better, honest, and direct communication.

Other Co-Victim Perspectives (as Stated in the "Forgotten Victims" Report) Include:

- A lack of notification of a change in case personnel caused them to question the veracity of the investigation.
- A concern that police believe the person's family member engaged in risky behavior and thus was at least partially responsible for his or her murder. This perception was expressed, above, by Sharron Bullis as "one 'n'er-do-well' doing away with another."
- A fear that a likely, but unconvicted, murderer will kill the victim's family if the family members push for case resolution.
- A belief that the police perceive their telephone calls as bothersome or problematic.
- A perception that nothing is being done, especially when communication between law enforcement and family members breaks down.[9]

Co-victims know that they have to be their family member's biggest advocate, which is very frustrating inasmuch as they do not have all of the pieces of the puzzle, that is, all of the information on the case. Most of the co-victims who participated in the study acknowledged that they are aware that law enforcement cannot share proprietary information, but they also reported that they would rather learn the truth—if the case were not being actively investigated—than falsely believe an active investigation was ongoing.

In agreement is Howard Morton, Executive Director of the grassroots organization, Families of Homicide Victims and Missing Persons (FOHVAMP), and also a parent of a murdered child. In an afterword to the study, Morton places "candor" and "active investigations" at the top of his want list.[10] Instead of being told that an agency is "working on a case," he wants to know if investigators have taken a passive approach, simply rereading the files, or if they are actively re-interviewing witnesses, have recently revisited the crime scene, and have checked to see if the evidence is still viable.

Morton also emphasizes recognition. Families of murder victims whose killers have been arrested and charged get to participate in the court system. Co-victims of unsolved murders, however, often have no contact with law enforcement for long periods of time, deepening their suspicion that nothing is being done. Ultimately, the families want resolution. Stated Morton:

> It is said that to murder a person is to murder that victim's whole family. The life of each person who felt close to the victim is abruptly and permanently changed. To help this co-victim, make an active effort to find and prosecute the killer. Communicate to the family what is being done. Recognize the effect of a cold case on a family versus the outcome experienced by the family of a victim whose killer is being prosecuted. Speak candidly.[11]

In addition, some of the families who believe that police are not doing their jobs have tried to solve their loved ones' cases themselves, only to find that they lacked adequate resources, protection, and support. Some were faced with job loss, extreme emotional distress, and may have placed themselves in dangerous situations that, potentially, could compromise the outcomes of their cases.[12]

What Law Enforcement Agencies Can Do (as Stated in the "Forgotten Victims" Report)

- Try to empathize with the co-victims' feelings of depression and despair.
- Explain that no matter what lifestyle the victim had, or the behavior he or she engaged in, no one deserves to be murdered.
- Instead of saying, "We know who did it, but we can't prove it," tell the family, "We believe we know who did it, but we are still trying to put together enough evidence to prosecute the suspect(s)."[13]
- Be honest, and do not hold out false hope. (Howard Morton prefers, "Be honest and forthcoming.")[14]

- If co-victims turn up new information, thank them. (The Metropolitan Police Department, in Washington, DC, goes a step farther and advises co-victims "to keep your eyes and ears open" and pass information on to police, adding that informed persons will frequently approach family members rather than go to the police.)[15]
- Acknowledge the family members' pain and fear.[16]

In addition, law-enforcement agencies, as well as district attorneys (if the cases go to court), need to make use of their victim advocates. But a friendly phone call to or from family members can be part of a coroner's or medical examiner's job, as well. Investigator Matthew Lunn, of the Arapahoe County Coroner's Office in Centennial, Colorado, says that coroners deal with families a lot, not surprising since they are the last people to know the victim. Lunn enjoys talking with families and can tell them, firsthand, what happened to the deceased. "One woman I know had a son who committed suicide," he stated. "Every year on the anniversary, she calls me to talk."[17]

Co-Victim Resources (A Sampling of Some Volunteer and Nonprofit Organizations)

National Center for the Victims of Crime

The National Center for Victims of Crime (NCVC, www.ncvc.org) is a nonprofit organization that advocates for victims' rights, trains professionals who work with victims, and serves as a trusted source of information on victims' issues. According to its website, the organization remains the most comprehensive national resource committed to advancing victims' rights and helping victims of crime rebuild their lives. The National Center is, at its core, an advocacy organization committed to—and working on behalf of—crime victims and their families. Rather than focus the entire organization's work on one type of crime or victim, the National Center addresses all types of crime. Its mission is to forge a national commitment to help victims of crime rebuild their lives. Through collaboration with local, state, and federal partners, the National Center:

- Advocates for laws and public policies that secure rights, resources, and protections for crime victims
- Provides current information and analysis on crime victims' needs and services to enhance awareness, outreach, services, and policies for supporting crime victims

- Serves as a trusted source of current information on victims' issues and plays a leading role in shaping the national discussion on victims' rights, protections, and services[18]

Parents of Murdered Children, Inc., National Organization of

Parents of Murdered Children, Inc. (POMC, www.pomc.com/index.htm) was founded in 1978, in Cincinnati, Ohio, for families and friends of those who have died by violence. Following the murder of 19-year-old Lisa, her parents, Robert and Charlotte Hullinger, were determined to survive and help others, so they opened their home to three other parents of murdered children. Now, POMC has more than 300 chapters in all 50 states as well as the District of Columbia, and provides individual assistance, support, and advocacy to more than 100,000 members.

One type of assistance offered by POMC is its Second Opinion Services (S.O.S) for unsolved cases. According to the organization's website,

> Volunteer medical, law enforcement, and investigative experts provide an independent objective viewpoint based on existing evidence and/or records submitted to POMC for review. Members of the S.O.S. evaluate materials, looking for evidence that needs to be followed up, findings that may have been misinterpreted, areas that need further investigation and inconsistencies or conflicting information. Although S.O.S. is not an investigative agency, its findings have caused many cases to be re-opened, provided valuable information and have solved several cold cases.[19]

Polly Klaas® Foundation

The Polly Klaas® Foundation (www.pollyklaas.org) was named for the 12-year-old girl who was abducted from her bedroom in 1993. The national organization helps to find missing children, prevents children from going missing, and promotes laws including AMBER Alert that help keep children safe. As of 2011, the organization has helped more than 7,500 families of missing children, counseling them on ways to find their children and work with law enforcement. According to the group's website, it makes and distributes posters of missing children for these families, has a national eVolunteer force that distributes posters of missing children in their communities, continues an around-the-clock hotline, publishes and distributes child safety information to people around the world, and distributes free Child Safety Kits and Internet Safety Kits that can be ordered or downloaded online.

Families of Homicide Victims and Missing Persons

Families of Homicide Victims and Missing Persons (FOHVAMP, http://unresolvedhomicides.org) is a Colorado-based organization, founded in 2001, for families and friends of cold case homicide victims and persons missing under suspicious circumstances. Howard Morton and his wife, and a handful of additional co-victims, held their first meeting in the Denver Pubic Library in 2002. During the next two years they held pot-luck dinners in a café owned by one of the members. Now, through generous donations from the Denver Police Foundation, they hold day-long annual meetings in comfortable conference facilities, complete with presentations, panel discussions, and luncheons.

The state has a backlog of approximately 1,500 unsolved murders dating from 1970, with nearly half of them in Denver. Throughout a six-year period, students and both paid and volunteer researchers (the author was one of them) assembled background case information, as well as current family contact information. The case information was derived, primarily, from original newspaper reports. (See Chapter 11.) The current contact information came from online people searches. (See Chapters 3 and 4.)

An important function of the organization is outreach to families; their circumstances are all different, but their pain is the same. In 2009, FOHVAMP, through Sarah Chaikin, found Bonita Raye Morgan's sister, Sharron Bullis. With a scholarship from the organization, Bullis was able to attend the annual meeting where she reconnected with (new) Denver Police Department personnel. Bullis was very appreciative, particularly to know that the organization has not forgotten Bonita, stating, "The feeling that someone cared is indescribable."[20] Even though Bullis again had to travel from out of state, she attended another FOHVAMP annual meeting in 2011 and was part of a panel in a workshop for law enforcement. Now, she is excited about participating in additional sessions in the future. "My high spot?" she asked, in e-mail correspondence with the author, then stated, "Actively being sought out by others (including Howard Morton and his family) after the workshop and being asked to assist in future projects. It not only showed that I was a valuable participant, but it validated my need to contribute."[21]

Missouri Missing

Missouri Missing (www.MissouriMissing.org) is a statewide organization representing more than 1,100 missing persons. The group's mission statement is, "To unite as one voice for our missing; create a support network for the loved ones of all missing persons, and to educate and create awareness for the families of all missing persons." In 2007, two mothers, Marianne Asher-Chapman of Holts Summit and Peggy Florence of Jefferson City, formed

Missouri Missing after suffering the losses of their adult daughters. Stated Asher-Chapman in a Missouri Missing media release, "There just isn't anything out there to tell you what to do next. It's like being spun into a world all by yourself without a single person to tell you what to do."[22]

Asher-Chapman's 28-year-old daughter, Michelle "Angie" Yarnell, went missing in October 2003. After more than five years, Angie's husband confessed, was arrested, and was convicted of her murder, but at the time of this writing, the woman's remains have still not been found. Similarly, Florence's daughter, 31-year-old Jasmine Sue Haslag, went missing in June 2007 after telling her three young children she would pick them up the following day. In her case, however, in February 2008, the police changed Jasmine's case from a missing person to a homicide, but her murder remains unsolved and her remains have not been found. With Victim Advocates Stephanie Clack and Alice Beverly (sisters of Paula Beverly Davis, see Chapter 6, "NamUs: Connecting the Missing and Unidentified"), and Executive Director Ra'Vae Edwards, Marianne Asher-Chapman, Peggy Florence, and other dedicated volunteers now supply the support that was previously lacking to these co-victims. Missouri Missing even supplies truckers with fliers of missing persons to distribute to truck stops across the country. In addition, the organization posts a county-by-county database of missing persons, with data provided by the Missing Persons Unit of the Missouri State Highway Patrol. [23]

Citizens Against Homicide

Citizens Against Homicide (CAH, www.citizensagainsthomicide.org) is a California-based nonprofit organization founded in 1994 to create a body of support and a voice for the survivors and friends of homicide victims. The majority of the organization's board members have lost a family member to murder. In addition to many links and resources, some of the services offered by the organization include:

- Helping to keep convicted murderers in prison with guidance on parole opposition letter-writing campaigns
- Honoring the deceased and attempting to generate new leads on cold and unsolved cases with victim profiles in the group's monthly newsletter
- Providing information on pending crime legislation in California
- Providing guidance, one-on-one, through the criminal justice system, including coroner, trial, and courtroom support
- Securing information on homicide reward funds and billboards
- Providing advice on writing presentencing letters, as well as a forum for sharing problems with the judicial system

Who Killed Our Kids

Who Killed Our Kids (WKOK, http://wkok.org) is a nonprofit organization for families of unsolved homicide victims in the greater Cincinnati, Ohio area. The group contacts family members to help them focus on information concerning the homicides in the hopes that they can be solved. Group members go out into the neighborhoods, ask questions, and pass out flyers to keep each unsolved case in the public eye. They also use reward posters, memorials, and exhibits, as well as television and radio broadcasts, to open up communication about homicides in their city.[24]

Outpost for Hope

The Outpost for Hope (www.outpostforhope.org) is a four-person, volunteer-run organization, founded in 1999. According to its website, the organization continues to work across the United States to help families and loved ones of missing persons, law enforcement agencies, forensics teams, mental health workers, and others find missing persons and "kids off the grid" in order to connect them to resources they may need.[25]

One Missing Link, Inc.

One Missing Link, Inc. (http://onemissinglink.org/omlindex.html) is designed to work in conjunction with the National Center for Missing and Exploited Children (NCMEC). Its purpose is to provide a link between families of the missing and existing systems in a cooperative effort to reunite the missing and their families. Its website states that the agency also "is dedicated to the provision of valid information regarding missing adults, children, parental abductions, stranger abductions, runaway and/or throwaway youth, and stalking victims."[26]

Let's Bring Them Home

Let's Bring Them Home (LBTH, www.lbth.org/ncma/index.php) operates a national missing adults program that provides services and coordination among various government agencies, law enforcement, media, and the families of endangered missing adults, as well as safety education for all ages.[27]

Victim Rights Act: Colorado as an Example

The Colorado legislation that provides for victims and co-victims (of homicides, as well as various other crimes) to receive annual written updates on their cases is a modification of the Colorado Victim Rights Act, passed in 1992.[28] According to the act, spouses, parents, children, siblings, grandparents, significant others, or other lawful representatives have the following rights:

- Treatment with fairness, respect, and dignity
- Information on all charges filed and assurance of swift and fair resolution of the proceeding
- Input into decisions regarding plea bargains and to be present and have input at sentencing and parole hearings
- Information regarding restitution or civil remedies
- Release of property within five days after the case is settled and the property is no longer needed as evidence
- Information about what steps can be taken if he or she is subjected to intimidation or harassment
- Assistance with employment problems resulting from being the victim of a crime.
- Notification of all case dispositions, including appeals
- Timely notification of all court dates
- Secured waiting area when available
- Information regarding community resources and other information that will assist recovery
- Notification of any change in the status or the release from custody of the accused[29]

Except for the first of the rights—treatment with fairness, respect, and dignity—all of the other rights were written for cases in which the perpetrators were arrested and prosecuted. The modification for yearly updates is appreciated by families of unresolved homicides and missing persons, but the majority of co-victims of cold cases do not believe that their needs have been met.[30]

Need for Kindness

One of the overlooked rights, and needs, of co-victims is kindness. In 1966, when the author was a student at the University of Colorado in Boulder, female botany student Elaura Jaquette was murdered on campus after a part-time custodian lured her into an organ practice room in a medieval-like tower in the gothic-style Macky Auditorium building. (It has been speculated that Elaura went to attend to an injured bird, but when asked, her now-deceased convicted killer continually refused to explain.) Tour buses now pause as they pass the building. And, nearly every Halloween, newspaper reporters trump up rumors of moaning sounds emanating from the "haunted" building, even though the victim's mother still lives, and grieves, in the same state. When society condones "ghost stories" of recent, or even not-so-recent, murder victims, it does not show kindness or respect for the victims or the co-victims.

Summary

Resources in this chapter include:

- The use of a victim advocate in a cold case unit
- Suggestions from co-victims on better communication from law enforcement
- Resources for co-victims

The Cold Case Unit of the Denver Police Department, in Denver, Colorado, employs a victim advocate who walks a fine line between being a voice for the victims while still protecting the integrity of the unit's cases.

- The murder, in 1979, of Bonita Raye Morgan is an example of a case that the police have not been able to solve or clear, and family members see no justice for the victim.
- According to a Colorado State University study, the biggest complaint of co-victims was the need for better, honest, and direct communication with law enforcement.
- Co-victim resources include several volunteer and nonprofit organizations at the national and state level. Included are the National Center for the Victims of Crime, the National Organization of Parents of Murdered Children, Inc., Colorado-based Families of Homicide Victims and Missing Persons, and Missouri-based Missouri Missing.
- Victim Rights Acts vary by state.

Endnotes

1. Chaikin, Sarah. Cold Case Program Coordinator. Interview with author, June 30, 2011.
2. Chaikin, Sarah. Cold Case Program Coordinator. Interview with author, June 30, 2011.
3. Chaikin, Sarah. Cold Case Program Coordinator. Interview with author, June 30, 2011.
4. Chaikin, Sarah. "Perspectives from the field," The National Center for Victims of Crime, www.ncvc.org/ncvc/main.aspx?dbName=DocumentViewer&DocumentID=48323 (accessed December 26, 2011).

5. Bullis, Sharron. Telephone interview with author, July 21, 2011.
6. Bullis, Sharron. Telephone interview with author, July 21, 2011.
7. Bullis, Sharron. Telephone interview with author, July 21, 2011.
8. Bullis, Sharron. Telephone interview with author, July 21, 2011.
9. Stretesky, Paul B.; Unnithan, N. Prabha; Shelley, Tara; and Hogan, Michael J. "Forgotten victims: What cold case families want from law enforcement" (Fort Collins: Center for the Study of Crime and Justice, Department of Sociology, Colorado State University, 2009), 4–6.
10. Morton, Howard. "Forgotten victims: What cold case families want from law enforcement" (Fort Collins: Center for the Study of Crime and Justice, Department of Sociology, Colorado State University, 2009), Afterword.
11. Morton, Howard. "Forgotten victims: What cold case families want from law enforcement" (Fort Collins: Center for the Study of Crime and Justice, Department of Sociology, Colorado State University, 2009), Afterword.
12. Stretesky, Paul B.; Unnithan, N. Prabha; Shelley, Tara; and Hogan, Michael J. "Forgotten victims: What cold case families want from law enforcement" (Fort Collins: Center for the Study of Crime and Justice, Department of Sociology, Colorado State University, 2009), 4-6.
13. Stretesky, Paul B.; Unnithan, N. Prabha; Shelley, Tara; and Hogan, Michael J. "Forgotten victims: What cold case families want from law enforcement" (Fort Collins: Center for the Study of Crime and Justice, Department of Sociology, Colorado State University, 2009), 7.
14. Morton, Howard. E-mail correspondence with author, November 1, 2011.
15. Metropolitan Police Department. http://mpdc.dc.gov/mpdc/site/default.asp (accessed December 26, 2011).
16. Stretesky, Paul B.; Unnithan, N. Prabha; Shelley, Tara; and Hogan, Michael J. "Forgotten victims: What cold case families want from law enforcement" (Fort Collins: Center for the Study of Crime and Justice, Department of Sociology, Colorado State University, 2009), 6–7.
17. Lunn, Matthew. Investigator. Interview with author, January 31, 2011.
18. National Center for Victims of Crime. Welcome page, www.ncvc.org/ncvc/main.aspx?dbID=DB_About189 (accessed December 26, 2011).
19. Parents of Murdered Children. www.pomc.com/index.htm (accessed December 26, 2011).
20. Bullis, Sharron. E-mail correspondence with author, July 28, 2011.
21. Bullis, Sharron. E-mail correspondence with author, October 11, 2011.
22. Missouri Missing. www.MissouriMissing.org (accessed December 26, 2011).
23. Missing Persons Unit, Missouri State Highway Patrol. www.mshp.dps.mo.gov/CJ51/index.jsp (accessed December 26, 2011).
24. Who Killed Our Kids. http://wkok.org (accessed December 26, 2011).
25. Outpost For Hope. www.outpostforhope.org (accessed December 26, 2011).
26. One Missing Link, Inc. http://onemissinglink.org/omlindex.html (accessed December 26, 2011).
27. Let's Bring Them Home. www.lbth.org/ncma/index.php (accessed December 26, 2011).
28. Colorado Victim Rights Act (VRA), Denver: Victim Assistance Unit. www.denvergov.org/dpdvau/ColoradoVictimRights/tabid/423633/Default.aspx (accessed December 26, 2011).

29. Colorado Victim Rights Act (VRA), Denver: Victim Assistance Unit. www.denvergov.org/dpdvau/ColoradoVictimRights/tabid/423633/Default.aspx (accessed December 26, 2011).
30. Morton, Howard. E-mail correspondence with author, November 1, 2011.

Review Teams and the Media

IV

Cold Case Review Teams and Information-Sharing Resources

15

Sometimes investigators working cold case homicides are so close to their cases that they can benefit from cold case reviews by objective well-skilled observers. These "think-tank" environments, free to law enforcement, provide opportunities for wide varieties of input, and they almost always furnish their presenters with new ideas and fresh perspectives. Cold case review teams also help satisfy the victims' families that law enforcement agencies are doing all that is possible, at least for the time being, to try to solve the homicides of their loved ones. In addition to review teams, there are many information-sharing resources available to investigators. This chapter includes a sampling of each; there are many more.

Cold Case Review Teams: A Sampling

- Vidocq Society
- Colorado Cold Case Task Force and Colorado Cold Case Review Team
- MACCHIA, Mid-Atlantic Cold Case Homicide Investigators Association
- Sheriffs' Association of Texas, Major Crimes Assessment Committee (MCAC) Cold Case Review Team
- Charlotte-Mecklenburg Police Department's Civilian Cold Case Review Team (See Chapter 2.)
- WAHI, Wisconsin Association of Homicide Investigators

Information-Sharing Resources: A Sampling

- CopLink
- Crime Stoppers International and Crime Stoppers USA
- NCAVC, National Center for the Analysis of Violent Crime, a component of the Federal Bureau of Investigation's (FBI's) Critical Incident Response Group (CIRG) that includes ViCAP (see below).
- IHIA, International Homicide Investigators Association
- LEO, Law Enforcement Online
- N-DEx, Law-Enforcement National Data Exchange

- NLETS, International Justice and Public Safety Information Sharing Network, formerly the National Law Enforcement Telecommunications System
- NCMEC, National Center for Missing and Exploited Children
- RISS, Regional Information Sharing System (including the Cold Case Locator)
- ViCAP and its collaboration with NamUs

Cold Case Review Teams

The Vidocq Society

Few organizations have namesakes as colorful as that of the Vidocq Society (www.vidocq.org) honoring Eugène François Vidocq, a French crook turned detective. James Steward-Gordon, the writer of the article, "World's First and Greatest Detective," described the notable historical figure as "a combination of Sigmund Freud, Giacomo Cassanova, Harry Houdini, and J. Edgar Hoover." In 1812, Vidocq created, and then headed, France's national police agency, the Sûreté Nationale, staffing it with a force of undercover reformed criminals like himself. Vidocq wrote his memoirs in four volumes, in which he claimed responsibility for the arrests of at least 20,000 criminals. His real-life exploits made him the model for fictional crime-fighters from Edgar Allan Poe's Chevalier Dupin and Agatha Christie's Hercule Poirot, to Sir Arthur Conan Doyle's Sherlock Holmes.[1]

Vidocq (1775–1857) is considered by historians and members of law enforcement to be the father of modern criminal investigation. Some of his accomplishments, and firsts, included:

- Introducing record-keeping (a card-index system), criminalistics, and the science of ballistics into police work
- Making plaster-of-Paris casts of foot/shoe impressions
- Being a master of disguise and surveillance
- Holding patents on indelible ink and unalterable bond paper
- Founding the first modern detective agency and credit bureau, Le Bureau des Renseignements[2]

Nearly every month in the stately Civil War-era Union League building a block from City Hall in downtown Philadelphia, approximately 100 forensic specialists and motivated private citizens from many parts of the country and overseas meet over lunch to listen and watch a law enforcement agency give a cold case presentation. Afterwards, the members bombard the presenter with comments and suggestions. At the end of the meeting, the locals return to their day jobs, and the out-of-town members often visit one-on-one with the presenter. In the months (and, sometimes, years) to follow, members continue to assist in the cases, pro bono and when needed. Although associate members and guests round out the banquet tables, full membership is limited to 82, a symbolic number depicting the number of years in Vidocq's life.[3]

The Society was founded in 1990 by three men: William Fleisher, a former Philadelphia Police Department officer and FBI special agent who later became the assistant special agent in charge of the U.S. Customs Service in Philadelphia; Richard Walter, a former forensic psychologist for the State of Michigan prison system and a crime scene analyst/profiler; and the late Frank Bender (see Figure 15.1), who called himself "the re-composer of the decomposed," an artist who was known for his uncanny ability to recreate facial reconstructions from partial and complete skulls.

Chairman of the Board and Case Management Director Frederick Bornhofen is a former director of security for an international energy company and is law enforcement's first contact. He also is responsible for lining up the monthly presentations.[4] Fleisher, one of the founders and now the organization's commissioner, came up with the Vidocq Society name. Speaking of Eugène François Vidocq to a British newspaper reporter, Fleisher once stated, "He [Vidocq]was the first really great detective. It seemed a shame to me that someone who had contributed so much to my field had largely been forgotten." The group's mission is "to act as a voice and a catalyst for all the people touched by a murder, particularly the victims' relatives."[5]

One of the Society's biggest success stories involves the facial reconstruction that Frank Bender created of John Emil List, a struggling Union County, New Jersey accountant who, on November 9, 1971, shot to death his wife

Figure 15.1 Vidocq Society co-founder, Frank Bender, posed in his studio in Philadelphia in July 2006. (Photo by author.)

Helen L. List, daughter Patricia M. List, and sons John F. List and Frederick M. List, along with his 84-year-old mother, Alma M. List. In a five-page letter John Emil List left for his pastor, he wrote that he had seen too much evil in the world, and that he had ended the lives of his family members in order to save their souls. Helen List and the children are buried together in the Fairview Cemetery, in Westfield, New Jersey. The inscription on their single gravestone reads, "There is peace in the eternal valley, Psalm 23."[6] Alma List is buried in the Saint Lorenz Lutheran Cemetery in Frankenmuth, Michigan.[7]

John Emil List then disappeared and built a new life for himself. In 1989, the producers of the television program, *America's Most Wanted,* asked Frank Bender and Richard Walter what List might look like 18 years later. They theorized that List would still be wearing horn-rimmed glasses—to make him look successful—and Bender sculpted him with the sagging facial features of an older man (see Figures 15.2 and 15.3). A woman watching the show in a suburb of Richmond, Virginia, recognized the bust as her neighbor, "Bob Clark." Agents went to the man's home, confronted List's stunned wife, and then obtained her help in filling in blanks from his past. Although he denied his identity, his fingerprints confirmed that he was John Emil List, and he was arrested at his office and later convicted of the murders. List died of complications of pneumonia in Trenton, New Jersey, in March 2008, at the age of 82.[8] He also is buried in the Saint Lorenz Lutheran Cemetery in Frankenmuth, Michigan.[9]

Although the Society has helped to solve and move forward many cases, its longest-standing and as yet unsolved challenge is the 1957 case of the Boy in the Box, "America's Unknown Child." Members discuss cases from all

Figure 15.2 When this unpainted copy of the bust of John Emil List was photographed in Frank Bender's studio, it was stuck on a shelf between another sculpture and a bicycle. (Photo by author.)

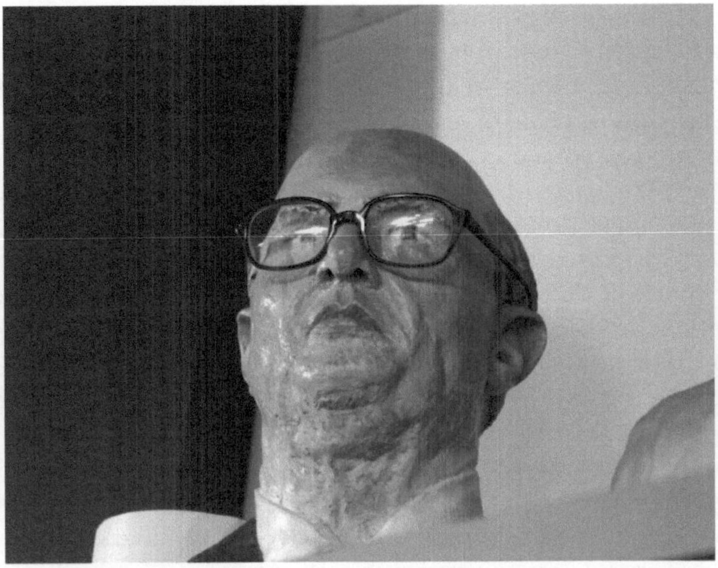

Figure 15.3 Horn-rimmed glasses were the finishing touch to the bust of John Emil List. (Photo by author.)

over the country, but, at the time of this writing, they still do not know who was responsible for the murder of the unidentified boy, aged four or five, found in a cardboard box in the woods on the north side of Philadelphia. The child died of a severe blow to his head, and he had numerous bruises on his body. In 1998, the boy's remains were exhumed from a potter's field near the Philadelphia State Hospital, and mitochondrial DNA was obtained from one of his teeth for future comparisons. After a special memorial service, he was then buried in Philadelphia's Ivy Hill Cemetery. Vidocq Society members were in attendance when a lone piper, on bagpipes, played "Going Home," from Czechoslovakian composer Antonín Dvořák's "New World Symphony."[10] The Vidocq Society maintains a "Boy in the Box" website with virtually all information available to the public on the case.[11]

Colorado Cold Case Task Force and Review Team

As noted in Chapter 5 under "State Clearinghouses," in 2007 the Colorado legislature created the Colorado Cold Case Task Force and Review Team (http://cdpsweb.state.co.us/coldcase), an advisory body comprised of law enforcement, victims' advocates, and family members of murder victims, as well as others who work with the group. A cold case, in this context, is defined as "a homicide investigation that is open for more than three years from the date of the commission of the crime and was committed since 1970." The Task Force was charged to "review and make recommendations on best practices related to cold case homicide investigation strategies and practices." After a survey of Colorado law enforcement agencies that indicated requests for more training, the Task Force developed an ongoing statewide two-day training course titled, "Cold Case Investigations: Strategies and Best Practices."[12]

In addition, Colorado's Cold Case Task Force was instrumental in facilitating the Colorado Cold Case Review Team. The 27-member unfunded team of law enforcement professionals is comprised of experts from a variety of associations including, but not limited to, the Colorado Association of Chiefs of Police (CACP), County Sheriffs of Colorado (CSOC), and the Colorado Organization for Victims Assistance (COVA), as well as several district attorneys and investigators. The review team first met on June 2, 2010 and continues to meet quarterly to review cold cases, but only at the request of law-enforcement agencies.[13] Currently, two or three cases are presented during each day-long meeting. After the agency concludes its presentation, the review team members, like those at Vidocq Society meetings, ask questions and offer suggestions. The presenting agency then is e-mailed an electronic account of the presentation, along with a list of the questions and suggestions made by the team. Each team member is required to sign a confidentiality agreement providing assurances to each presenting agency that the information will be kept confidential within law enforcement.[14]

Tim Lewis, Commander for the Longmont Police Department in Longmont, Colorado, speaks highly of the process. After one of his agency's three-year-old cases—the murder, in 2007, of Dana Pechin—was deliberated by the review team, the victim's boyfriend was charged in the woman's beating and strangulation. "I got to the point where I wanted to see if we missed something," Commander Lewis told a *Denver Post* reporter. "I wanted a lot of eyes to look at this. I'm totally sold on this concept and how it went."[15]

Mid-Atlantic Cold Case Homicide Investigators Association

The Mid-Atlantic Cold Case Homicide Investigators Association (MACCHIA, www.coldcasehomicide.org), along with similar associations in other parts of the country, provides training, networking, and information-sharing services. MACCHIA also holds biyearly roundtable cold case reviews. The purpose of the Mid-Atlantic Cold Case Homicide Investigators Association is:

- To establish an esprit de corps among cold case homicide investigators within the Mid-Atlantic region, as well as nationally
- To provide a forum to discuss and exchange information related to homicide case management and operational strategy, to discuss and exchange information on the latest advancements in forensic technology and laboratory sciences, and to discuss and exchange

information on improving training for police, investigators, prosecutors, laboratory personnel, and any other person or organization who may assist in a cold case homicide investigation
- To conduct seminars, conferences, and training opportunities related to all phases of a cold case homicide investigation
- To open lines of interagency communication, as well as promote, encourage, and foster the controlled exchange of need-to-know information among all agencies who may be involved in multijurisdictional investigations[16]

Sheriffs' Association of Texas, Major Crimes Assessment Committee (MCAC) Cold Case Review Team

Since 1985, the Sheriffs' Association of Texas, Major Crimes Assessment Committee (MCAC) Cold Case Review Team (www.txsheriffs.org/comm_coldcase.htm) has been providing assistance to law enforcement agencies statewide on unsolved major crimes. The team meets quarterly and consists of sheriffs, deputies, officers from city police departments, the Texas Department of Public Safety (DPS), DPS Crime Laboratory, DPS Special Crime Services, Texas Rangers, and a medical doctor. The team's objective is to bring together a wide variety of seasoned investigators with a tremendous amount of expertise in different areas to provide assistance with unsolved cases. All members have extensive training and experience in criminal investigations, criminal profiling, and analysis of violent crimes.[17]

Items required by the MCAC for Case Assessment include:

- All investigative reports
- Photographs of the crime scene, the victim with the body positioned at different angles, a residence (if involved) with a crime scene sketch, and, if possible, photographs of the area to include an aerial shot to show the relationship of the body placement to its area
- Racial, ethnic, and social data on the neighborhood and complex
- The medical examiner's report (autopsy protocol), with photographs to show the full extent of damage to the body (including stabbing, gun shot, bruises, and lividity)
- Laboratory reports, if available
- An explanation of whether wounds are postmortem
- The opinion of the medical examiner that may not be committed to the report
- A map of the victim's travel prior to death, along with place employed, residence, where last seen, crime scene location, county, and city[18]

Charlotte-Mecklenburg Police Department's Civilian Cold Case Review Team

(See Chapter 2, "Agency Organization: Cold Case Units" and Chapter 13, "Volunteers: How They Can Help.")

Wisconsin Association of Homicide Investigators

The Wisconsin Association of Homicide Investigators (WAHI, www.wi-homicide.org) was founded in 1996 in response to requests for specialized training in the area of death investigation. Since then, they have instituted a Cold Case Review Team, with the following criteria:

- Only the agency in control of the case can request a review.
- The case must be at least three years old.
- All evidence has been processed and reports have been received.
- The complete file, including still photographs, as well as videos, must travel with the requesting investigator.

Prior to the review, the investigating agency contributes a chronological case history. Then, on the day of the review, the presenter gives a 40–60-minute PowerPoint presentation that includes case particulars including victim information, as well as crime scene and autopsy photographs. Team members offer feedback and will provide a written report in approximately 14 days, when requested. According to WAHI's website, "In no way is the cold case review team attempting to 'take over the case.' They are simply offering one more resource to bring some type of justice to those whose loved ones have been murdered."[19]

Information-Sharing Resources

CopLink

CopLink (www.i2group.com/us/products/coplink-product-line) is a nationwide network that allows officers to follow up on investigative leads by accessing each other's files on suspects and cases from their computers. Developed through a 1996 pilot program between the Tucson Police Department in Tucson, Arizona, and the University of Arizona, also in Tucson, it can instantly make connections between suspects and phone numbers, addresses, bunkmates in prison, co-workers, and other known associates. Its software, already referred to as "Google for police," allows law enforcement agencies to share warrant information from out-of-state jurisdictions, as well as crime data that include descriptions of tattoos, nicknames, or partial license plate numbers. The structure of CopLink has been compared to that of bicycle wheels, each with a regional agency as its hub. Along CopLink's "spokes" are vast quantities of structured and seemingly unrelated data, including data currently housed in various incompatible databases and records management systems, to be organized, consolidated, rapidly analyzed, and shared over a highly secure intranet-based platform.[20]

The Person Search is the default search screen. Other search categories, including phone, vehicle, and firearm tabs are then accessible on the screen. The "Incident Analyzer" and the "Visualizer" are impressive mapping tools. The Incident Analyzer displays geographic relationships between incidents, and it animates the progression of incidents over time using mapping, analytical, graphing, and charting tools. The Visualizer organizes information into visual layouts to help users understand patterns in the data. Included (for a fee) is Face Match photo recognition software, in which users input a probe image and receive back a list of images considered to be a close match in appearance.[21]

In August 2011, at the Jefferson Parish Sheriff's Office in Metairie, Louisiana, investigators working on a homicide relied on CopLink software to search for witnesses, contacts, vehicles, and other relevant information. Sheriff Newell Normand told a *Times-Picayune* reporter at the time, that in less than one hour his detectives had assembled information that would have taken three deputies six hours each to collect. "In my 33 years of law enforcement, this is the single endeavor that I am most excited about," Normand said at a news conference, while announcing a new Criminal Intelligence Center, staffed each day by 40 officers from six different law enforcement agencies.[22]

Crime Stoppers International and Crime Stoppers USA

Crime Stoppers (www.csiworld.org/sites/default/files/CSI%20BROCHURE.pdf) directly engages citizens to aid in community crime-fighting efforts by giving people the opportunity to share information anonymously. Since its inception in 1976, tips to Crime Stoppers have aided all branches of law enforcement in the United States. The organization has apprehended 510,000 felony suspects, helped solve 840,000 criminal cases, and recovered $4 billion in stolen property, cash, and illicit drugs. (See Chapter 16 for Crime Stoppers' role in Florida's cold case playing cards.)

National Center for the Analysis of Violent Crime, a Component of the FBI's Critical Incident Response Group (CIRG) That Includes ViCAP

The National Center for the Analysis of Violent Crime (NCAVC, www.fbi.gov/about-us/cirg/investigations-and-operations-support) provides behaviorally based and analytical support to local, state, federal, and international law enforcement agencies investigating unusual or repetitive violent crimes, communication threats, terrorism, and other matters of significant interest to law enforcement. It consists of four units:

- Behavioral Analysis Unit 1 (counterterrorism/threat assessment)
- Behavioral Analysis Unit 2 (crimes against adults)
- Behavioral Analysis Unit 3 (crimes against children)
- ViCAP, Violent Criminal Apprehension Program (See separate listing at the end of the chapter.)

The special agents and other professionals on the NCAVC staff provide advice and support for a range of cases, including child abduction or mysterious disappearance of children; serial, spree, mass, and other murder cases; serial rape; extortion; threats; kidnapping; product tampering; arson and bombing; weapons of mass destruction; public corruption; cyber crime; and domestic and international terrorism. NCAVC services are provided during on-site case consultations, telephone conference calls, and phone consultations, and are organized through a network of NCAVC coordinators located in every Federal Bureau of Investigation field office in the United States. Law enforcement requests for NCAVC assistance are referred to the coordinator in the appropriate field office.[23]

International Homicide Investigators Association

The International Homicide Investigators Association (IHIA, www.ihia.org) was founded during a 1988 Violent Criminal Apprehension Program (ViCAP) International Homicide Symposium that was sponsored by the Federal Bureau of Investigation at Quantico, Virginia. This symposium brought together an elite group of professionals from around the world that represented all disciplines involved in death investigation. The organization is now the largest and fastest-growing organization of homicide and death investigation professionals in the world and has representation from the United States as well as 16 other nations. Although not specifically involved with cold cases, the association offers training, networking, and other support for homicides in general. Its mission is "to provide active support to law enforcement death professionals through leadership, training, networking, and provision of resources and expertise to resolve cases."[24]

Law Enforcement Online

Law Enforcement Online (LEO, www.leo.gov) is a seven-days-a-week, 24-hours-a-day online (realtime) controlled-access communications and information-sharing data repository. It provides a secure website for law enforcement and offers a service for investigators to send documents, photos, and other sensitive data by secure e-mail. LEO also has message boards and allows investigators to set up Law Enforcement Online Special Interest Groups (LEOSIGs) in order to trade information. For instance, a region can set up a cold case SIG for all the members in that region to post topics of mutual interest.[25]

Law-Enforcement National Data Exchange

The Law-Enforcement National Data Exchange (N-DEx, www.fbi.gov/about-us/cjis/n-dex) is like a national edition of CopLink. The FBI database brings together data from law enforcement agencies throughout the United States, including incident and case reports, booking and incarceration data, and parole/probation information. N-DEx "connects the dots" between data that are not seemingly related by detecting relationships between people, vehicles/property, location, or crime characteristics. It also supports multi-jurisdictional task forces, enhancing national information sharing, links between regional and state systems, and virtual regional information sharing.

The International Justice & Public Safety Network (Formerly National Law Enforcement Telecommunications System)

The International Justice & Public Safety Network (NLETS, www.nlets.org/who-we-are) links together and supports every state, local, and federal law-enforcement, justice, and public safety agency for the purposes of sharing and exchanging critical information. The types of information being exchanged include out-of-state motor vehicle and drivers' license data (important in cold case research for photographs and signatures), as well as state criminal history records and corrections images, and Canadian and Interpol databases. (According to Interpol's website, www.interpol.int, the international police organization is the world's largest, with 190 member countries.)

NLETS was invaluable following the August 2009 murder by an Alabama man of both his parents. The suspect fled the state, but Alabama detectives tracked him through his credit card purchases, then sent an all-points bulletin (APB) over NLETS to every control terminal agency on the NLETS system. The South Dakota Control Terminal Agency (Department of Public Safety dispatch center) picked up the information on the suspect and sent it to officers on the street. Because the dispatch center relayed the locations of the credit card purchases, and Alabama detectives were able to communicate with investigators in other states, officers on Interstate 90 in South Dakota quickly apprehended the suspect.[26]

National Center for Missing and Exploited Children

The National Center for Missing and Exploited Children (NCMEC, www.missingkids.com) is a quasi-government agency that helps law-enforcement authorities track down missing and exploited persons under the age of 21. As discussed in Chapter 5, its website includes a database with a variety of parameters. In addition to the Center's main office in Alexandria, Virginia, a branch office is located in TLO's facility. (See Chapter 3.) NCMEC also aids law enforcement with technical assistance, training, and investigative and technological resources that include:

- 9-1-1 Call Center Partner Program
- Attempted abductions
- AMBER Alert (disseminating AMBER Alert messages to secondary communications distributors)
- Case analysis
- Forensic assistance
- Family advocacy services
- Family reunification assistance
- Hotline: 1-800-THE-LOST
- Infant abduction prevention program
- International family abduction services
- Photo and poster distribution
- Project ALERT (America's Law Enforcement Retiree Team), which can provide the personnel, for instance, in tracking down and obtaining data such as DNA and dental records to help populate the NamUs Missing Person database (See Chapter 7.)
- Missing-child clearinghouse program
- Team Adam[27]

Regional Information Sharing System

The Regional Information Sharing System (RISS, www.riss.net) is a nationwide program of regionally oriented services designed to enhance the ability of local, state, federal, and tribal criminal justice agencies to:

- Identify, target, and remove criminal conspiracies and activities spanning multi-jurisdictional, multi-state, and sometimes international boundaries
- Facilitate rapid exchange and sharing of information among the agencies pertaining to known suspected criminals or criminal activity

- Enhance coordination and communication among agencies that are in pursuit of criminal conspiracies determined to be inter-jurisdictional in nature

RISS is comprised of a collection of six regional centers:

- NESPIN—New England State Police Information Network (Connecticut, Maine, Massachusetts, New Hampshire, Rhode Island, and Vermont, as well as parts of Canada)
- MAGLOCLEN—Middle Atlantic–Great Lakes Organized Crime Law Enforcement Network (Delaware, Indiana, Maryland, Michigan, New Jersey, New York, Ohio, Pennsylvania, and the District of Columbia, as well as Australia, Canada, and England)
- ROCIC—Regional Organized Crime Information Center (Fourteen southeastern and southwestern states, Puerto Rico, and the U.S. Virgin Islands)
- MOCIC—Mid-States Organized Crime Information Center (Illinois, Iowa, Kansas, Minnesota, Missouri, Nebraska, North Dakota, South Dakota, and Wisconsin, as well as parts of Canada)
- RMIN—Rocky Mountain Information Network (Arizona, Colorado, Idaho, Montana, Nevada, New Mexico, Utah, Wyoming, and Canada)
- WSIN—Western States Information Network (Alaska, California, Hawaii, Oregon, Washington, as well as Canada and Guam)[28]

The MOCIC operates the Cold Case Locator System, a homicide mapping system designed to target traveling killers by connecting investigators throughout the country who work similar homicides. Investigators enter homicide locations that are mapped on Google Earth. Clicking on a mapped location displays the entered victim/homicide details, including contact information for the officer and the agency responsible for the investigation of the selected homicide.[29] Additionally, MOCIC can loan materials (such as surveillance equipment) and can help build timelines and link charts for prosecutors.

ViCAP and Its Collaboration with NamUs

As discussed in Chapter 5, the Violent Criminal Apprehension Program (www.fbi.gov/about-us/cirg/investigations-and-operations-support/vicap-brochure-1) is the nation's largest repository of detailed information on major violent crimes. In addition, ViCAP has always been proactive with missing person and unidentified human remains cases; but, in early 2010, it escalated its position by entering into a collaborative initiative with NamUs. Since that time, a NamUs staff member has been working in ViCAP with the goal of cross-referencing ViCAP missing and unidentified human remains cases by entering them in the NamUs database. The ViCAP cases are quality controlled and compared against the NCIC record prior to creating the NamUs case. No ViCAP or NCIC case information is used without the express permission of the "owner of the record."[30] (For more on NamUs, see Chapters 6 and 7.)

A NamUs staff member emphasizes that there are three main databases where law enforcement should ensure that their missing person and unidentified human remains cases are entered:

- NCIC: First and foremost. This is especially critical with missing person cases, as this is the system that law enforcement uses multiple times a day. Every time a missing person record is entered in NCIC, it is automatically searched against the unidentified human remains cases.
- NamUs: The goal is to get all missing and unidentified cases into one central database and give the family and friends of a missing person the opportunity to enter their own records and conduct their own database searches. As discussed in Chapters 6 and 7, NamUs is the only one of the three systems that can be accessed by the general public. "It cannot be stated enough the importance of having all of the missing and unidentified person records entered into *one* central database," stated the staff member in correspondence with the author. "It is the only way to find the missing and give a name to the unidentified."[31]
- ViCAP: Cases are entered if foul play is indicated. If a case is in ViCAP, law enforcement can request analysis on its case. As part of the analysis, the crime analyst will query the national database to look for similar cases.

"We're hoping that someday all three systems will 'talk' to one another," added the NamUs staff member who stated:

> It's critical to let law enforcement know that these investigative tools are there for them to use—free of charge. It is also important to educate the family and friends of those who go missing what is out there and assist law enforcement to ensure that the information is entered in the appropriate databases. With these three databases, the missing persons and unidentified remains cases will never go cold.[32]

Summary

Resources in this chapter include:

- A description of where to find cold case review teams, and what they do
- A guide to some of the information-sharing resources that may be helpful in cold case research

Cold case review teams give law enforcement fresh sets of eyes, pro bono. There are many review teams all over the country, but perhaps the most well-known is the Vidocq Society. Named for a French crook turned detective, the organization meets monthly in Philadelphia to listen to cases presented by law enforcement, and then offers suggestions and continues, sometimes for years, to aid investigators in their work. Some other review teams include:

- Colorado Cold Case Task Force and Colorado Cold Case Review Team
- MACCHIA, Mid-Atlantic Cold Case Homicide Investigators Association
- Sheriffs' Association of Texas, Major Crimes Assessment Committee (MCAC) Cold Case Review Team
- Charlotte-Mecklenburg Police Department's Civilian Cold Case Review Team
- WAHI, Wisconsin Association of Homicide Investigators

The list of information-sharing resources for law enforcement is long, but it includes:

- CopLink
- Crime Stoppers International and Crime Stoppers USA
- NCAVC, National Center for the Analysis of Violent Crime—a component of the FBI's Critical Incident Response Group (CIRG) that includes ViCAP (see below)
- IHIA, International Homicide Investigators Association
- LEO, Law Enforcement Online
- N-DEx, Law-Enforcement National Data Exchange
- NLETS, International Justice and Public Safety Information Sharing Network, formerly the National Law Enforcement Telecommunications System
- NCMEC, National Center for Missing and Exploited Children
- RISS, Regional Information Sharing System (including the Cold Case Locator)
- ViCAP and its collaboration with NamUs

Endnotes

1. Steward-Gordon, James. "World's first—and greatest—detective," *The Reader's Digest*, (October 1977) 129–133.
2. The Vidocq Society. "La Vie de Monsieur Vidocq." www.vidocq.org/vidocq.html (accessed December 26, 2011).
3. Pilkington, Ed. "Vidocq Society—The Murder Club," *Guardian.co.uk*, March 3, 2011.
4. Vidocq Society. www.vidocq.org/who.html (accessed December 26, 2011).
5. Pilkington, Ed. "Vidocq Society—The Murder Club," *Guardian.co.uk*, March 3, 2011.
6. Find A Grave, Memorial #23081 (Helen List). www.findagrave.com/cgi-bin/fg.cgi?page=gr&GRid=23081 (accessed December 26, 2011).
7. Find A Grave, Memorial #23085 (Alma M. List). www.findagrave.com/cgi-bin/fg.cgi?page=gr&GRid=23085 (accessed December 26, 2011).
8. Stout, David. "John E. List, Killer of 5 Family Members, Dies," *New York Times* (March 25, 2008).
9. Find A Grave, Memorial #25511539 (John Emil List). www.findagrave.com/cgi-bin/fg.cgi?page=gr&GRid=25511539 (accessed December 26, 2011).
10. Pulham, Mark. "The boy in the box: America's unknown child," *Crime Magazine* (February 2, 2011).
11. "America's unknown child, the boy in the box mystery." http://americasunknownchild.net (accessed December 26, 2011).
12. Department of Regulatory Agencies (DORA), Office of Policy, Research, and Regulatory Reform, "2011 Sunset Review: Colorado Cold Case Task Force," October 14, 2011 (4, 5, 14).
13. Department of Regulatory Agencies (DORA), Office of Policy, Research, and Regulatory Reform, "2011 Sunset Review: Colorado Cold Case Task Force," October 14, 2011 (13).
14. Colorado Department of Public Safety, *Annual Report—Cold Case Task Force to the Colorado House and Senate Judiciary Committees* (Section 24.33.5-109(8), C.R.S.), October 1, 2011 (3).
15. Mitchell, Kirk. "Law-enforcement experts' work helps Longmont police file charges in a 2007 murder investigation," *The Denver Post* (May 9, 2011).
16. MACCHIA, www.coldcasehomicide.org/MACCHIA%20Membership%20Information%20Sheet.htm (accessed December 26, 2011).
17. Sheriffs' Association of Texas. www.txsheriffs.org/comm_coldcase.htm (accessed December 26, 2011).
18. Sheriffs' Association of Texas. www.txsheriffs.org/comm_coldcase.htm (accessed December 26, 2011).
19. Wisconsin Association of Homicide Investigators. www.wi-homicide.org/index.php?option=com_frontpage&Itemid=1 (accessed December 26, 2011).
20. Woodfill, D.S. "Arizona crime data shared by police through network," *The Arizona Republic* (July 27, 2011).
21. CopLink, www.i2group.com/us/products/coplink-product-line (accessed December 26, 2011).
22. Ross, Bob. "Criminal Intelligence Center in Metairie promises added efficiency," *The Times-Picayune* (August 25, 2011).

23. NCAVC. www.fbi.gov/about-us/cirg/investigations-and-operations-support (accessed December 26, 2011).
24. IHIA. www.ihia.org (accessed December 26, 2011).
25. LEO. www.leo.gov (accessed December 26, 2011).
26. Tipton, Delton. "Getting the Word Out," undated, NLETS, www.nlets.org/our-impact/in-their-own-words/suspect-identification (accessed December 26, 2011).
27. NCMEC. Resources for Law Enforcement, www.missingkids.com/missingkids/servlet/PageServlet?LanguageCountry=en_US&PageId=184 (accessed December 26, 2011).
28. RISS. www.riss.net (accessed December 26, 2011).
29. RISS, "MOCIC provides resources to support cold case investigations," www.riss.net/Documents/RISS.Insider.2009.07.pdf, (accessed December 26, 2011).
30. Stiltner, Suzanne. E-mail correspondence with author, November 28, 2011.
31. Stiltner, Suzanne. E-mail correspondence with author, November 28, 2011.
32. Stiltner, Suzanne. E-mail correspondence with author, October 28, 2011.

Taking Advantage of the Media

16

The media showed rapt attention when Vidocq Society co-founder Frank Bender unveiled his facial reconstruction of Boulder Jane Doe at a press conference at the Boulder County Sheriff's Office in Boulder, Colorado, in 2005. (Photo by author.)

As indicated in previous chapters, investigators in law enforcement agencies and coroner and medical examiner offices across the country are solving cold cases with the latest tools and techniques, combined with old-fashioned police work. This chapter discusses ways that law enforcement agencies can use the media to their advantage to disseminate information and bring in new leads. In its broadest definition, media refer to all forms of mass communication, from traditional newspaper articles and television broadcasts to innovative information-sharing and investigative techniques that include agency websites, social media, and cold case playing cards.

- Print and broadcast media (augmented with websites)
- Web-based/social media (information for the public and for investigators)
- Cold case playing cards

Print and Broadcast Media (Augmented with Websites)

Law enforcement agencies are often leery about using the media. But, as shown in the following case history on a Marin County, California, John Doe case, Joseph Coogan's remains would still be unidentified if a coroner's investigator had not reached across the country to a newspaper reporter in Erie, Pennsylvania.

Perhaps the most recurring complaint that investigators have about the media is that they have been misquoted in the past and do not want to be misquoted again. Instead of stewing about it, a simple request to the reporter during the interview, such as "Could you please read back my quote?" and then gently correcting any erroneous information, will result in a much better story. Taking the time to develop a good working relationship or rapport with a reporter, as well as gaining a reputation for being a stickler for accuracy, does not hurt either (Setting up a "Google Alert" [see Chapter 4] will keep one informed as to when the article is in print, online, or on the air.) If the reporter did a good job, be sure to thank him or her with a phone call or e-mail.

Larger agencies have public information Officers (PIOs) who write press releases, arrange press conferences, and interface with the media. But not all news accounts need to come at the request of newspapers or television stations. Investigators and PIOs who want to raise awareness of their cold cases, to get new leads or new witnesses, have found that print and broadcast reporters are eager to publicize unsolved homicides, missing persons, and unidentified remains if they are provided with a new "hook" on which to base their stories. (And sometimes it helps to seek out an alternative lifestyle publication more apt to reach one's target audience.) But, unless the reporters are true investigative reporters, and there are fewer and fewer these days, they usually are unaware of what that hook might be.

When soliciting a story from the media, consider basing one's pitch on the following, or come up with a creative hook of one's own:

- Anniversary of the date a body was found or a crime occurred
- Anniversary of the date a person was reported missing
- Anniversary of the date of the discovery of unidentified remains
- Birthday of a homicide victim or missing person
- Change in status of a co-victim, provided the co-victim is willing to be interviewed
- Previously unreleased information, with an appeal to the public for help (see the following case history on Darrell Harris and John Doe Number 3/Joseph Coogan).

Years ago, when Sergeant David Rivers of the Metro-Dade (now Miami-Dade) Police Department, wrote his report on the formation of his agency's cold case squad, he made it clear that he was a proponent of the media, and his advice holds true today. "Use—do not be used by—the media," he wrote, emphasizing that good press can be as beneficial as bad press can be damaging. Murders make headlines in any city in the nation, but Sergeant Rivers stated that publicity on cold cases is always positive because it helps the agency as a whole, shows the general population that police officers care about older, seemingly forgotten cases, and it may generate additional phone calls on other cold cases.[1]

Case History: John Doe Identified as Joseph Coogan

Darrell Harris, an investigator with the Marin County Sheriff's Office–Coroner Division, in San Rafael, California, found the answers to a decades-old John Doe case with the same methodology used by an earlier Bay Area resident, Edward O. Heinrich. Called "America's Sherlock Holmes" and the "Wizard of Berkeley," Heinrich worked independently as an investigative consultant and is credited with solving more than 2,000 West Coast cases from the 1920s until his death in 1953. He would have liked the set of keys that literally unlocked Harris's John Doe case, but he might not have thought of using the media to break it open.

On February 20, 1983, a badly decomposed torso and legs of a male clad in Calvin Klein blue jeans and entwined in fishing line washed up on a seaweed-covered beach at Point Reyes National Seashore in Marin County, California. An anthropologist hired at the time by the coroner's office determined that "John Doe Number 3" was a Caucasian male in his mid-to-late twenties. The anthropologist estimated that the partial remains were that of a five-foot-eleven-inches-to-six-foot tall man with a stocky build and had been in the water for three to four weeks.[2]

Surprisingly, still wedged in the pockets of the torso's blue jeans (secured with a brown leather belt) was a keychain with four keys and a small orange and white rubber commercial-type key fob that read, "Shades Auto Sales, 2315 West 12th, Erie, PA, Ph. 452-6441" (see Figure 16.1). In addition, there was one dime, a black plastic lens cap to a Canon camera, and two small keys that dangled from a rusted paperclip. Starting with the most obvious clue, the coroner's office's investigators contacted authorities in Erie, Pennsylvania, but no one with the man's description had been reported missing. Teletypes were sent to law enforcement agencies up and down the coast of California, but no agencies responded to this particular missing man.[3]

Four months later, Marin County authorities buried John Doe Number 3 in an unmarked grave in Valley Memorial Park in Novato, California.

Figure 16.1 Depicted here are the keys found in the jeans pocket of the partial remains of Joseph Coogan, washed up on a beach in Marin County, California, in 1983. (Photo courtesy of Darrell Harris.)

The keys, fob, lens cap cover, and the dime were placed in an evidence envelope and filed away with pencil sketches of the scene and photographs of the man's remains. Long before the launching of the NamUs System, which enabled Dr. James Davis in Montgomery County, Ohio, to quickly identify "Englewood Jane Doe" (see Chapter 6), Marin County's John Doe Number 3 was entered into a California missing and unidentified persons database, the Missing and Unidentified Persons Section (MUPS), administrated by the California Department of Justice. Then the case was filed away and all but forgotten.

Meanwhile, also filed away at the Monterey County Sheriff's Office (125 miles to the south) was a one-page report stating that, on January 23, 1983 (one month before the torso and legs were found by a beachcomber in Marin County), a man named Joseph Coogan had fallen from some rocks on the coastline and had been swept out to sea. Members of the United States Coast Guard had spotted his body lifeless in the water, but due to stormy weather they were unable to recover him. The recovery was abandoned, and the incident was recorded as an accidental death.[4] "Since the Monterey County Sheriff's Office considered Coogan deceased, rather than missing," stated Harris in a telephone interview with the author, "it did not issue a missing person's report, nor did they respond to the description of the recovered remains."[5] In 1983, no one made the connection between Marin County's John Doe and the Monterey County Sheriff's Office's accidental death. In addition, neither of the agencies at the time thought to contact the media. Media attention, along with the keys, would prove to be essential when Harris reopened the case nearly 22 years later.

On December 1, 2004, coroner's office volunteer Mark Friedman handed Investigator Darrell Harris an evidence envelope for John Doe Number 3. At the time, Friedman, a successful building inspector, offered his time one day per week to organize old John and Jane Doe cases (see Chapter 13). Harris, then 34 years old, had grown up in the Bay Area and had come from the Alameda County Coroner's Office in Oakland, California, to Marin County in 2003.

Harris had recently solved several other John Doe cases and also has a missing person in his own family, so he was highly motivated to take a fresh look at John Doe Number 3. When Harris and Friedman spread out the evidence to examine it, they both were struck with the same fact: no one had really dug deeply for information on the keys. As they studied them, the men came up with these clues and dead ends:

- One of the keys had a stamp on it that read "Bundy." Unlike Harris's predecessors, he worked in the Internet age, so he entered "Bundy" under the "license look-up page" of the website of the California Department of Consumer Affairs.[6] There, he found Bundy's Lock and Key Company (aka Bundy's Lock and Safe Company, Inc.) in West Los Angeles, but, on the telephone, an employee told Harris that although the lock shop occasionally stamped keys when they copied them for customers, there was no way to trace who did it or when it was done.
- The remaining keys were small. One was labeled "Hawthorn" (a filing cabinet manufacturer) and the other "American Tourister," a luggage manufacturer.
- Harris called the telephone number for Shades Auto Sales (as stamped on the key fob) in Erie, Pennsylvania, but it no longer was in business.[7]

Harris then followed up on a missing person report from Erie, Pennsylvania. The report turned out to be another dead-end, but it got him talking with Detective Jim Skindell of the Erie Police Department. The detective knew a reporter at the *Erie Times* and offered to see if the newspaper would appeal to the public on John Doe. Harris realized that media coverage could aid in his investigation, so he agreed to share what information he had on the case. The resulting article, "Keys Could Unlock Mystery Death," was published in the *Erie Times* on December 8, 2004. "It doesn't hurt to release information to the public," stated Harris. "I'm a believer in using the media, or whatever is available. If you let the streets do the talking, the family calls you."[8]

In this case, finding the identity of the Marin County John Doe was not quite that simple, but the *Erie Times* story became a turning point in the investigation. Only one person called in response to the reporter's plea for information, but the reader, Dan Veith, relayed the following:

- Veith had a college roommate named Joseph Coogan who had traveled to California on a business trip in late 1982 or early 1983. He never came home.
- The informant added that Coogan was terrified of water and did not know how to swim.[9]

Harris then contacted every California police agency with a beach-line jurisdiction south of Marin County, requesting a records search for any case involving a Joseph Coogan from 1982 to 1983. A few days later, Harris received the one-page report from the Monterey County Sheriff's Office, revealing the following facts:

- On January 23, 1983, 28-year-old Joseph Coogan and a business partner (initially misspelled as Michael Koridibin, but later determined from a Christmas card to Coogan's mother, to be Michael Kardibin) had climbed on some rocks at the beach to take photographs.
- The business partner told police that he was photographing Coogan standing on a rock. Suddenly, Coogan was knocked down by a wave, and then he was wedged between two rocks before a second wave swept him out into the ocean.
- The Pacific Grove Marine Rescue and the United States Coast Guard were unsuccessful in recovering Coogan. A helicopter crew spotted him floating lifeless in the water.
- Coogan's mother, Blanche, was reportedly informed of her son's death by her private physician, due to her state of ill health.[10]

As noted above, the years 2004 and 2005 were during the pre-NamUs days, and they also were prior to the launching of TLO and the advanced people-searching capacities that investigators have today. However, Harris found in the Social Security Death Index the name of a Pennsylvania man, Francis Coogan. He had died in 1990, but widows often retain their late husbands' names in telephone directories, and Francis Coogan was still listed. (See Chapter 4 for information on the Social Security Death Index and Chapter 12 for telephone and city directories.)

When Harris called the number, he was hoping to get someone who might have known the family, but instead, an elderly woman picked up the telephone. She just happened to be Blanche Coogan, Joseph's mother. In an emotional telephone call for both of them, the investigator in California and the mother in Pennsylvania compared descriptions and came to the same conclusion: John Doe Number 3 was Joseph Coogan.[11] Before the conversation was over, Blanche stated, "Oh, Darrell. I know it's him; that's my Joe. I just knew there was a reason God let me live this long. It's so I could get this phone call."[12]

Next, Harris talked with one of Coogan's sisters who filled in several gaps. First of all, the sister confirmed that her missing brother had purchased his last car at Shades Auto Sales in Erie, Pennsylvania, and that he had an American Tourister briefcase, with a missing key. The Coogan family also put Harris in contact with the man who witnessed Coogan being swept out to sea. The two men had rented a car and driven along the coast. Coogan asked his friend to take his photograph to show his family back home. Coogan handed his friend his Canon camera, slipped the lens cover into his pocket, and climbed down to the beach, and then back up and on top of a large rock. The friend took one photograph, and when he looked up from the camera, Coogan was gone. The film was developed, and the sister still had a copy of the photo. Coogan was wearing blue jeans.[13] The pieces of the puzzle were fitting together.

As an investigator, the last task Harris had to do was prove his case. Today, when the Marin County Sheriff's Office–Coroner Division buries the remains of an unidentified person a long bone and all of the person's teeth are held as evidence. That was not done in the pre-DNA days of 1983. Harris received authorization to have Coogan's remains exhumed so that his DNA could be profiled, then compared with a family reference sample from Coogan's mother. Both Harris and Friedman, his volunteer, attended the exhumation, but the grave was so water-logged and the bones too degraded to yield a positive identification. However, the DNA comparisons did not rule out Joseph Coogan as John Doe Number 3. With all of the other evidence in place, Marin County Coroner Ken Holmes identified the remains as Joseph Coogan's.[14]

Now, the only unsolved part of the mystery is how Coogan's body got swept from south to north. Normally, the currents along the California coast between Monterey and Marin counties move floating objects from the north to the south. "I guess we'll never know how his body got pulled against the current," Coroner Holmes told a newspaper reporter in 2005. "He could have got hooked up in nets or dragged by lines."[15] In April 2005, Coogan's remains were sent home for a private burial next to his father in the Calvary Cemetery, in Pottsville, Pennsylvania. A year and a half later, on November 20, 2006, the father and son were joined by

Blanche Coogan, who died at the age of 88.[16] The man lost on one beach and found on another is finally back on solid ground, with his family and with his own name on his grave.

(For two additional stories of drowning victims, in very different circumstances, see "Special Circumstances" in Chapter 6 about the recovery of the partial remains of Gary Mayo, as well the underwater sonar recovery of Scot Glover, under "Ralston & Associates" in Chapter 13.)

Web-Based Media: Agency Use of Cold Case Websites and Social Media

Agency Use of Cold Case Websites

An increasing number of agencies with multiple cold cases are posting them on agency websites. One that has led the way is the Clark County Office of the Coroner/Medical Examiner (CCOCME), in Las Vegas, Nevada, with its listing of the "Las Vegas Unidentified." Clark County Coroner P. Michael Murphy states (on the website), "When I accepted the post of Clark County Coroner in 2002, our office had a total of 182 John and Jane Doe cases. Immediately, I began to work with staff to create a cold case unit task force to bring resolution to as many families as possible by positively identifying their loved ones. To date, we have identified thirty people as a result of the task force." At the time of this writing, there still are 152 unidentified remains, from 1969 to the recent past, all listed with vital statistics and brief case histories. All are also on the NamUs database, which Coroner Murphy helped to bring to fruition.[17] (For more on NamUs, see Chapters 6 and 7.)

In Denver, Colorado, the Denver Police Department Cold Case Unit has a dedicated webpage for each of its 700 unsolved (since 1970) homicides. Administering the agency's website is part of the job of Sarah Chaikin, Cold Case Program Coordinator of the Victim Assistance Unit (see Chapter 14). "On each page, we post a photo and other information that we might receive from the families," stated Chaikin, who added:

> On the older homicides, we usually have only a few lines of information about the crime, so I ask the families to make a personal statement about the victim. Posting that information gives the families support and a connection to us, which starts a dialogue that in some cases can lead to some useful information. It may also lead to a dead end, but we can tell the families truthfully: this is where we are. We let them know why the case isn't on the detective's desk or why there is no further work at the lab.[18]

Social Media: Information for the Public—and for Investigators

Many law enforcement agencies are discovering that:

- Social media provide information to the public.
- Social media are investigative tools.

Social Media Provide Information to the Public

Since February 2011, the Dallas Police Department in Dallas, Texas, has had a full-time social media officer. At a time when the city was cutting back positions, the police department realized that a social media position was needed to maintain control over the information being released. One less officer on the street translated into an officer who spends all of her time on the agency's Facebook, Twitter, and other social media accounts, connecting with thousands of people at the same time. The department's posting of surveillance videos on YouTube recently led to the arrests of several criminals.[19] "The world is changing," stated Dallas Police Lieutenant Ches Williams, in a television interview. "When I was a young man, we contacted people via telephone, and if we saw them on the street we would talk to them. But nowadays people are using their cell phones. They're using the Internet. They're using other means of communication, electronic means of communication, and this is our effort to just reach out."[20]

Another agency that uses Facebook to disseminate information with the added bonus of bringing in clues is the Huntington Beach Police Department in Huntington Beach, California. In 2011, when the department reopened the homicide of a Jane Doe from 1968, investigators posted photographs of the decedent's white purse, along with photographs found inside it, of a man, woman, and several children. Although, at the time of this writing, the woman remains unidentified and case is still unsolved, the brief case history and the photographs of the victim's friends or relatives posted on Facebook have led to new leads.[21]

The Kentucky State Police also posted a Jane Doe on its Facebook page. Investigators included photographs of a forensic facial reconstruction and the woman's distinctive rose tattoo, as well as a silver ring found with the body when it was discovered in 2001. In return, Facebook users provided the police with additional information. At one time, the State Police used mass faxing to disseminate information to as many people as possible. Then the agency sent out multiple e-mails. Now, with an active Facebook page with more than 35,000 fans, the State Police are using the popular webpage to reach out to thousands of people in an instant. "Social media is a handy tool for law enforcement to communicate to, and solicit information from, the public," stated Captain Lisa Rudzinski, Kentucky State Patrol Post 3 commander, in a newspaper interview. "I am confident that its use in law enforcement will grow significantly in the future."[22]

An excellent resource for law enforcement is the International Association of Chiefs of Police (IACP) Center for Social Media. The Center serves as a clearinghouse of information and no-cost resources to help law enforcement personnel develop or enhance their agencies' uses of social media.[23] In the Center's online publication, "Building Your Presence with Facebook Pages: A Guide for Police Departments," it lists five top tips, as follows:

- Be timely and topical with your information. Crime and public safety information can be the most important information that people can get.
- Showcase and promote local events and citizens.
- Remind your citizens where they should contact you in an emergency.
- Let them know when to look out for suspects and when they have been apprehended.
- Post fun content, too. Not everything has to be serious.[24]

Social Media Are Investigative Tools

Only a few years ago, cops on patrol got the "word from the street." Now, in order to keep up with all the latest activities such as gang violence and flash mobs, law enforcement agencies have found that they have to participate in social media. With the click of a mouse, police can often learn who the subjects' friends are, where they spend their time, what their hobbies are, and what music they listen to, plus, literally, an embarrassing amount of other information that some people decide to post on themselves. For instance, the Bowling Green Police Department in Bowling Green, Kentucky, was able to identify and arrest a local graffiti tagger because he took photographs of his artwork and posted them on his Facebook profile page. As Bowling Green Detective Tim Wilson stated to a reporter, "Solving crime is like putting together a puzzle, and sometimes, Facebook might have an outside piece of the total picture of the investigation."[25]

Unless the social media website users choose to keep their profile pages private, Facebook and the other websites can be goldmines for investigators. In addition to tracking down criminals and their activities, the websites are also used in cold case research, particularly when putting together witness lists. Some people post and tag (identify) photographs of themselves, very valuable if they are the only photographs a law enforcement agency can find. In addition, many users allow viewers to access the pages of their "friends," even spelling out the ages and locations of family members. This is extremely helpful in people searching when it is necessary to determine family relationships or subjects' associates.

As noted above, the IACP Center for Social Media actively supports the needs of law enforcement. In September 2011, the Center released its findings from its recent survey of 800 agencies throughout the country. When asked about their most common use of social media, 71.1% stated that they use it for investigations, and Facebook is by far their first choice. More than half stated that social media helped them solve crimes in their jurisdictions. Of the agencies not yet using social media, the barriers holding them back were time and personnel constraints.[26] Other popular social media websites include MySpace, BlackPlanet.com, Reunion.com, Classmates.com, Twitter, and LinkedIn.

Some investigators have had luck creating Facebook accounts for fictional individuals and then attempting to "friend" that person in order to access his or her "wall" (the portion of a Facebook page that displays user updates and comments). Then, once on the wall, the investigators can read the same "chatter" that anyone else can read, which may include (like the graffiti tagger) bragging about crimes committed, statements about conflicts between people (or gangs), or threats of future crimes.

Profile: Special Agent Tommy Ray Has Ace Up His Sleeve

Media, from the Latin plural of "medium," includes every means of information that can be conveyed to a mass audience. Detectives in the Pocatello Police Department in Pocatello, Idaho, use billboards to display photographs of victims of unsolved homicides, along with pleas to the driving public for help.[27] In many other parts of the country, prisoners are shown similar photographs—with brief write-ups on missing persons and victims of homicides—on cold case playing cards. The reasoning behind the use of the cards creatively combines the concepts of prisoners playing cards with the fact that prisoners are the segment of the population that is constantly in contact with criminals.

Law enforcement's use of cold case playing cards to attempt to solve cold missing persons and cold homicide cases originated in Polk County, in central Florida. Each standard deck of 52 cards displays a photograph of a victim and factual information on that individual's case. The idea was the brainchild of Tommy Ray (see Figure 16.2), a native of Auburndale, Florida, who started working cold case homicides in 1982 for the Polk County Sheriff's Office and is now a special agent with the Florida Department of Law Enforcement (FDLE). "Before I retire," Special Agent Ray said in e-mail correspondence with the author, "I would like to see the Cold Case Card Program spread to every state in the United States and every cold case homicide unit possible."[28]

In 2005, Ray initiated the organization called the Polk County Cold Case Assessment Team (CCAT), a group of crime-solving professionals

Figure 16.2 Special Agent Tommy Ray came up with the idea of producing cold case playing cards in his native state of Florida. (Photo courtesy of Tommy Ray.)

who meet monthly to collaborate on the county's many unsolved murders. The organization also maintains a website that lists more than 150 Polk County cases of unsolved murders and unidentified bodies, as well as missing persons whose cases may have turned into homicides. The team had been impressed with playing cards distributed by the U.S. military in 2003 to U.S. troops in Iraq. Those cards featured Iraq's most wanted fugitives, in which Saddam Hussein (executed in December 2006) was the ace of spades.[29]

The first deck of cold case playing cards depicting Polk County homicides was one of the CCAT's major projects. The group distributed the cards in the Polk County Jail and had almost immediate success. In November 2005, local officials arrested two individuals for the 2004 fatal shooting of Thomas Wayne Grammar. The tip came from an inmate who saw Grammar's playing card and remembered another individual confessing to the crime, but until the inmate saw the card, he had not believed that the crime actually occurred.[30] "Jails are the Internet of unsolved crimes," *CBS News* correspondent Mark Strassmann said in a television news report outside the Polk County Jail in March 2006. "Prisoners know things, they hear things, and sometimes they talk."[31]

Spurred on by success at the local level, Ray took the idea to the state. In July 2007, the Florida Department of Law Enforcement (FDLE), Florida Department of Corrections (DC), and the Florida Attorney General's Office announced that the agencies had teamed up with the Florida Association of Crime Stoppers and developed two statewide decks of cards featuring 104 unsolved cases. At first the cases were assigned to the card by how old the crimes were (aces and kings for the oldest) but now the numbers and suits on the cards are randomly assigned. According to the FDLE's press release, at the time approximately 100,000 decks of cards were distributed to 93,000 inmates in 129 state prison facilities, beginning with the Wakulla Correctional Institution.[32]

The cards were funded by the Crime Stoppers Trust Fund, administered by the Florida Attorney General. The Trust Fund was created in 1998 when the Florida Crime Stoppers Act was passed by the state legislature.[33] A toll-free number is listed on each card, and offenders are given access to telephones so they can call in new information. As with all Crime Stoppers initiatives, no identifying information is obtained from the callers; the callers are free to remain anonymous. According to Ray, the playing cards are well received by the prisoners (see Figures 16.3 and 16.4). "The inmates are fascinated by them," he said. "They've told me that if the cards were about drugs or thefts, they would keep their mouths shut, but unsolved murders and missing persons are different, as the victims could be one of their family members."[34]

Figure 16.3 Prisoners in maximum security at the Polk City Correctional Facility in Polk City, Florida, enjoy a game of cards. (Photo courtesy of Tommy Ray.)

Figure 16.4 Tips from Florida prisoners using the cold case playing cards have already contributed to at least three homicide arrests and convictions. (Photo courtesy of Tommy Ray.)

Within months, two murder cases were solved as a result of the first edition of the statewide decks: James Foote and Ingrid Lugo. Foote, the seven of clubs, was the first. He had been found dead on November 15, 2004, from a single gunshot wound to his chest. His killer was arrested in October 2007, after an inmate at the Columbia Correctional Institution Annex in Lake City, Florida, saw Foote's cold case playing card and alerted authorities. "This arrest is a good example of just how far creative-out-of-the-box thinking can go toward fighting and solving crime in our communities," stated Florida Attorney General Bill McCollum in a FDLE press release at the time.[35]

Lugo, the second statewide case solved, was the six of spades (see Figure 16.5). She was murdered on December 13, 2004, nearly a month later than Foote, and was strangled in a retention pond in Manatee County. An inmate at the Cross City Correctional Institution in Cross City, Florida, saw the cold case playing card featuring Lugo and contacted Crime Stoppers to report the involvement of the victim's ex-boyfriend, a former inmate (on forgery charges) at the same institution.[36] Another card features homicide victim Starsky Garcia (see Figure 16.6).

Ongoing tips from the playing cards continue to be received. A second statewide edition followed the first, and, it too, was funded by the Crime Stoppers Trust Fund.[37] In August 2008, the original founding agencies teamed up with Florida sheriffs and police chiefs to create a third deck of cards. The third edition, funded by a federal Edward Byrne Memorial Justice Assistance Grant, features an additional 52 of Florida's unsolved homicide and missing person cases. These new

Figure 16.5 Ingrid Lugo's case was solved after her photograph and a description of her murder were published on a Florida cold case playing card. (Photo courtesy of the Florida Department of Law Enforcement.)

decks have been distributed to all of the approximately 65,000 inmates in all 67 county jails and to all of the approximately 141,000 supervised offenders reporting in through the state's 156 probation offices. "This is a creative and well-crafted approach to investigating some of Florida's toughest cases," stated FDLE Commissioner Gerald Bailey in a press release. "I'm proud of the collaboration between law enforcement agencies to put this program in place. It's worked before and we're betting it will work again."[38]

Following the Florida model, cold case playing cards have been produced in states including Texas, South Carolina, California, Washington, Kansas, Oregon, New York, Kentucky, Minnesota, Oklahoma, Maryland, and Virginia, as well as the state of Queensland, Australia. One of the most recent states to produce its own cards is Wisconsin, distributing them to prisons in September 2011.[39] In Florida, Tommy Ray is in the process of collecting the data on the total number of cases solved with cold case playing cards. At the time of this writing, he has counted 12 cases throughout the United States, with three of those in Florida. "Working cold case homicides is the most challenging as well as the most rewarding thing I have done in my 39 years of law enforcement," he said. "Coming up with the idea of the unsolved homicides and missing persons on these

Figure 16.6 The Florida case of Starsky Garcia remains unsolved. (Photo courtesy of the Florida Department of Law Enforcement.)

cards shows that you're never too old or too young to think of new ideas in solving these most heinous of crimes."[40]

Summary

Resources in this chapter include:

- How law enforcement can use the media to bring in new leads
- An example of the use of media in solving a John Doe case
- A discussion of the increasing number of agencies (with multiple cold cases) that are posting the cases on their own websites
- A description of how several agencies now use social media to provide information to the public, while also using it creatively as an investigative tool
- A description of how cold case playing cards are solving homicides

Media, the plural of medium, includes every means of information that can be conveyed to a mass audience. Law enforcement agencies use the media to their advantage to disseminate information and to bring in leads. Print and broadcast media (augmented with websites) are eager to publicize unsolved homicides, missing persons, and unidentified remains if they are provided with a "hook" on which to base their stories. Because of one newspaper article, the identification of "John Doe Number 3" as Joseph Coogan was made by investigator Darrell Harris of the Marin County Sheriff's Office–Coroner Division nearly 22 years after Coogan's partial remains washed up on a California beach.

Cold case playing cards originated in Polk County, Florida. The concept is spreading throughout the United States and Australia and has already been successful in contributing to several arrests and convictions in cold case homicides.

Endnotes

1. Rivers, David W. Sergeant. "Cold case squads" (unpublished and undated report, Metro-Dade Police Department, circa 1988–1997).
2. Harris, Darrell. Investigator. E-mail correspondence with author, August 19, 2011.
3. Harris, Darrell. Investigator. E-mail correspondence with author, August 19, 2011.
4. Koopman, John. "Cold case on the coast: A dogged investigator uses DNA to identify remains of a man who fell into the surf off Monterey in 1983," *San Francisco Chronicle* (April 14, 2005).
5. Harris, Darrell. Investigator. Telephone interview with author, August 23, 2011.
6. California Department of Consumer Affairs, Contractors State License Board. http://consumerwiki.dca.ca.gov/wiki/index.php/Contractors_State_License_Board (accessed December 26, 2011).
7. Harris, Darrell. Investigator. E-mail correspondence with author, August 19, 2011.
8. Harris, Darrell. Investigator. Telephone interview with author, August 23, 2011.
9. Harris, Darrell. Investigator. E-mail correspondence with author, August 19, 2011. Also, Horowitz, Donna. "At Last, Closure for a Mother," *Los Angeles Times* (May 15, 2005).
10. Harris, Darrell. Investigator. E-mail correspondence with author, August 19, 2011.
11. Harris, Darrell. Investigator. E-mail correspondence with author, August 19, 2011.
12. Harris, Darrell. Investigator. E-mail correspondence with author, August 19, 2011.
13. Harris, Darrell. Investigator. E-mail correspondence with author, August 19, 2011.
14. Harris, Darrell. Investigator. Telephone interview with author, August 23, 2011.
15. Harris, Darrell. Investigator. E-mail correspondence with author, August 19, 2011. Also, Wolfcale, Joe. "Mystery Solved," *Marin Independent* (April 5, 2005).
16. Staff. "Blanche A. Coogan Obituary," *Pottsville Republican and Evening Herald* (November 22, 2006).

17. Las Vegas Unidentified, Clark County Nevada Coroner-Medical Examiner, www.clarkcountynv.gov/Depts/coroner/unidentified/Pages/default.aspx (accessed December 26, 2011).
18. Chaikin, Sarah. "Perspectives from the field," The National Center for Victims of Crime, www.ncvc.org/ncvc/main.aspx?dbName=DocumentViewer&DocumentID=48323 (accessed December 26, 2011).
19. Dallas Police Department. http://dallaspolice.net/index.cfm?page_ID=11656 (accessed December 26, 2011).
20. Kawano, Lynn. "Dallas police hire social media officer," myFoxdfw.com, February 25, 2011.
21. Huntington Beach Police Department Facebook page, Jane Doe 1968.
22. Highland, Deborah. "KSP Turns to Facebook as Investigative Tool," *Bowling Green Daily News* (KY; April 3, 2011).
23. IACP Center for Social Media. www.iacpsocialmedia.org (accessed December 26, 2011).
24. IACP Center for Social Media. www.iacpsocialmedia.org, (accessed December 26, 2011). See "Building Your Presence With Facebook Pages: A Guide for Police Departments," www.iacpsocialmedia.org/SiteSearchResults.aspx?cx=010726981603076586402:9zh0rgaljuc&cof=FORID:10&ie=UTF-8&q=Building%20your%20presence%20with%20facebook (accessed December 26, 2011).
25. Highland, Deborah. "KSP Turns to Facebook as Investigative Tool," *Bowling Green Daily News* (KY; April 2, 2011).
26. IACP Center for Social Media. www.iacpsocialmedia.org
27. O'Connell, John. "Police use billboards to generate cold case tips," *Idaho State Journal*, 22 March 2011.
28. Ray, Tommy. Special Agent. E-mail correspondence with author, September 26, 2011.
29. Suzie Schottelkotte, "Special Team Rethinks Cold Crimes," *The Ledger*, April 24, 2005. Also, Polk County Cold Case Assessment Team, http://coldcaseteam.com (accessed December 26, 2011). Also, Zucco, Tom. "Troops Dealt an Old Tool," *St. Petersburg Times* (FL; April 12, 2003). Also "Hussein Executed with Fear in His Face," *CNN World*, December 29, 2006.
30. Florida Department of Law Enforcement. "Attorney General and Department of Corrections Bet Playing Cards Will Solve Cold Cases," www.fdle.state.fl.us/Content/News/July-2007/FDLE,-Attorney-General-and-Department-of-Correctio.aspx July 24, 2007 (accessed December 26, 2011).
31. *CBS Morning News*. "Cold Case Answers in the Cards?" March 30, 2006.
32. Florida Department of Law Enforcement. "Attorney General and Department of Corrections Bet Playing Cards Will Solve Cold Cases," www.fdle.state.fl.us/Content/News/July-2007/FDLE,-Attorney-General-and-Department-of-Correctio.aspx July 24, 2007 (accessed December 26, 2011).
33. Florida Department of Law Enforcement. "Attorney General and Department of Corrections Bet Playing Cards Will Solve Cold Cases," www.fdle.state.fl.us/Content/News/July-2007/FDLE,-Attorney-General-and-Department-of-Correctio.aspx July 24, 2007 (accessed December 26, 2011).
34. Ray, Tommy. Special Agent. E-mail correspondence with author, August 16, 2011.

35. Florida Department of Law Enforcement. "First Cold Case Playing Card Case Solved; Man Arrested in Fort Meyers," October 19, 2007, www.fdle.state.fl.us/Content/News/October-2007/First-Cold-Case-Playing-Card-Case-Solved;-Man-Arre.aspx (accessed December 26, 2011).
36. Florida Department of Law Enforcement. "Cold Case Playing Cards Help Solve Second Case; Riverview Man Arrested," November 8, 2007, www.fdle.state.fl.us/Content/News/November-2007/Cold-Case-Playing-Cards-Help-Solve-Second-Case;-Ri.aspx (accessed December 26, 2011).
37. Florida Department of Law Enforcement. "FDLE, Attorney General and Department of Corrections Bet Playing Cards Will Solve Cold Cases," July 24, 2007, www.fdle.state.fl.us/Content/News/July-2007/FDLE,-Attorney-General-and-Department-of-Correctio.aspx (accessed December 26, 2011).
38. Florida Department of Law Enforcement. "Third Edition Deck of Statewide Cold Case Playing Cards Unveiled," August 29, 2008, www.fdle.state.fl.us/Content/News/August-2008/Third-Edition-Deck-of-Statewide-Cold-Case-Playing-.aspx (accessed December 26, 2011).
39. Brueck, Dana. "Investigators Hope Cold Case Playing Cards in Prisons Solve Crimes," http://nbc15.com (Madison, Wisconsin), September 7, 2011.
40. Ray, Tommy. Special Agent. E-mail correspondence with author, September 26, 2011.

17 Conclusion

A simple cross on a fence post marks the entrance to the Caribou Cemetery in Caribou, Colorado. (Photo by author.)

"What's in a name?" asked Tom Adair, a retired senior criminalist with the Westminster, Colorado, Police Department in an article on Boulder Jane Doe in *Evidence Technology Magazine*. Adair then answered his own question by explaining that it originally was written by English poet and playwright William Shakespeare and was obviously never directed at him. But, if given the opportunity to answer, Adair said he would reply with one word: identity.

"I am not talking about an arrest number or a date of birth as we commonly identify people in law enforcement," stated Adair. "I am talking about a person's selfhood." He then went on to explain that our names represent a fundamental gateway as to who we are and where we came from. For many of us, it is something we often take for granted. But to a homicide detective, a victim's name is perhaps the most crucial component to an investigation. It is the foundation upon which tangible facts are discerned and leads are developed. "Without it," added Adair, paraphrasing Shakespeare in *Romeo and Juliet* "A rose is just a rose."[1]

This book, *Cold Case Research: Resources for Unidentified, Missing, and Cold Homicide Cases*, as its name implies, combines cold case homicides with cases of the missing and unknown that have also gone cold. The reason they are lumped together is simple: they do not neatly separate into one group or another. A murder victim may be found with no name, and a missing person's case can "turn into" a homicide. The case of a missing-and-presumed-dead person can even be prosecuted as a "no-body" homicide.

The purpose of *Cold Case Research* is to aid in jump-starting stalled investigations and to help to keep others from going cold in the future. As Detective James Trainum noted in the Foreword, the book will, it is hoped, open up a world of new opportunities for cold case unit managers: "the opportunity to expand the capacities of their units, take advantage of free resources, and to institute changes that address the outdated attitudes, policies, and procedures that, in the past, prevented some cases from being solved."

Why is reopening (and, we hope, solving) cold cases important? We do it:

- For the victims, to bring them justice
- For the families, to bring them "resolution" (a term they prefer to "closure")
- For society (reflecting a mutual recognition that each of us counts)
- To arrest and convict murderers who think they are never going to get caught

Dedicated investigators agree on never taking "no" for an answer and never giving up. But, they also agree that if cases take longer to solve than they wish, it is important to leave paper trails and case files the way they would want their successors to find them in the future. Highlights of resources from each chapter are outlined below.

Section I Tools and Techniques

1. Challenges and Checklist

- Changing relationships can bring forward new witnesses.
- A new witness was instrumental in solving the murder of Surette Clark. Detective Ed Reynolds of the Phoenix Police Department brought justice to the Navajo child formerly known as "Little Jane Doe."
- In cold case investigations, time is an ally, as it can give people an opportunity to mature, to overcome former fears, and to develop a different sense of right and wrong.

2. Agency Organization: Cold Case Units

Resources in this chapter include:

- Descriptions of formations of cold case squads or units, with current examples of law enforcement at work
- Current practices for reopening cold cases
- Qualities of a good cold case investigator

Murders increased dramatically between 1960 and 1995. Facing a backlog of unsolved cases, agencies began to tackle the problem by forming cold case squads, or units. Leading the way were the Metro-Dade (now Miami-Dade) Police Department, in Miami, Florida; the Metropolitan Police Department, in Washington, DC; and the Phoenix Police Department, in Phoenix, Arizona.

- Investigator Cheryl Moore's "Unit of One" at the Jefferson County Sheriff's Office, in Golden, Colorado, identified a Jane Doe and brought justice to her and to another victim, both murdered by the same man.
- Detective Ron Lopez, the only sworn officer in the Homicide/ Missing Persons Unit of the Colorado Springs Police Department, proactively tackles and solves cold missing persons cases.
- According to recent surveys by the Rand Corporation and by Colorado State University, the main reason behind clearing cold case homicides was new information from witnesses or information from new witnesses.
- A good cold case investigator has a passion for his or her work; is persistent and highly motivated; keeps an open mind and is non-judgmental; is patient, detail-oriented, and tenacious; is creative, an independent thinker, and uses deductive reasoning; is discreet and keeps information confidential; is skilled in conducting interviews; has strong research skills; and is proactive and keeps up to date with developing trends and investigative tools.

3. TLO: The Latest Investigative System

Resources in this chapter include:

- A law enforcement profile that explains how TLOxp® was used to solve a case
- User tips on the TLOxp online investigative system

TLOxp is not the only online investigative system, but as part-time Chief Chad Weaver of the Hutsonville Police Department in Hutsonville, Illinois, discovered when he was able to quickly track down a fugitive in a cold case, the new tool has revolutionized the way his agency does its research.

- For its product, TLOxp, TLO gathers information from courthouses and news and Internet sources, and also purchases data from data suppliers. The company was founded by Hank Asher, who had also founded Seisint, Inc., where he developed ACCURINT® for Law Enforcement.
- Investigators reap the rewards, all at no cost to law enforcement. (In order to keep it free, the company charges its other subscribers.)
- New data are continuously being added to TLOxp. According to CEO Ken Hunter, each day the data are different, have increased and, one hopes, are more accurate, more current, and more complete. He states, "Investigators should never stop checking to see if a new bit of knowledge provides the missing clue, the missing link, or the missing puzzle piece."[2]
- The search capabilities and functionalities of TLOxp are only as good as knowing how to use the system. To gain its full advantage, users are encouraged to contact Customer and Tech Support, live chat, and e-mail, as well as watch the company's e-training videos.
- For more information on TLOxp, and how to sign up, go to www.tlo.com.

4. Additional Options for People Searches

Resources in this chapter include:

- The use of Google in cold case research
- Other people-searching options in addition to Google and TLO (see Chapter 3)

For effective people searching, investigators have found that it helps to become familiar with as many online tools as possible, find the ones that work best, and bookmark them to keep them handy.

- Google (one of several search engines) can be the easiest of searches or the most frustrating, depending upon how one goes about performing a search. Tips include putting search terms in quotes in order to keep a search focused.
- A researcher's creative use of keywords located a missing woman who had lived under a false identity for 50 years.
- Printing (or taking screen shots) of search results that contain sensitive data is recommended, as the web page may suddenly disappear.

- "Google Alerts" are helpful in keeping up to date on media coverage of an individual, a specific agency, a developing case, or even oneself.
- Various websites, such as veromi.net, have people-search options that can help in determining family relationships.
- The Social Security Death Index has some limitations, but it can determine if a person is dead or alive.
- Ancestry.com requires a subscription, but this premier family history research tool provides additional people-searching options.
- Several fee-based data aggregators are available to law enforcement.

5. Dealing with Databases

Resources in this chapter include a guide to some of the databases that may be helpful in cold case research. Investigators use many databases in cold case research. Among them are the following:

- CODIS: Combined DNA and National DNA Index Systems, along with a discussion of the services of the University of North Texas Center for Human Identification (UNTCHI)
- IAFIS: Integrated Automated Fingerprint Identification System
- NamUs System (See Chapters 6 and 7.)
- NCMEC: National Center for Missing and Exploited Children
- NCIC: National Crime Information Center (including its historical database)
- NIBIN: National Integrated Ballistic Information Network
- State clearinghouses, for example, CBI: Cold Case Files of the Colorado Bureau of Investigation
- The Doe Network: International Center for Unidentified & Missing Persons (and a sampling of other privately funded databases)
- ViCAP: Violent Criminal Apprehension Program
- Individual agency cold case websites (See Chapter 16.)

Section II Missing, Murdered, and Unidentified

6. NamUs: Connecting the Missing and Unidentified

Resources in this chapter include:

- An explanation of the NamUs System that connects a Missing Persons database with an Unidentified Persons database, along with a case study on its application

- Descriptions of free forensic services available to law enforcement and medical examiners/coroners
- A medical examiner/coroner example of how to handle a partial remains case

New, in 2009, the NamUs System is a powerful investigative tool that links two databases: NamUs-MP, on missing persons and NamUs-UP, on unidentified persons. A good example is the identification, 22 years later, of Englewood Jane Doe (found in Montgomery County, Ohio) as Paula Beverly Davis (who went missing from Kansas City, Missouri).

- NamUs was formed by combining the Unidentified Decedent Reporting System (UDRS) with the Missing Persons System (a missing persons database created in 2007 and 2008).
- NamUs provides—to law enforcement and medical examiner/coroners' offices—free forensic services, including odontology, anthropology, and fingerprint and DNA analysis.
- Special circumstances include archiving solved missing persons' cases, as well as keeping those missing persons' cases active in which partial, and forensically identified, remains have been found. The discovery, in Delaware, of the skull belonging to drowning victim Gary Mayo is a good example of the handling of a partial remains case.

7. Entering and Searching in the NamUs System

Resources in this chapter include:

- Tips for law enforcement to enter cases in the NamUs Missing Persons database
- Tips for medical examiners/coroners to enter cases in the NamUs Unidentified Persons database
- How law enforcement, medical examiners/coroners, and also the public can enter and search

As valuable as the NamUs databases are, they are only as good as the information that is provided. Before entering data, it is recommended that all forensic work and expert opinions be re-examined. For best results, investigators need to search from both sides of the system by manipulating the parameters of both NamUs-MP, on missing persons, and NamUs-UP, on unidentified remains.

- To make the system effective, law enforcement agencies need to enter their cold missing person cases, and medical examiners/coroners are encouraged to input information on their unidentified remains.
- Data on missing persons cases can be entered by any registered user, including the public, but the data will not go live until they are vetted by the appropriate law-enforcement agency.
- In addition to investigators, the public is encouraged to search the site, as well as enter additional information such as jewelry regularly worn by the missing person.

8. PKU Cards Retain Overlooked DNA

Resources in this chapter include:

- An explanation of PKU/Guthrie cards as sources of direct reference DNA samples
- Retention of these samples listed by state

PKU/Guthrie cards have been on file since 1966, but their use in missing persons cases is a new tool for law enforcement agencies. The identification of Ben Maurer in New Jersey in 2009 may have been the first case in which DNA extracted from a drop of blood on a PKU card was used to find a missing person and make a positive identification of an unidentified person.

- These direct DNA samples are retained by all 50 states, but each health department varies widely in the amount of time the dried blood is kept on file.
- PKU/Guthrie cards may prove especially helpful for missing children who were adopted and no biological parents are known or available for family reference samples.

9. The Plight of the Missing and Unknown

Resources in this chapter include:

- One scenario—the missing person is presumed dead.
- Prosecuting no-body homicides.
- Examples of missing person cases. In addition to missing under suspicious circumstances and presumed dead, other scenarios include a motive to disappear, walking away, committing suicide, and natural and accidental deaths.

- Suggestions for reconstructing case files of John and Jane Does, starting with newspaper articles and then followed by database searches.

There are many reasons why individuals disappear. Some go missing under suspicious circumstances and are murdered. In some instances their bodies or skeletal remains are found, whereas other times they are not. The ones whose remains are not found present a particular challenge to investigators and prosecutors. If there is a suspect and enough evidence, the cases can be tried as no-body homicides. As former Assistant United States Attorney, Thomas A. "Tad" DiBiase stated, "Don't treat the case like a missing person case; treat it like a homicide where the best evidence of the crime is missing—the body."

Missing persons with a motive to disappear or who chose to walk away may be alive and may not want to be found. Other missing persons may have committed suicide or died natural or accidental deaths. The case history, "Joseph Halpern Disappeared into Thin Air" illustrates a case in which the missing person may have died an accidental death or may have walked away. A nephew has taken up the search and has found a surprising amount of information in the National Archives and in FBI files. Readers interested in cold missing persons cases can join the ranks of those who follow the stories of Glen and Bessie Hyde (missing from the Grand Canyon in 1928) and Everett Ruess (missing from southern Utah in 1934).

Section III Resources for Expanded Research

10. Historical and Geographical Context

Resources in this chapter include:

- An explanation of the importance of historical and geographical context and perspective
- A guide to finding maps, photographs, and weather conditions at the time of the crime, and other historical resources helpful in reconstructing a case file
- Two case histories showing the applications of historical and geographical context

Investigators benefit from historical and geographical context. Historical context is mentally going back in time to place the victims in the eras in which they lived. Geographical context involves physically revisiting the crime scenes, canvassing the neighborhoods, and taking a lot of photographs.

- A Connecticut researcher and historian used both historical and geographical contexts to connect three previously unrelated missing persons cases in New England.
- Social changes from the 1950s to the present day contributed to a rise in homicide rates.
- Historical United States Geological Survey maps, Google Earth historical imagery maps, original newspaper photographs, weather reports from the day of the crime, and bus and train maps and timetables are just a few of the many resources available to researchers.
- Both historical and geographical contexts were used when the author located a long-forgotten crime scene by comparing the scene with historical photographs.

11. Newspaper Research: Online and Off

Resources in this chapter include:

- Information on locating historical newspaper articles online for context, to find new witnesses and missing persons, and to aid prosecutors
- How to find the same information when the newspaper articles are not online

Historical newspaper articles can be accessed both online and off. Either way, they can help to locate new witnesses, reveal lifestyles and opinions, put crimes in historical context, and provide new names for missing persons lists. Articles from the time of a crime can also aid the prosecution, for instance, to confirm whether a suspect or witness was telling the truth when he or she claimed to have acquired a particular item of information by reading about it in a newspaper.

Newspaper accounts, however, are secondary sources and the facts need to be independently verified. Obituaries are an excellent source for determining family relationships, but current-day obituaries are paid advertisements and may be less accurate than their traditional counterparts. The following newspaper resources are available to researchers and investigators:

- NewsBank
- ESBCO Host
- Google News Newspapers
- Subscription-based online newspaper access
- Individual newspaper archives
- Microfilmed newspapers
- Clipping files

12. Published and Public Records

Resources in this chapter include:

- A description of public records and where to find them
- The use of public records in determining family relationships
- The use of public records in tracing name changes of women

The information on most online people-searching resources, including investigative systems such as TLO, dates from the mid-1980s. Public records, however—and many are online—go back many decades. Whatever the time period, they can help investigators identify family relationships and trace name changes of women.

- Loosely defined, public records are records from government entities that receive public funds.
- Federal public records include the National Archives and Social Security applications for deceased individuals.
- State public records include statewide secretary of state offices and licensing boards, as well as state archives.
- Local public records include recorded documents offices (the names vary by state), police departments and sheriffs' offices, district attorneys' offices, coroners' and medical examiners' offices, and court records.
- Published records, such as telephone and city directories, are available in many local libraries.
- Public records can be missing and, in rare cases, they can also be inaccurate.

13. Volunteers: How They Can Help

Resources in this chapter include:

- A description of the Volunteers in Police Service (VIPS) Program that aids law enforcement agencies in their use of volunteers
- Profiles of volunteers and how they can help in cold case research

Volunteers include individuals, students, and retired law enforcement officers, and they all bring different skills and perspectives to cold case investigations. They may also have time to do background research, they work for free, and most are passionate about their work or they would not be doing it.

- In its Cold Case Unit, the Charlotte-Mecklenburg Police Department in Charlotte, North Carolina, combines volunteers with experienced investigators and is a model for the country.

- Milli Knudsen's work in the Cold Case Unit of the New Hampshire Department of Justice, Office of Attorney General is an outstanding example of the use of a volunteer in law enforcement.
- Specialized and independent volunteers aid in cold case research, too. Examples include Texas EquuSearch, NecroSearch, and Ralston & Associates.

14. Contact with Co-Victims

Resources in this chapter include:

- The use of a victim advocate in a cold case unit
- Suggestions from co-victims on better communication from law enforcement
- Resources for co-victims

The Cold Case Unit of the Denver Police Department in Denver, Colorado, employs a Victim Advocate who walks a fine line between being a voice for the victims while still protecting the integrity of the Unit's cases.

- The murder in 1979 of Bonita Raye Morgan is an example of a case that the police have not been able to solve or clear, and family members see no justice for the victim.
- According to a Colorado State University study, the biggest complaint of co-victims was the need for better, honest, and direct communication with law enforcement.
- Co-victim resources include several volunteer and nonprofit organizations at the national and state level. Included are the National Center for the Victims of Crime, the National Organization of Parents of Murdered Children, Inc., Colorado-based Families of Homicide Victims and Missing Persons, and Missouri-based Missouri Missing.
- Victim Rights Acts vary by state.

Section IV Review Teams and the Media

15. Cold Case Review Teams and Information-Sharing Resources

Resources in this chapter include:

- A description of where to find cold case review teams, and what they do

- A guide to some of the information-sharing resources that may be helpful in cold case research

Cold case review teams give law enforcement fresh sets of eyes, pro bono. There are many review teams all over the country, but perhaps the most well known is the Vidocq Society. Named for a French crook turned detective, the organization meets monthly in Philadelphia to listen to cases presented by law enforcement, and then offers suggestions and continues, sometimes for years, to aid investigators in their work. Some other review teams include:

- Colorado Cold Case Task Force and Colorado Cold Case Review Team
- MACCHIA, Mid-Atlantic Cold Case Homicide Investigators Association
- Sheriffs' Association of Texas, Major Crimes Assessment Committee (MCAC) Cold Case Review Team
- Charlotte-Mecklenburg Police Department's Civilian Cold Case Review Team
- WAHI, Wisconsin Association of Homicide Investigators

The list of information-sharing resources for law enforcement is long, but it includes:

- CopLink
- Crime Stoppers International and Crime Stoppers USA
- NCAVC, National Center for the Analysis of Violent Crime—a component of the FBI's Critical Incident Response Group (CIRG) that includes ViCAP (see below).
- IHIA, International Homicide Investigators Association
- LEO, Law Enforcement Online
- N-DEx, Law-Enforcement National Data Exchange
- NLETS, International Justice and Public Safety Information Sharing Network, formerly the National Law Enforcement Telecommunications System
- NCMEC, National Center for Missing and Exploited Children
- RISS, Regional Information Sharing System (including the Cold Case Locator)
- ViCAP and its collaboration with NamUs

16. Taking Advantage of the Media

Resources in this chapter include:

- How law enforcement can use the media to bring in new leads

- An example of the use of media in solving a John Doe case
- A discussion of the increasing number of agencies (with multiple cold cases) that are posting the cases on their own websites
- A description of how several agencies now use social media to provide information to the public, while also using it creatively as an investigative tool
- A description of how cold case playing cards are solving homicides

Media, the plural of medium, includes every means of information that can be conveyed to a mass audience. Law enforcement agencies use the media to their advantage to disseminate information and to bring in leads. Print and broadcast media (augmented with websites) are eager to publicize unsolved homicides, missing persons, and unidentified remains if they are provided with a "hook" on which to base their stories. Because of one newspaper article, the identification of "John Doe Number 3" as Joseph Coogan was made by investigator Darrell Harris, of the Marin County Sheriff's Office–Coroner Division, nearly 22 years after Coogan's partial remains washed up on a California beach.

Cold case playing cards originated in Polk County, Florida. The concept is spreading throughout the United States and Australia and has already been successful in contributing to several arrests and convictions in cold case homicides. As FDLE Special Agent Tommy Ray noted, "You're never too old or too young to think of new ideas in solving these most heinous of crimes."[3]

Endnotes

1. Adair, Tom. "Long ago lost: How a local historian's knowledge, skills, and tenacity served to identify the victim of a homicide that had grown cold over 55 years," *Evidence Technology Magazine* (January/February 2010) 16–19.
2. Hunter, Ken. E-mail correspondence with author, November 20, 2011.
3. Ray, Tommy. Special Agent. E-mail correspondence with author, September 26, 2011.

Selected References

Books

Block, Eugene B. *The Wizard of Berkeley: The Extraordinary Exploits of America's Pioneer Scientific Criminologist, the World-Famous Edward Oscar Heinrich* (New York: Coward-McCann, 1958).

Branson, Jack and Branson, Mary. *Delayed Justice: Inside Stories from America's Best Cold Case Investigators* (New York: Prometheus Books, 2011).

BRB Publications. *The Sourcebook to Public Record Information: The Comprehensive Guide to County, State, and Federal Public Records Sources* (Tempe, AZ: BRB Publications, 2009).

Capuzzo, Michael. *The Murder Room: The Heirs of Sherlock Holmes Gather to Solve the World's Most Perplexing Cold Cases* (New York: Gotham Books, 2010).

Jackson, Steve. *No Stone Unturned: The True Story of NecroSearch International, the World's Premier Forensic Investigators* (New York: Kensington Books, 2002).

Dooling, Michael C. *Clueless in New England: The Unsolved Disappearances of Paula Welden, Connie Smith and Katherine Hull* (CT: The Carrollton Press, 2010).

Moomaw, Jack C. *Recollections of a Rocky Mountain Ranger* (Estes Park, CO: YMCA of the Rockies, 1994).

O'Harrow, Robert, Jr. *No Place to Hide* (New York: Free Press, 2006).

Pettem, Silvia, *Someone's Daughter: In Search of Justice for Jane Doe* (Lanham, MD: Taylor Trade, 2009).

Walton, Richard H. *Cold Case Homicides: Practical Investigative Techniques* (Boca Raton, FL: Taylor & Francis/CRC Press, 2006).

Documents and Reports

Allord, G.J. and Carswell, W.J., Jr. 2011. Scanning and geo-referencing historical USGS quadrangles: U.S. Geological Survey Fact Sheet 2011–3009. http://pubs.usgs.gov/fs/2011/3009 (accessed December 26, 2011).

Bonner County Sheriff's Office Press Release, September 28, 2010, www.bonnerso.org/pressreleases.html (accessed December 26, 2011).

Chaikin, Sarah. "Perspectives from the field," The National Center for Victims of Crime, www.ncvc.org/ncvc/main.aspx?dbName=DocumentViewer&DocumentID=48323 (accessed December 26, 2011).

Colorado Department of Public Safety. "Annual report—Cold case task force to the Colorado House and Senate Judiciary Committees (Section 24.33.5-109(8), C.R.S.)," October 1, 2011 (3).

Davis, Robert C.; Jensen, Carl; and Kitchens, Karin E. "Cold case investigations: An analysis of current practices and factors associated with successful outcomes" (Arlington, VA: Rand Center on Quality Policing, 2011).

Department of Regulatory Agencies (DORA), Office of Policy, Research, and Regulatory Reform. "2011 sunset review: Colorado Cold Case Task Force," (October 14, 2011) 4, 5, 14.

DiBiase, Thomas A., "Tad." "How to successfully investigate and prosecute a no body homicide case," 19 March, 2010. www.nobodymurdercases.com/tips.html (accessed December 26, 2011).

Dickson, Warden F.R. California State Prison at San Quentin, "Cumulative case summary on condemned inmate Harvey Murray Glatman" (February 25, 1959).

FBI. "When offline is better: Another way to search crime records," www.fbi.gov/news/stories/2010/january/ncic_010410 (accessed December 26, 2011).

Florida Department of Law Enforcement. "Cold case playing cards help solve second case; Riverview man arrested," November 8, 2007, http://www.fdle.state.fl.us/Content/News/November-2007/Cold-Case-Playing-Cards-Help-Solve-Second-Case;-Ri.aspx (accessed December 26, 2011).

Florida Department of Law Enforcement. "FDLE, attorney general and department of corrections bet playing cards will solve cold cases," July 24, 2007, www.fdle.state.fl.us/Content/News/July-2007/FDLE,-Attorney-General-and-Department-of-Correctio.aspx (accessed 26 December 2011).

Florida Department of Law Enforcement. "First cold case playing card case solved; Man arrested in Fort Myers," October 19, 2007, www.fdle.state.fl.us/Content/News/October-2007/First-Cold-Case-Playing-Card-Case-Solved;-Man-Arre.aspx (accessed 26 December 2011).

Florida Department of Law Enforcement. "Third edition deck of statewide cold case playing cards unveiled," August 29, 2008, www.fdle.state.fl.us/Content/News/August-2008/Third-Edition-Deck-of-Statewide-Cold-Case-Playing-.aspx (accessed December 26, 2011).

IACP Center for Social Media. "Building your presence with Facebook pages: A guide for police departments," www.iacpsocialmedia.org/SiteSearchResults.aspx?cx=010726981603076586402:9zh0rgaljuc&cof=FORID:10&ie=UTF-8&q=Building%20your%20presence%20with%20facebook (accessed December 26, 2011).

Morton, Howard. "Forgotten victims: What cold case families want from law enforcement," (Fort Collins: Center for the Study of Crime and Justice, Department of Sociology, Colorado State University, 2009) Afterword.

Naday, Alexandra; Unnithan, N. Prabha; Shelley, Tara; and Hogan, Michael. "Analysis of the cold case survey of law enforcement for the Colorado Bureau of Investigation" (Fort Collins: Colorado State University, Center for the Study of Crime & Justice, Department of Sociology, 2009).

National Sheriffs' Association, Justice Solutions, and National Organization of Parents of Murdered Children. "A compilation of cold case resources: Literature review and survey of cold case units; summary report," April 6, 2010.

O'Neill, Ann. *CNN Justice*, "Students narrow suspects in Levy case to one," February 27, 2009, http://articles.cnn.com/2009-02-27/justice/levy.campus.crime.club_1_ingmar-guandique-chandra-levy-susan-levy?_s=PM:CRIME (accessed December 26, 2011).

Pettem, Silvia. Epilogue to *Someone's Daughter: In Search of Justice for Jane Doe*, (Lanham, MD: Taylor Trade, 2009) www.silviapettem.com/JANE%20DOE%20 articles/Epilogue.html (accessed December 26, 2011).

Priest, Jonathyn W. "Cold case investigation: Protocol for reviewing unresolved cases," *Cold Case Homicide Investigation: Strategies & Best Practices Participant Manual* (September 22, 2006).

Rivers, Sergeant David W. "Cold case squads" (unpublished and undated report, Metro-Dade Police Department, circa 1988–1997).

Taylor, Michael. March 4, 1998, Obituary—Pierce Brooks. http://articles.sfgate.com/1998-03-04/news/17715701_1_serial-killers-mr-brooks-onion-field (accessed December 26, 2011).

Tipton, Delton. "Getting the Word Out," undated, NLETS, www.nlets.org/our-impact/in-their-own-words/suspect-identification (accessed December 26, 2011).

U.S. Department of Justice, Office of Justice Programs. "NamUs: National Missing and Unidentified Persons System; A guide for users," 2010.

Walton, Richard H. and O'Toole, Mary Ellen. "Workshop #3, They're alive! Breathing new life into the investigation and prosecution of cold case homicides," *American Academy of Forensic Sciences 61st Annual Meeting*, February 16, 2009.

Wells, Bonnie M. "The Beginning of EquuSearch," posted 2007, http://starlightinnerprizes.com/TheBeginningOfEquusearch.htm (accessed December 26, 2011).

Writer unknown, 2002, Ben Maurer Obituary: June 1, 1985–June 26, 2002, Piscataway, New Jersey. www.tributes.com/show/Ben-Maurer-86342216 (accessed December 26, 2011).

Interviews

Asher-Chapman, Marianne (Missouri Missing)

Brown, Hal G. (Deputy director of the Delaware Office of the Chief Medical Examiner & Forensic Sciences Laboratory)

Bulllis, Sharron (Sister of Bonita Raye Morgan)

Chaikin, Sarah (Cold case program coordinator of the Victim Assistance Unit at the Denver Police Department)

Clack, Stephanie (Sister of Paula Beverly Davis)

Clark, Steven, C., PhD. (Occupational Research and Assessment)

Davis, James H., MD. (Coroner of Montgomery County, Ohio)

DiBiase, Thomas A. "Tad" (Former assistant U. S. attorney)

Dooling, Michael C. (Historical researcher and writer)

Furr, Detective Stephen (Charlotte-Mecklenburg Police Department)

Hall, Officer Tom (Cold Case Cowboys)

Halpern, Roland (Nephew of Joseph Halpern)

Hanzlick, Randy, MD. (Chief Medical Examiner, Fulton County, Georgia)

Harris, Darrell. (Investigator with the Marin County Sheriff's Office–Coroner Division)

Hunter, Ken (CEO of TLO)

Knudsen, Milli (Cold Case Unit of the New Hampshire Department of Justice, Office of Attorney General)
Lavigne, Micki (Historical researcher)
Lopez, Ron. Detective. (Colorado Springs Police Department)
Lunn, Matthew. Investigator. (Arapahoe County Coroner's Office)
Mayo, Regina (Widow of Gary Mayo)
Moore, Cheryl. Investigator. (Jefferson County Sheriff's Office)
Morton, Howard (Families of Homicide Victims and Missing Persons)
Parmelee, Kevin. Investigator. (Somerset County Prosecutor's Office, and formerly with the Piscataway Police Department, in New Jersey)
Racioppo, Steve (COO of TLO)
Ralston, Gene (Ralston & Associates)
Ray, Tommy. Special Agent. (Florida Department of Law Enforcement)
Reynolds, Ed. Detective. (Phoenix Police Department, retired)
Rinker, Marcey. Victim Advocate. (United States Attorney's Office)
Sister of Wayne Clifford Roberts (name withheld upon request).
Somershoe, Stuart. Detective. (Phoenix Police Department)
Stiltner, Suzanne (ViCAP NamUs Coordinator, FBI)
Trainum, James. Detective. (Metropolitan Police Department, retired)
Weaver, Chad. Part-time Chief. (Hutsonville Police Department; also school resource officer for the Robinson Police Department)

Magazine and Journal Articles

Adair, Tom. "Long ago lost: How a local historian's knowledge, skills, and tenacity served to identify the victim of a homicide that had grown cold over 55 years," *Evidence Technology Magazine* (January/February 2010).

Dooley, Danette. "Volunteers travel North America finding the dead," *Blue Line Magazine* (December 2007).

Gunn, Charlotte. "Drowning victim recovered from Beardsley Reservoir after 3 years; side-scan sonar mission, February 27–March 1, 2002," *Rescue: Idaho Mountain Search and Rescue Unit, Inc.*, 35: 2 (March 2002).

Heurich, Charles, "Cold cases: Resources for agencies, resolution for families," *NIJ Journal, 260* (July 2008).

Lord, Vivian B. "Implementing a cold case homicide unit: A challenging task," *FBI Law Enforcement Bulletin,* 74: 2 (February 2005).

Lyford, G. and Wood, U. "National Crime Information Center: Your silent partner," *FBI Law Enforcement Bulletin* 52: 3 (March 1983).

McLaughlin, John S. "A report on the disappearance of Joseph Laurence Halpern," Rocky Mountain National Park Chief Ranger's report, National Archives (August 23, 1933).

Parmelee, Kevin. "PKU card: A new tool in the search for missing and unidentified individuals," *UNT Health Science Center, Forensic Services Unit Newsletter,* 2: 3 (May/June 2011).

Pettem, Silvia. "Out of the past: A fresh look at cold cases," *Evidence Technology Magazine* 8: 2 (March-April 2010).

Pulham, Mark. "The boy in the box: America's unknown child," *Crime Magazine* (February 2, 2011).

Ralston, Gene and Pinksen, Junior. "Underwater technology used to bring closure to families of drowning victims," *Journal of Ocean Technology 2010*, 5: 3 (2010).

Reed, Pamela. "Direct DNA references for missing persons," *UNT Health Science Center, Forensic Services Unit Bulletin* (July 2010).

Regensburger, Derek. "Law enforcement volunteers: An essential tool in the investigation of cold case homicides," *Sheriff Magazine* (May/June 2011).

Regini, Charles L. "The cold case concept," *FBI Law Enforcement Bulletin* (August 1997).

Ritter, Nancy. "Missing persons and unidentified remains: The nation's silent mass disaster," *NIJ Journal*, 256 (January 2007).

Schuster, Beth. "Cold cases: Strategies explored at NIJ regional trainings," *NIJ Journal*, 260 (July 2008).

Steward-Gordon, James. "World's first—and greatest—detective," *The Reader's Digest* (October 1977) 129–133.

Turner, Ryan and Kosa, Rachel. "Cold case squads: Leaving no stone unturned," *Bureau of Justice Assistance Bulletin* (July 2003).

Newspaper Articles and Radio and Television Broadcasts

Anas, Brittany. "Mystery solved: Boulder sheriff IDs 'Jane Doe' as Dorothy Gay Howard," Boulder *Daily Camera* (CO; October 28, 2009).

Brown, Robin. "Weather and dark water hamper efforts by rescuers," *The News Journal* (Wilmington, DE; November 23, 2007).

Brueck, Dana. "Investigators hope cold case playing cards in prisons solve crimes," nbc15.com, Madison, WI (September 7, 2011).

CBS Morning News. "Cold case answers in the cards?" (March 30, 2006).

Globe Wire Services. "Retired teacher's contribution to Cold Case Unit is priceless," *Boston Globe* (April 26, 2010).

Highland, Deborah. "KSP turns to Facebook as investigative tool," *Bowling Green Daily News* (KY; April 3, 2011).

Horowitz, Donna. "At last, closure for a mother," *Los Angeles Times* (May 15, 2005).

Hutchins, Ryan. "DNA test leads family to missing teenager found dead in N.Y.C.," *The Star-Ledger* (Newark, NJ; 15 July 2009).

Kawano, Lynn. "Dallas police hire social media officer," myFoxdfw.com (February 25, 2011).

Keilman, John. "Markers for the nameless," *Dayton Daily News* (December 12, 1999).

Koopman, John. "Cold case on the coast: A dogged investigator uses DNA to identify remains of a man who fell into the surf off Monterey in 1983," *San Francisco Chronicle* (April 14, 2005).

Lindsay, Sue. "Jeffco investigator brings drive to job of solving cold cases," *Rocky Mountain News* (Denver; January 26, 2009).

Lohr, David. "TV drama helps family find missing loved one," AOLNews (February 9, 2010).

Meltzer, Erica. "CU-Boulder prof acknowledges DNA mistake in case of poet Everett Ruess," Boulder *Daily Camera* (CO; October 21, 2009).

Mitchell, Kirk. "Law-enforcement experts' work helps Longmont police file charges in a 2007 murder investigation," *The Denver Post* (May 9, 2011).
Nelson, Katie. "Little victim still without an identity," *Arizona Republic* (Phoenix, AZ; July 1, 2005).
O'Connell, John. "Police use billboards to generate cold case tips," *Idaho State Journal* (March 22, 2011).
O'Harrow, Robert, Jr. "LexisNexis to buy Seisint for $775 Million," *Washington Post* (July 15, 2004).
Ober, Gail. "Gloddys plea for cold case unit," *The Citizen of Laconia* (NH; May 1, 2009).
Page, Doug. "Englewood 'Jane Doe' pending exhumation, reburial," *Dayton Daily News* (OH; May 5, 2010).
Pilkington, Ed. "Vidocq Society—The murder club," *Guardian.co.uk* (London; March 3, 2011).
Ross, Bob. "Criminal Intelligence Center in Metairie promises added efficiency," *The Times-Picayune* (New Orleans, LA; August 25, 2011).
Russell, Dana Benton. "UNT Health Science Center awarded NamUs grant," *Wall Street Journal*, (New York; November 11, 2011).
Russo, Stephanie. "Tempe police identify child's body after 40 years," *Arizona Republic* (Phoenix, AZ; August 5, 2010).
Schottelkotte, Suzie. "Special team rethinks cold crimes," *The Ledger* (Lakeland, FL; April 24, 2005).
Staff. "Blanche A. Coogan obituary," *Pottsville Republican and Evening Herald* (Pottsville, PA; November 22, 2006).
Staff. "Body of murdered, unidentified girl found near Boulder Creek," Boulder *Daily Camera* (CO; April 9, 1954).
Staff. "Body of unidentified man found near Leadville, *Leadville Times* (CO; November 3, 1958).
Staff. "Child's skeleton found in Tempe," *Arizona Republic* (Phoenix, AZ; March 27, 1979).
Staff. "Foltz gets 10 years for child pornography," *WTAY/WTYE-TOC 1570 AM radio*, Robinson, IL (April 11, 2011).
Staff. "Hope abandoned for Joe Halpern's life," *The Estes Park Trail* (CO; August 25, 1933).
Staff. "Hussein executed with fear in his face," *CNN World* (December 29, 2006).
Staff. "Lost face reappears; Expert reconstructs unknown victims," *Arizona Republic* (Phoenix, AZ; May 10, 1997).
Staff. "Police extend hunt for girl missing 3 days," Albany *Times Union* (New York; April 5, 1936).
Staff. "Searchers comb Vermont region for Paula Welden," *Stamford Advocate* (CT; May 24, 1947).
Staff. "Serial killer sentenced for killing 2 women," *TheDenverChannel.com* (December 11, 2008).
Staff. "Slayer once abducted Boulder mother; also suspected of killing mystery girl whose body was found," Boulder *Daily Camera* (CO; October 31, 1958).
Stout, David. "John E. List, killer of 5 family members, dies," *New York Times* (March 25, 2008).
Wilber, Del Quentin. " 'Freeway Phantom' slayings haunt police, families—Six young D.C. females vanished in the '70s," *Washington Post* (June 26, 2006).

Wolfcale, Joe. "Mystery solved," *Marin Independent* (San Rafael, CA; April 5, 2005).
Woodfill, D.S. "Arizona crime data shared by police through network," *The Arizona Republic* (Phoenix, AZ; July 27, 2011).
Zachariah, Holly. "Families of missing can find answers through online networks," *The Columbus Dispatch* (OH; March 21, 2011).
Zucco, Tom. "Troops dealt an old tool," *St. Petersburg Times* (FL; April 12, 2003).

Websites

America's Unknown Child, The Boy in the Box Mystery, http://americasunknownchild.net (accessed December 26, 2011).
Ancestry, www.ancestry.com (accessed December 26, 2011).
California Department of Consumer Affairs, Contractors State License Board, http://consumerwiki.dca.ca.gov/wiki/index.php/Contractors_State_License_Board (accessed December 26, 2011).
Charlotte-Mecklenburg Police Department, Homicide Cold Case Unit, http://charmeck.org/city/charlotte/CMPD/organization/investigative/ViolentCrimes/Homicide/ColdCase/Pages/home.aspx (accessed December 26, 2011).
CODIS, www.dna.gov/dna-databases/codis (accessed December 26, 2011).
Colorado State Archives, Colorado Laws Concerning Public Records, www.colorado.gov/dpa/doit/archives/open/00openrec.htm (accessed December 26, 2011).
Colorado Victim Rights Act (VRA), Denver: Victim Assistance Unit, www.denvergov.org/dpdvau/ColoradoVictimRights/tabid/423633/Default.aspx (accessed December 26, 2011).
Coplink, www.i2group.com/us/products/coplink-product-line (accessed December 26, 2011).
Correction Department, City of New York, City Cemetery, www.correctionhistory.org/html/chronicl/nycdoc/html/hart.html (accessed December 26, 2011).
Dallas Police Department, http://dallaspolice.net/index.cfm?page_ID=11656 (accessed December 26, 2011).
Denver Police Department, Victim Assistance Unit www.denvergov.org/dpdvau/ColoradoVictimRights/tabid/423633/Default.aspx (accessed December 26, 2011).
Doe Network, The, www.doenetwork.org (accessed December 26, 2011).
Evergreen Cemetery Records, Lake County Library, www.lakecountypubliclibrary.org/Cemetery%20Records.htm (accessed December 26, 2011).
Family Search, www.familysearch.org (accessed December 26, 2011).
FBI Records, www.fbi.gov/foia/requesting-fbi-records (accessed December 26, 2011).
Find A Grave, Memorial #23081 (Helen List), www.findagrave.com/cgi-bin/fg.cgi?page=gr&GRid=23081 (accessed December 26, 2011).
Find A Grave, Memorial #23085 (Alma M. List), www.findagrave.com/cgi-bin/fg.cgi?page=gr&GRid=23085 (accessed December 26, 2011).
Find A Grave, Memorial #25511539 (John Emil List), www.findagrave.com/cgi-bin/fg.cgi?page=gr&GRid=25511539 (accessed December 26, 2011).

Huntington Beach Police Department Facebook page, Jane Doe 1968, www.facebook.com/HuntingtonBeachPolice (accessed December 26, 2011).

IACP Center for Social Media, www.iacpsocialmedia.org (accessed December 26, 2011).

IHIA, www.ihia.org (accessed December 26, 2011).

Internet Archive Wayback Machine, www.archive.org/web/web.php (accessed December 26, 2011).

Justice Solutions: A Web Site by Crime Victim Professionals for Crime Victim Professionals, www.justicesolutions.org/index.htm (accessed December 26, 2011).

Las Vegas Unidentified, Clark County Nevada Coroner-Medical Examiner, www.clarkcountynv.gov/Depts/coroner/unidentified/Pages/default.aspx (accessed December 26, 2011).

LEO, www.leo.gov (accessed December 26, 2011).

Let's Bring Them Home, www.lbth.org/ncma/index.php (accessed December 26, 2011).

LexisNexis, www.lexisnexis.com/government/solutions/investigative/accurint-le-features.aspx (accessed December 26, 2011).

MACCHIA, www.coldcasehomicide.org/MACCHIA%20Membership%20Information%20Sheet.htm (accessed December 26, 2011).

Maricopa County Recorder, http://recorder.maricopa.gov/recdocdata (accessed December 26, 2011).

Meteor showers online, http://meteorshowersonline.com/perseids.html (accessed December 26, 2011).

Metropolitan Police Department, http://mpdc.dc.gov/mpdc/site/default.asp (accessed December 26, 2011).

Miami-Dade Police Department, www.miamidade.gov/mdpd (accessed December 26, 2011).

Missing Persons Unit, Missouri State Highway Patrol, www.mshp.dps.mo.gov/CJ51/index.jsp (accessed December 26, 2011).

Missouri Missing, www.missourimissing.org (accessed December 26, 2011).

National Archives, www.archives.gov/research (accessed December 26, 2011).

National Center for Victims of Crime, Welcome page, www.ncvc.org/ncvc/main.aspx?dbID=DB_About189 (accessed December 26,2011).

NCAVC, www.fbi.gov/about-us/cirg/investigations-and-operations-support (accessed December 26, 2011).

NCIC, www.fas.org/irp/agency/doj/fbi/is/ncic.htm and www.fbi.gov/about-us/cjis/ncic/ncic (accessed December 26, 2011).

NCMEC, www.missingkids.com (accessed December 26, 2011).

NecroSearch, www.necrosearch.com/index.html (accessed December 26, 2011).

NLETS, www.nlets.org/who-we-are (accessed December 26, 2011).

No Body Murder Cases, http://nobodymurdercases.com/index.html (accessed December 26, 2011).

One Missing Link, Inc., http://onemissinglink.org/omlindex.html (accessed December 26, 2011).

Outpost For Hope, www.outpostforhope.org (accessed December 26, 2011).

Parents of Murdered Children www.pomc.com/index.htm (accessed December 26, 2011).

Polk County Cold Case Assessment Team http://coldcaseteam.com/ (accessed December 26, 2011).
Ralston & Associates, http://gralston1.home.mindspring.com/Sidescan.html (accessed December 26, 2011).
RISS, www.riss.net (accessed December 26, 2011).
RISS, "MOCIC provides resources to support cold case investigations," www.riss.net/Documents/RISS.Insider.2009.07.pdf, (accessed December 26, 2011).
Royal Canadian Mounted Police, ViCLAS, www.rcmp-grc.gc.ca/tops-opst/bs-sc/viclas-salvac-eng.htm (accessed December 26, 2011).
Sheriffs' Association of Texas, www.txsheriffs.org/comm_coldcase.htm (accessed December 26, 2011).
Social Security Administration, Number allocations, www.socialsecurity.gov/employer/stateweb.htm (accessed December 26, 2011).
Social Security Administration, Randomization, www.socialsecurity.gov/employer/randomization.html (accessed December 26, 2011).
Sunshine Review, Colorado Open Records Act, http://sunshinereview.org/index.php/Colorado_Open_Records_Act (accessed December 26, 2011).
Texas EquuSearch Mounted Search and Recovery Team, http://texasequusearch.org (accessed December 26, 2011).
The History of World Expositions, www.expo2000.de/expo2000/geschichte/detail.php?wa_id=12&lang=1&s_typ=21 (accessed December 26, 2011).
TLO, "Welcome to TLO" video, www.tlo.com (accessed December 26, 2011).
UNTCHI, www.hsc.unt.edu/departments/pathology_anatomy/dna/Forensics/Initiative/Information.cfm (accessed December 26, 2011).
ViCAP (Violent Criminal Apprehension Program), www.fbi.gov/wanted/vicap and http://www.fbi.gov/about-us/cirg/investigations-and-operations-support/vicap-brochure-1 (accessed December 26, 2011).
VicePresidents.com, www.vicepresidents.com/theysaidIT.html (accessed December 26, 2011).
Vidocq Society, www.vidocq.org/who.html (accessed December 26, 2011).
Volunteers in Police Service, www.policevolunteers.org/resources (accessed December 26, 2011).
Who Killed Our Kids, http://wkok.org (accessed December 26, 2011).
Wisconsin Association of Homicide Investigators, www.wi-homicide.org/index.php?option=com_frontpage&Itemid=1 (accessed December 26, 2011).

Index

D

G

H

I

O

P